POLISCIDE

COAUTHORS

ELLIOT J. FELDMAN

GREGORY J. NIGOSIAN

JONATHAN POOL

ALLAN ROSENBAUM

CARLYN ROTTSOLK

MARGARET STAPLETON

JUDITH VAN HERIK

JULIA VITULLO-MARTIN

THOMAS VITULLO-MARTIN

POLISCIDE

THEODORE J. LOWI

BENJAMIN GINSBERG

CORNELL UNIVERSITY

Macmillan Publishing Co., Inc.
NEW YORK

Collier Macmillan Publishers
LONDON

Macmillan Publishing Co., Inc.
866 Third Avenue, New York, New York 10022

Collier Macmillan Canada, Ltd.

Library of Congress Cataloging in Publication Data

Lowi, Theodore J
  Poliscide.

  Includes index.
  1. Science and state—United States—Case studies.
2. Particle accelerators—Case studies.   3. Eminent
domain—Weston, Ill.—Case studies.   4. Weston, Ill.
I. Ginsberg, Benjamin, joint author.   II. Title.
Q127.U6L68   333.7'7   75-12629
ISBN 0-02-372140-5

Printing: 1 2 3 4 5 6 7 8   Year: 6 7 8 9 0 1 2

ACKNOWLEDGMENT

Theodore J. Lowi and Margaret Stapleton, "Congress, the Atom, and Civil Rights: A Case Study in Civil Wrongs," in Theodore J. Lowi and Randall B. Ripley (eds.), LEGISLATIVE POLITICS U.S.A., 3d ed., pp. 290–313. Copyright © 1973 by Little, Brown and Company (Inc.). Reprinted and adapted by permission.

Preface

When the Atomic Energy Commission decided in late 1966 to locate its new accelerator in Weston, Illinois, the Weston villagers congratulated each other on a job well done. Optimism exuded from the place. Along the highway approaching Weston's main entrance the villagers constructed a billboard characterizing their home as an "atomic town," host of the largest atom smasher in the world.

The villagers' optimism was based on a pattern of illusions: (1) the illusion that governmental institutions concerned themselves with the welfare of those they governed; (2) the illusion that science was synonymous with the public good; (3) the illusion that politics on the metropolitan fringe was anything other than unconditional and total; (4) the illusion that their village would survive the coming of the accelerator.

The reality masked by the villagers' illusions was a politics of conquest. Conquest began when local interests used every governmental and political trick to rid themselves of Weston, an urban threat to their suburban way of life. Conquest ended in "poliscide," as state and county interests used the accelerator to rid themselves of the village. The villagers' illusions, in part externally fostered to prevent them from opposing the accelerator, were themselves part of the reality of conquest.

Our book is a cluster of case studies centering upon the single problem of the coming of the accelerator. Each of our cases tells part of the same story—from the national perspective, the state perspective, the metropolitan perspective, the county perspective, the perspective of the villagers, and the perspective of the farmers included in the site area. The technique resembles that used in the classic Japanese film, *Rashomon*, in which the same crime is described several times from the standpoint of each of the persons involved.

Many aspects of the Weston story are distressing, but the most distressing part to us is the fact that scientists involved in the development, design, and location of the accelerator were unaware of the characteristics of the area and of the local issues surrounding the village and the affected farms. The scientists were, without any question, dedicated to the public good. So were virtually all of the state and county public officials, and so were the Weston village officials. It was this very sincerity and dedication—coupled with ignorance at the top and devastating manipulation at the bottom—that made the story for us such a significant one. We found ourselves facing what Reinhold Niebuhr must have meant by moral man and immoral society, because we found institutions that were virtually the enemy of individuals.

For us the larger picture has become one in which political behavior arises out of narrowly defined and formal perspectives. In the absence of a prevailing official definition to the contrary, each actor sees his own reality from the standpoint of his individual obligations, and he behaves accordingly. In the Weston story each of our role players viewed the accelerator as a means of fulfilling his own responsibilities, but because those responsibilities were defined strictly in terms of *job* responsibilities, the overall results were wasteful from a national standpoint and are disappointing to anyone who harbors hope that politics will be different in an age of sophisticated science and technology. The results of our study lead us to wonder whether this hope may not be based as much on illusion as the optimism of the Weston villagers.

Eleven authors have shared in the field research and the writing for this book. No single chapter escaped collective scrutiny, to a point where, despite some specific disagreements over interpretation, the book is a common product. The two senior authors took responsibility for the final drafts, and Elliot Feldman and Thomas Vitullo-Martin deserve special mention as project directors. In all other respects the book can be said to have eleven authors.

Singly and collectively, the authors wish to express their gratitude to the many persons and institutions that gave us support. Harvey Shapiro, John Will, and Edward Hayes participated effectively in various stages of the project but for different reasons did not stay with us until the end. Professor Jack Meltzer of the University of Chicago's Center for Urban Studies provided encouragement in a number of respects, as did his research associate, John Gardner. We would also like to thank Professor Boyd Keenan, of the University of Illinois–Circle Campus, for giving us the benefit of his extensive experience in the politics of science.

However, our heaviest debt of gratitude is to those participants who allowed themselves to be used as research sources. It would be neither useful nor fair to identify them by name. But they include over one hundred villagers; almost as many local farmers and farm families; scores of county, state, metropolitan, and national officials; and at least two dozen participating scientists. Our job could not have been done without their cooperation, and we deeply appreciate it.

There continue to be moments when we regret our critical posture; but we feel the facts warranted it and hope that the participants understand that nothing personal is intended. If there is to be any improvement in public morality, public efficiency, or public responsibility, we could expect no less of ourselves than a dedication to exhaustive analysis and thorough criticism. And we will expect no less of our readers when their opportunity comes, as surely it must, when our message reaches them.

T. J. L. and B. G.
Ithaca, New York

Contents

Introduction to a Science Project   1

PART I   **Science—The Politics of Public Works**

1. Federal Government and Science as a
   Social Problem   21
2. Disorder in the Scientific Establishment   33
3. Politicization of Science   57
4. The Quest for the Golden Smasher   87
5. Congress, the Atom, and Civil Rights:
   A Case Study in Civil Wrongs   109

PART II   **The Realpolitik of the Metro**

6. Weston, the Past and the Future   131
7. Poliscide: The Two Histories Collide   159
8. County Governments Know How to Plan
   —And Do   175

9. The People of Weston and the Dilemmas
   of Understanding   195

PART III The Politics of Conquest

10. The Accelerator as a Political Issue
    in Weston   215

11. Public Acquisition—In Private   235

12. Enemy of the People   261

13. Aftermath and Afterthoughts: Building on a
    Solid Base of Ignorance   281

   Index   297

Introduction to a Science Project

On December 15, 1966, Chicagoans learned they would soon be neighbors of the world's largest atom smasher. After a widely publicized, nationwide site selection competition, the Atomic Energy Commission (AEC) had selected a 6,800-acre site 30 miles due west of Chicago's Loop. At the end of 1966, these "6,800 desirable acres" contained 71 farms and the 100 houses that composed the village of Weston, Illinois. Twenty months later, all of the farmers and all but one of the Weston families had been removed, and construction of the billion-dollar, 200 billion electron volt (bev) accelerator was in full swing. No legal trace of the village or farms remained. National Accelerator Laboratory (NAL) personnel occupied the village and farmhouses while supervising construction of the underground ring, 2 miles in diameter, in which atoms would be accelerated, shot at, and smashed.

This is neither the beginning nor the end of the story. It is the middle, the point of impact of Washington on Weston. Two points could hardly be farther apart than the community of national scientists and the rural and suburban community around Weston. Yet they are the two main points of contention in the story of the accelerator and its effects. The lines that connect the two points are multiple and roundabout. But careful observation

1

and assessment of the factors that brought the accelerator to that place at that time will shed a great deal of light on two forces in American life that could become central public problems of the 1970s and 1980s: the structure of federalism and the operations of big science.

Two tales need to be told. One is the history of the decision to build an enormous accelerator and to locate it in the suburbs of Chicago. Although many Chicagoans participated in this story, by and large the terrain is national and the constituencies and jurisdictions of the participants are national. It involves the national community of scientists and their accustomed arenas of operation—the Atomic Energy Commission, the National Academy of Sciences, the United States Congress and its Joint Committee on Atomic Energy, the White House, and the president's science advisors.

The second history is focused almost entirely on the Chicago area, particularly DuPage County, one of America's most prosperous counties. The participants were almost entirely nonscientists who were concerned primarily with implementing Washington's decisions and using Washington to further their own interests.

The Fellowship of the Ring

Big science is essentially a post–World War II phenomenon. Governments and industries have been exceedingly generous during the past 25 years; however, the supply of research and development (R and D) monies has always been outstripped by imaginative and exciting scientific demands. An ever-expanding R and D budget made possible the avoidance of many conflicts; and many choices were among totally incommensurable things—as between new accelerators and space probes, or cancer versus molecular biology research, and so on. Although there occasionally have been heated controversies across the subdisciplines of science, the most consistent controversy probably has been within the individual subdisciplines. Within each subdiscipline, the alternatives are highly comparable, the sense of victory and defeat is easier to measure, and there is intense competition as well as fellowship. Conflicts have been intense enough to involve scientists and their political supporters in mutual suspicions, character assassinations, loyalty and security charges, and permanent animosities. Nonetheless, there are strong fraternal bonds within each of these competitive subdisciplines.

High-energy physics is very possibly the preeminent example. The long history of competition in this field arises out of the extraordinarily successful collaboration among scientists to build the atomic bomb during World War II. Following the war, "centers of excellence" in particle physics emerged at the Lawrence Radiation Laboratory on the West Coast, at Argonne National Laboratory outside Chicago, and, shortly thereafter, in the East at Brookhaven. Competitive balance was maintained among the facilities by allowing the expansion of one while the next level of expansion was being planned at another.

Equilibrium was upset during the 1950s by the shortcomings of Argonne and the clear emergence of Lawrence and Brookhaven as the favored facilities. This convinced many that the Midwest was suffering a scientific brain drain, brought on by the growing concentration of R and D on the two coasts.

The pattern of coast-to-coast logrolling was ultimately broken, and it was broken through politicization. Midwest scientists organized a professional lobby—Midwest University Research Associates (MURA). Congressional delegations, mayors, and business interests were brought in, and the activity intensified after MURA lost in its first major effort to become the third member of the logrolling cycle with its proposal for an accelerator in Madison, Wisconsin.

Despite MURA's initial failure, the cycle was broken, and the process of decision making in the area of publicly financed physics facilities was permanently altered. Political intensification meant that the AEC had to find another basis for balance and harmony among the fellowship of physical scientists. The agency sought such a balance by opening the accelerator site selection process to a public competition. Immediately the AEC was deluged with over 200 proposals from 46 states. To narrow the field in a way that appeared to be fair, the AEC contrived a two-point plan. First, it entered into an agreement with the National Academy of Sciences to set up a site selection committee. Second, the AEC enunciated several "hard criteria" according to which the NAS committee should make its decisions. These hard criteria included such obvious requirements as a minimum parcel of geologically adequate land (3,000 acres), a minimum amount of available electric power and water, and accessibility to transportation, commercial, and industrial services. But the AEC eventually accepted a basket of additional "soft criteria." These included requirements that the site be close to communities with the proper kind of housing, cultural, and educational facilities for scientific personnel and their families. All of this introduced a considerable amount of discretion, and it also revealed a great deal about the character of the decision that would ultimately be made.

Still another influence that reveals something about the character of the decision was the political agreement at the highest levels that the prize would go to the Midwest, assuming a site could be produced there that satisfied the "hard criteria." This understanding, which involved President Lyndon Johnson, prevailed despite the fact that 3 years prior to that time a panel of the President's Science Advisory Committee had decided that the 200-bev machine ought to be built at Berkeley.

Finally, the process was further complicated by the fact that the AEC was strapped for funds. In this context the introduction of an open—or a semiopen—decision process of competitive bidding among states and metropolitan areas was an ingenious move. It accomplished several important things for the AEC and the scientists. First, it took the onus of final decision off the AEC and spread it over a process that would look eminently legitimate to the public. Second, it forced the serious contenders to offer the AEC more land and facilities at lower prices. (The final site was given over without any federal expenditure; it included more than twice the acreage called for in the original specifications, and it included housing and utilities, which lowered the AEC's vital cash outlays.) Third, it committed Congress and the president to the principle of building the accelerator; facing over 200 hopeful contenders spread across the continent, no national figure would have risked an attempt to veto the facility.

A *Site to Behold—History #2*

The site was simply an abstract parcel of land to the scientists and to the national and Illinois officials involved in the site selection. But to any local observer it was as heterogeneous and improbable a combination of attributes as one could imagine; and it was populated by real people. The 3,000, then 5,000, then 6,800 acres included farmers, tenant farmers, gentlemen farmers, ordinary white-collar commuters who loved open country, blue-collar workers who could buy a cheap house, and land speculators waiting to subdivide or to be subdivided.

History #2 begins in 1959, when one such subdivision began to take place. At that time Mrs. Julia Krafft, a millionairess who some years earlier had bought a 420-acre farm for speculative purposes, found herself an appropriate buyer in one DeSoto McCabe. McCabe was convinced that the maturation of the offspring of the postwar baby boom and the convergence of appropriate transportation and services in this heretofore remote area would make it viable as a housing site for Chicago-bound commuters. The idea of the village of Weston was born.

McCabe soon learned that the biggest enemy of land development in any metropolitan area is the county government with its building code, its zoning code, and its various other protective laws. These codes are particularly strict in DuPage County. Ninety feet is minimum frontage in the area around Weston, and in the early 1960s this virtually dictated minimum new-home values near $30,000. This in turn dictated a particular social, racial, and class composition and explains the unusually high median family income (one of the top five counties in the United States) as well as the unusually low proportion of blacks residing in the county (below 1 per cent in DuPage County). But strict zoning requirements were not even the most important check against urbanization and proletarianization where the Weston development was concerned. Here the county officials made a very special case. Opposition to Weston was of three types and was mounted at three different stages in Weston's development.

First, in contrast to the usual hospitality shown to suburban developers, the county officials applied building codes with devastating severity. The county also used informal techniques of obstruction during this first stage, including efforts to close off the developers from access to Chicago financing. The result was not to kill Weston but to turn developers to less legal forms and sources of financial backing.

The second type of obstruction began after the county failed to prevent construction of the village. This was done primarily by a legal battle to prevent Weston's incorporation. Unincorporated places are governed by county zoning powers, but with incorporation these powers devolve upon the local government. With that power, the developers would be able to carve three 60-foot lots out of each original pair of 90-foot lots. It was because of this plan that the developers had been able to offer homes in Weston at prices well below the market.

Third, the county sought to block the expansion of Weston through suits against annexation and through the efforts of the Chicago Better Business Bureau to prevent the promotion of Weston homes or investment in future Weston developments. In this they were aided by the local offices of several federal agencies whose *modus operandi* has always been cooperation with local authorities. Federal Housing Administration and Veterans Administration officials refused to provide insured mortgages for Weston—much as they have done in urban slums.

Four and Eighty Mailboxes All in a Row

When completed, the exterior ring of houses in the village of Weston sat several hundred feet away from the county highway. At the conjunction of the county highway and the main entrance road to Weston there were stretched, during most of Weston's brief history, more than 80 rural letterboxes, one for each Weston household. Through various pretexts and powers, the county had kept the U.S. Post Office at bay. These boxes symbolized the grim determination of the county to maintain a hostile environment.

It is no wonder the village survived only with the help of crime syndicate money. It is no mystery that it failed to survive a federal atomic project involving an initial outlay of $500 million, backed by an impressive scientific purpose. It is also no mystery why the county worked so hard to eradicate Weston. What we ponder is how it was possible to enlist federal aid in pursuit of this local purpose.

There were two twins of Weston in the Chicago metropolitan area, and both had been financed and built by the same savings and loan corporations and businessmen; yet neither had been seriously opposed by the county. Why Weston? Weston was distinguished by the fact that it was a development in the middle of open country previously slated by county and regional planners for clean industry and other low-density uses. To the county officials, Weston represented a threat to their very significant power over who would pick up the options in the development of the entire metropolitan fringe. If Weston could establish itself, the pattern could spread. Even if there were no land speculators already holding certain of those tracts, the farmers themselves constituted a menace. They were already under considerable financial pressure, because the county itself had redefined that land as industrial for purposes of county taxation. There was no telling when an elderly farm couple without heirs would accept the inducements of a very large purchase price in contrast to the meager cash income they were enjoying from the operation of their farms during the twilight of their lives. The development of Weston had redefined the situation so extraordinarily that the great farming tradition itself had become part of the enemy camp in the eyes of the DuPage County suburbanites and their government.

From their perspective, the county and the state officials would have been derelict if they had not used every available power to block or, failing that, to inhibit Weston. The developers' plan to carve a third lot from each pair of lots foreshadowed an intensive land use that was deeply contrary to the goals of the DuPage County leaders. Moreover, in order to carry out this plan, the developers would need to rent, rather than sell, most of the houses, thereby retaining proprietary rights during Weston's formative years. Rentals meant transiency, and intense land use meant low-income families and greater demands on county services. Taking all these things together, the situation was unconscionable to the *suburban* outlook that dominated DuPage County. The Weston model gave an initial impression of being an *urban* model. That was the sticking point. The villagers themselves were on the verge of middle-class respectability, but their village was an urban phenomenon, and it had to go.

The Real Federal System and Science Public Works

LEVEL OR LOCATION OF PARTICIPANT	RESPONSIBLE OFFICIAL OR POSITION	DEFINITION OF GENERAL RESPONSIBILITIES	PERSPECTIVES	POLICIES
			LEADS TO →	WHICH GUIDE →
1. Atomic Energy Commission	Site selection committee NAL director	Advance pure science. Stay ahead of the Russians in pure and applied science. Make life better for scientists and the universities.	What's good for science is good for America. Everyone wants an accelerator in his neighborhood. Nonscientists generally share our perspective.	Build the biggest accelerator at least cost. Serve a maximum number of scientists. Provide maximum amenities for scientists' families. Find some added social benefits *after* site is chosen and project is built. Remain ignorant about acquisition process.
2. Congress	State delegations Joint Committee on Atomic Energy	Preserve U.S. technological and military supremacy. Spread benefits from science projects to entire country.	What's good for R&D is good for America. AEC requests are by and large good for R&D.	Lose gracefully to AEC and president. Get assurances on open housing. Reelect Paul Douglas but don't hurt

		Deal with conflict so as to minimize it. Reelect as many incumbents as possible.	Benefits from a big site are so great that local governments will want to share costs.	Pat Brown. Remain ignorant of specific "spillover effects" of site acquisition and construction.
3. President	President Johnson Science advisor	Same as 2, except reelect as many Democrats as possible.	What's good for R&D is probably good for America. AEC decisions are politically problematic. The Midwest needs and deserves help.	Guide AEC gracefully toward Chicago. Help Paul Douglas, liberal hawk. Remain ignorant of specific effects of site acquisition. Get assurances from Daley that site is desirable.
4. State of Illinois	Governor Kerner Department of Business and Economic Development	Build prestige of newly established Department of Business and Economic Development. Get the accelerator to stop the scientific brain drain. Keep the Chicago metropolitan area alive.	What's good for Illinois is good for America. What's good for science in Illinois is good for Illinois. What's good for Chicago suburbs is good for Chicago.	Get the accelerator regardless of cost. Displace the costs during the acquisition. Leave acquisition to professionals and the county. Remain ignorant of county plans.

The Real Federal System and Science Public Works—Continued

LEVEL OR LOCATION OF PARTICIPANT	RESPONSIBLE OFFICIAL OR POSITION	DEFINITION OF GENERAL RESPONSIBILITIES	LEADS TO → PERSPECTIVES	WHICH GUIDE → POLICIES
5. City of Chicago	Mayor Daley Semipublic business council	Maintain the metropolis as a viable economic region. Maintain the prestige of Chicago and its universities.	What's good for the suburbs is better than nothing for Chicago. Science public works produce valuable side effects. Science public works don't cost Chicago anything.	Use local clout on AEC via president and House delegation. Cooperate with financial community to speak with one voice. Remain ignorant of AEC plans and state and county activities regarding site acquisition and construction.
6. Chicago financial community	Area development vice-presidents	Gain and maintain a favorable competitive relation with other regions. Develop suburbs in light of downtown financial needs.	What's good for Chicago business is good for America. Science is clean industry, Chicago's highest priority.	Create pools of Ph.D.'s and other skilled people through the accelerator. Cooperate with DuPage County by (1) supporting accelerator and

		Large facilities breed more business.		(2) remaining ignorant of DuPage plans. Stay on good terms with Mayor Daley.
7. DuPage County	County board	Preserve land values. Maintain the suburban way of life. Keep government services to a minimum. Keep the city out of the suburbs.	DuPage County *is* America. Science is clean industry, which is good for DuPage County. Urban patterns are evil and unnecessary.	Eliminate the village of Weston. Create a large preserve to prevent future Westons. Use state authority and professional expertise to acquire the land. Develop other clean industry and a university in the area.
8. Farm families on the site	Individuals. Abortive ad hoc defense organizations	Enjoy life in the open country. Survive tax pressure.	What's good for farms used to be good for America. What's good for science is a threat to large tracts of land.	Oppose the accelerator. Cooperate with state and county if opposition fails.

The Real Federal System and Science Public Works—Continued

LEVEL OR LOCATION OF PARTICIPANT	RESPONSIBLE OFFICIAL OR POSITION	DEFINITION OF GENERAL RESPONSIBILITIES	PERSPECTIVES	POLICIES
9. Developers of Weston	Various corporations and dummy corporations	Make maximum profit for selves and investors. Use legal means, whenever possible. But don't investigate investors too carefully.	The metropolitan fringe is a mass of high-profit opportunities. Farm owners are about ready to throw in the towel.	Build Weston, in-corporate it, then sub-subdivide it. Cultivate an illusion of a new town.
10. Village of Weston	Village board	Build and maintain an inexpensive dream city.	What's good for science may be good for a new Weston.	Get the accelerator. Adopt open housing to prove good will. Annex land for the new town near the site. Cooperate with NAL directors.

LEADS TO → DEFINITION OF GENERAL RESPONSIBILITIES → PERSPECTIVES

WHICH GUIDE → POLICIES

How the Two Tales Become One

It is a far, far better thing we do . . .

The Washington decision makers were not in the least aware of
the local dimensions and implications of their accelerator decision.
And the physicists were probably least of all aware—of Weston,
what it meant to the villagers, what it meant to the neighboring
farmers, and what its elimination meant to the rest of the county.
The concern of the scientists for the project and the site constituted a pair of blinders. But, in a sense, each of the other participants also worked with blinders on.

The preceding table should help introduce the characters
as well as elucidate the pattern and meaning of the narrow and
isolated perspectives carried by those participants most concerned
with the accelerator. The table is a picture of a federal system
based on relationships of mutual ignorance and mutual noninterference among all the layers. Two important cases, the perspectives of the scientists and the state officials, can best illustrate in
detail the general pattern captured in the table and well documented in succeeding chapters for all the participants.

The Fellowship and the Ring

Scientists tend to make their collective decisions regarding
projects through a process they sometimes call "consensual assessment." That is, they allow themselves to be influenced rather
heavily by the status of the science leader who is pushing the
project. This is their way of personifying some fairly clear and
well-understood notions about the state of the art.

At the level of decision making on individual projects, it
would probably be very difficult to improve upon consensual
assessment, although in recent years many younger scientists have
attacked this as part of what they call the scientific establishment.
But even if consensual assessment is accepted as the best means
by which scientists make collective decisions on individual projects
—and even if they are allowed without too much opposition to
use government to ratify and implement these decisions—the

decisions are nonetheless concerned overwhelmingly with the projects themselves and not with the ramifications, the "spillover effects."

As the decision moves from whether to have the project to where the project shall be installed, for example, the real involvement of the scientists drops off precipitously. As the criteria become softer and more political, the scientist tends to wash his hands. Or if he participates, his participation begins to resemble that of any interested lay citizen.

Regarding Weston, there seems to have been widespread scientific consensus that a 200-bev accelerator ought to be built—although the man who ultimately became the NAL director had at an earlier point pushed for a cheaper and smaller variant. There also seems to have been consensus on the hard criteria governing site selection. However, the scientists' soft criteria left open a vast area of discretion, first because these soft criteria were concerned only about amenities for scientists and their families, and, second, because no criteria, hard or soft, were concerned with broader social values that might be affected by a scientific facility of such size and expense. In effect, the scientists were saying, "Give us our site, but don't tell us how you got it."

The State, the Site, and the Strength of Illusion

The State of Illinois, to serve its citizens in the Chicago area, came out of the site competition with a very costly commitment, a commitment far in excess of original plans. During the course of the competition the land commitment moved from 3,000 to 5,000 to 6,800 acres. And the specifications escalated from an undefined tract with water and utilities to a built-up area with dozens of houses ready for immediate occupancy by AEC-NAL employees.

To carry out these commitments, the Illinois Department of Business and Economic Development (DBED) received $30 million from the state legislature, a sum far below the obvious value of the farms alone, much less the village of Weston. This meant that the DBED would have to set artificially low limits on acquisition prices. There was, however, a way to smooth the skids. The Weston villagers could be fed a diet of hope and the illusions of selfish gain.

Over half the Westoners accepted the village's accelerator candidacy with elation. Another segment felt mildly positive or apathetic, and only a scant few were doubtful or opposed to it. This reaction was based on an expectation that the village facilities and houses would be physically moved to a neighboring tract of land that was already being annexed by the newly incorporated village. The Weston developers were going to spend over $50,000 to plan a new town.

State and federal officials did little, if anything, in public to dispel that illusion. Privately, DBED officials vowed there would be no new town as defined by the villagers. Even the scientists opposed it; to them it would look too much like a compound. But publicly all of them were more evasive. Indeed, Governor Kerner at one point gave the distinct impression that there would be a new Weston. Publicly, no one denied it.

Cultivation of this illusion was the only way the Weston site could have been selected and acquired. The locals would have to be for the accelerator or the AEC might well choose some other spot, perhaps outside Illinois altogether. Ultimately the farmers worried about the potential impact of a site, but the Westoners themselves gave the distinct impression that there was enthusiastic consensus for it. As a result, Weston was up, and Barrington, the second possible Illinois site for the accelerator, was down. In most respects, Barrington was a far more desirable location, in terms of the status of the residents, the proximity to the city and the airport, and the general look of the housing. But when a few leading spokesmen went to Springfield to object for Barrington, the state and the AEC agreed to withdraw Barrington's candidacy.

Eventually the locals would find that their plans for a new town were based on false assumptions. But by the time they did, the site had been committed and the villagers and farmers had too little time or knowledge to organize opposition to the site or to the acquisitions under eminent domain. Having kept the property holders divided and confused, the state then sent in its appraisers and negotiators with powers that are almost unique in the history of eminent domain proceedings in Illinois. Through eminent domain—the power to take private property for a public purpose—billions of dollars' worth of property have been transferred to public agencies for highways, utilities, urban redevelopment, and so on and so forth. Constitutions require that "just compensation" be rendered, and this generally has come to mean "fair market value." However, 6,800 acres of metropolitan land, housing, and public facilities for $30 million is not market value. In any case, whenever transactions are made under duress, fair market value is a myth.

Later documentation will show how the state carried off this coup. The important point here is that it was carried off zealously and sincerely in pursuit of the public interest. State officials defined their responsibility solely in terms of Illinois' commitment to the AEC. To them it was unnecessary to know the AEC position, which was, as one AEC official put it, to "take what we could get." Indeed, that was the AEC way of sincerely fulfilling its own responsibilities. Nor was it necessary for the state officials to know the motives of the county. Delivery of 6,800 acres, despite a heavy reduction of the tax rolls, was the county's way of carrying out what it saw as its obligation to county citizens.

So, indeed, it goes through all the participants. Preservation of America's strategic atomic supremacy by authorizing the project was Congress's job. Implementation of the entire matter belonged to agents of Congress and could be as remote from Congress as Congress wished. Each of the other participants worked about the same way, by pushing the implications of their acts off as someone else's responsibility. For each official, responsibility meant fulfillment of obligations to serve his clientele. That defined the public interest, without looking at responsibility in terms of some larger whole.

This, it seems to us, is a route to poliscide on a national scale. Corruption and incompetence are far less likely to do it. Selfishness is far less efficient. Poliscide can best be done through zealous pursuit of the public interest. Sincere and competent people—and nearly all the participants in the Weston story were sincere and competent—are not necessarily fit to serve the public. "Public-regardingness," however desirable, is not statecraft. Power corrupts; specialization of power, zealously applied along specialized lines, corrupts absolutely.

The story of Weston reveals a great deal about the requirements of proper exercise of power. It is a case of how public good can be accidental whereas the bad can be virtually foreordained. It is an illustration of how institutions can be the enemy of rational men of good will, because it is a story of how such rational men of good will were led, by their own responsibilities, to abuse public authority or to allow for its abuse on their behalf.

PART I

Science–The Politics
of Public Works

Federal Government and Science as a Social Problem

The metropolitan fringe is America's most recent last frontier. Society can shape its own future only where substantial options are available, and most of the major options in the last third of the twentieth century are in the expanding outer circle of the suburbs. The pattern and promise of development in the metropolis tend to contradict an old and respected geopolitical principle. In the metropolis, it must now be said that whoever holds the fringe will ultimately control the heartland. The stakes are tremendously high, the political struggle correspondingly intense. Politics at the fringe of the metropolis is not normal politics. It is a politics of conquest.

Conquest, like war, justifies strategies and methods that would, under conditions of normal politics, be considered undemocratic and unfair. These methods might be employed in normal politics, but they would be indirect, hidden, covert; and, after the fact, the participants would tend to deny the involvement of these noncompromise strategies. They tend even to deny that the other side resorts to such methods, in a silent conspiracy to maintain the myth of compromise politics, and in a tacit agreement not to contribute to each other's embarrassment. In contrast, for example, during and after the fight over Weston every participant was frank and open about his own role and usually dispassionate about the parts played by others. There was nothing to be ashamed of. Everyone was doing his duty as he saw it. Everyone was a good guy. It is the sincerity and zeal of all parties that makes the entire story so fascinating. It is that same intensity, pride, and zeal that exposes for any observer a virtually total record of events.

The real problem of distortion, therefore, comes not from poor documentation but from the superabundance of good information that requires cutting, simplification, and organization. Nevertheless, it is compellingly clear that the many fundamental issues raised by the story, the many fundamental political patterns on which the story throws bright light, can be brought most meaningfully together within three easy-to-define areas.

The first of these is the politics of building the metropolis. Society will rise or fall on it, and Weston suggests some ways that politics will contribute to the one or the other.

Second, the cases lead to some lasting insights into the politics of large contemporary government in general and of large federal systems in particular. We will continue to be optimistic but will nevertheless always wonder whether a federal government can keep itself viable in face of such national problems as modern technology, warfare, conglomerate capitalism, and race and class conflict. We wonder if government does not produce more of today's problems than it solves. And we hope to maintain our optimism in some small way precisely by defining federalism as a social problem that needs attention for its own sake.

The third area is the politics of science, or scientists. We wonder with increasing intensity about what the role of scientists will be in the government and politics of the future. And we ponder with abiding puzzlement why such good men with such extraordinary powers of analysis seem to bring us no further than lay politicians along the road toward just rule.

Metro Building and the Viability of Vestigial Organs

As social scientists bringing urban, national, and international orientations to this project, we were jolted by our rediscovery of county government and how much it can influence the development of the metropolis. Considered an anachronism and almost totally neglected in contemporary political writing, the county government seems always to have been strong in many rural areas and is finding its own peculiar kind of renaissance as suburban sprawl obliterates the rural. Even where strong and up to date, rural county governments are almost universally more conservative than their urban and suburban cousins; and this is particularly ironic and troublesome because of the frequency with which these old-fashioned institutions and points of view can dominate the new and dynamic developments out at the metropolitan fringe. The politics of conquering open country and converting it to suburb involves basic conflicts of cultures.

The rise and fall of the village of Weston is perhaps more than anything else a story of efforts to mix different types of people who ultimately do not mix. The confrontation was not between people of different races or classes. It was a confrontation of competing models of community life—the urban, the suburban, the small town, the rural, and the exurban. Each model was very real for those who held it; either it already existed as a reality, or it was an ardently sought-after ideal.

The intrusion of the Weston development reveals an ugly struggle among these models for domination. Competing ideals became the basis for an intense power struggle. This competition among persons holding very different models is a good route to understanding fully the role played by major influentials and ultimately by public authority. No small victories were sought. There was no question here of normal competition and peaceful bargaining among persons willing to adjust to incremental differences of opinion and demands. A whole way of life appeared to be at stake. This was not the kind of politics described in contemporary studies of stable democratic, pluralistic orders. Because it was a politics of conquest there was ultimately no way to avoid bringing the direct, coercive powers of government into play. Coexistence seemed out of the question. These odds favored the suburban model; it won out, and in the process obliterated the rural and urban models around it.

Perhaps the suburban model is, according to the hackneyed phrases of the determinists, the wave of the future, or with the grain of history. Certainly it is a very fashionable model in our day. Nevertheless, in the Weston area it did not win out by a natural process of development or through the accepted processes of bargaining. It won out because county government officials in the area, helped by state and central city interests, came to concern themselves with the future of the fringe, saw the issue as a serious confrontation, and conquered competing models by committing themselves to using every available mechanism of public control to help the suburban model in its conquest of the fringe.

The county government was, of course, influenced by many processes, many forces, and many powerful interests. But *direct* power to resolve issues of conquest among the alternative models of community life resided solely with the county board. Actually, little direct play of power and influence had to be exercised on the board. The county board members and their agents were good suburbanites. They had not only come to share the suburban model by and large, but more importantly they defined their public responsibilities in those terms. The public interest required the particular uses of governmental power we shall observe. In a very important sense, the influence of the suburbanites, the financial interests, the commuting executives, and so on was working *in* rather than *on* the members of the board.

The official commitment against Weston, and ultimately against the farmers in that area, was probably natural and inevitable. It was there before the decision to build the accelerator in the area; the accelerator simply made conquest feasible and antagonistic county government involvement justifiable.

Our studies indicate the impressive array of powers available to the county board and the manner in which they can be used. Powers over zoning, powers over incorporation, powers over certain essential services, powers regarding health and construction codes constitute a formidable list of opportunities for those who have the position and the inclination to use them. These are powers that can be directly and coercively exercised over persons and property. They are also powers that can encourage or prevent private initiatives. This gives the suburban county official a far greater influence over his territory than any other type of power holder has, even including the infamous "economic influentials" operating out of the central city. We can admit that such influentials as the corporate heads of the major utilities, the major banks, and the major newspapers are formidable. But in no way does this detract from the still more formidable, yet less appreciated, power of the county board.

It is through its formal powers that the county has shaped and continues to shape the new metropolitan frontier. DuPage County failed to prevent the development of Weston, and that failure threatened to bring on a highly undesirable urbanization of part, if not all, of the fringe. But the county lost only a few early skirmishes, not the war. The county succeeded in delaying the growth of Weston until the developers were in deep trouble and until Weston's troubles conveyed a poor impression. The county ultimately won the war because it had the power to fulfill its own prophecies regarding the character of urbanized land.

Evaluation of metrobuilding would of course be incomplete without consideration of state government, because county government is, after all, a unit of state government. But our studies suggest that more often than not it is a case of tail wagging dog. The power of the state of Illinois seems so often to amount to little more than the power to embrace local values and local demands. No effort was made to counteract or counterbalance the obvious direction in which DuPage County was going. On the contrary, the state officials viewed county plans as overwhelmingly consistent with state needs and central city needs.

As a result, the state lent to the county the additional powers and resources the county needed to carry out its Weston policy, eradication. Examples abound in later chapters.

Nevertheless, it should be added that, even when in the act of slavishly tending goal for the counties, the state proves how formidable and effective it can be. The state government in our federal system offers opportunities for effective control and change rarely realized, especially in the past half century. As the Weston case amply illustrates, the problem is not the lack of power; the problem is attributable to an unfortunate interpretation of the ideal of local self-government, an interpretation that has led state officials to see their sacred responsibility as one of embracing local values, especially the deeply conservative values of old-line members of county boards and new main-line executives who use the suburban fringe as a bedroom, country club, and bridle path.

Policy makers have an awesome task. They must play Plato. They must carry to each decision a vision of a very much larger ideal. If they do not, someone else will, and when someone else does public powers are being wielded irresponsibly. This is the basic problem raised by the patterns and practices of carrying out the accelerator project. Smaller units of government, like interest groups, cannot take fully into account the consequences of their own actions. A context larger than themselves must be involved, and a full balancing of all spillover effects, negative and positive, must eventually be made at more inclusive levels of government. This is the farthest cry from servile embrace of local actions. Precisely this consideration is what makes federal government seem so systematically remiss in the literally thousands of policy issues like Weston. It is not county governments that are anachronistic; their resources, powers, and organizations are commensurate to contemporary tasks. It is the national view of the allocation of functions that is anachronistic. National policy decisions that simply express a sentiment and then appropriate some money on behalf of that sentiment are inevitably going to be implemented farther and farther down the line, farther and farther away from original intentions. This kind of permissive, open-ended delegation of power empties into state and local tributaries where directions are determined by local pilots. It is a tragedy that so many grand national schemes have become local failures because of the opportunities for local subversion offered by vague federal enabling legislation. The Weston decision is a significant case in point.

Let us emphasize the situation this way: if the decision makers in this case had been offered the Weston results as a series of propositions on a referendum, they would almost surely have voted most of the propositions down. This is no paradox. It is built into the way Washington makes policy; it is built into the national policy approach to federalism. Thus the value judgments we have brought in to criticize the major participants and the processes of policy making and implementation are largely those of the national policy makers themselves. This gives us a fair basis for judgments; it also enables us to assess the extent to which institutions and processes may interfere with the best men and the best intentions.

Divided We Stand

Federalism in the United States has become responsibility's escape route. Because of the federal structure of government and the institutional consequences that flow directly from that federal structure, when federal policies are carried out by those with local responsibilities, the policies become, as Swift would put it, "but a ball bandied to and fro, and every man carries a racquet about him to strike it from himself among the rest of the company."

In a federal system, several layers—not merely two layers—are interposed between national goals and local implementation. As a result of the autonomy of the states, American cities and counties also come to have more autonomy than most of their European counterparts. Local traditions, local interests, and local political parties spring up to reinforce local idiosyncracies, and all of this provides most of our localities with a healthy lust for independence. Cities, even small towns, develop a great deal of "home rule" even when it is not granted in a state constitution.

To these layerings must be added the federal structure within many of the most important administrative agencies. The Army Corps of Engineers, the Forest Service, the Soil Conservation Service, the Extension Service, most of the welfare agencies, and virtually all of the Housing and Urban Development agencies are examples of federal bureaucracies deliberately built to parallel federal, state, and local principalities. To this structure are usually added a policy and a tradition of cooperation between the locally installed federal agents and the local interests. The AEC merely aped these patterns in the Weston project.

This presents a very peculiar and very significant spectacle. The true picture departs very far from the formal model of federalism. But the true picture also departs from more recently established formulations of federal reality, such as the idea of the "marble cake" and the sharing of functions formulated by Morton Grodzins. These notions suggest a more natural interdependence and a happier outcome than reality will support. The typical case, and that includes the building of the accelerator, is one in which the federal government authorizes a project or an activity and then leaves all of the details to the personnel in the field and to the local officials and interests concerned with that activity or project.

And in these instances, as all of our cases show in various ways, the relationships among the layers are relationships of mutual noninterference and mutual ignorance. The outcome of this is one in which the periphery usually exploits the center.

Having layer after layer of official responsibility is tantamount to the multiplication of access points and opportunities for influence. Indeed, this guarantees local variation in national programs that, on principle, may sound extremely attractive. This euphoric condition is expressed in such rhetoric as "putting power close to the people" on the left and "states' rights" on the right. But what is close to the people? What kinds of people and purposes does this kind of government actually come close to? One of the major sources of illegitimacy in our country is a lack of congruence between nationally expressed commitments and locally implemented practices. The more levels of government there are between the point of decision and the point of implementation, the greater the likelihood of incongruence between intention and result, *unless the intention is spelled out in some fairly clear guidelines*. Federal officials are probably closer to the people than most state and local officials. The typical citizen can name his congressman well before he can name his state senator or county board member. Remoteness is something that develops wherever the representative gives away his powers to a long line of unknown and irresponsible agents. They end up making the real decisions in their own way, and their physical proximity matters little if their authority to make the decision came very indirectly from a long chain of unguided delegations and subdelegations. There is probably a Malthusian principle involved here: as the subdelegations increase arithmetically, the actual distance between government and citizen increases geometrically.

The accelerator project presents a just illustration of this problem. The appropriation of vast sums of federal revenue for pure science has at its foundation the faith that pure science serves national interests. But the federal government has other policy commitments that will also be served by the construction of so large a facility as the National Accelerator Laboratory. When policy makers remained silent as to how the project would serve those other commitments, this did not mean neutrality. It meant that the lower-line officials would be free to use the project money to pursue their own commitments instead. These commitments could simply be irrelevant to such national policies as aggregate growth, racial integration, environmental protection, health, and the redistribution of wealth. But these local commitments could also be in opposition to national goals and yet would still be directly under federal sponsorship.

The national policy makers involved in this case were all honorable and sincere people, dedicated to an honorable job and cause. Yet if the outcome was in so many respects contrary to their own values and to national social priorities—if they would actually have voted against these outcomes in a referendum—then something is quite evidently wrong with the institutions and practices of policy making that intervene between power holders and power users.

Federal Government and Science:
From Panacea to Problem

Americans have tended to look at science as the New Providence. In a period of crisis, when the established bases of confidence have been shaken, government may, through science, build the archway through which we shall escape into the twenty-first century.

Europeans such as C. P. Snow tend to be much more pessimistic. They concern themselves with such problems as the "two cultures," scientists and laymen, much as Americans tend to be concerned about the "two nations," white and black. Americans have hardly begun to develop appropriate concepts for dealing with science or technology as a social problem.

A casual review of almost any federal or state science advisory commission report will convey some sense of how Americans view the intermingling of government and science. The attitude can be characterized for its optimism, its trust, its faith, and its confidence.

Americans are optimistic that science, pure and applied, means progress. To reduce public support before all of the logical implications of a piece of research have been exhausted constitutes a veritable infringement on the civil liberties of scientists and also an irrational submaximal use of national resources.

The emerging American ideology toward science is also characterized by trust in the view that science is efficient and efficacious wherever it is applied. That is to say, science is always worth doing; it is always worth the cost. Science not only provides the shortest distance between two points but also establishes the means by which to determine what points ought to be connected. And this trust in science is combined with a faith in scientists, a faith that scientists are always independent, disinterested, and perhaps even omnicompetent.

Finally, science helps perpetuate the traditional American confidence that the future is always manageable. Scientific method and scientific research can always provide the One Best Way to answer "What is to be done?" whether the question is asked by Lenin or by the president of the United States.

This optimistic outlook has a great deal of documented support. American history is full of experience with using science as a spectacularly successful instrument for public good. However, in recent years the rate and scale of expansion of government R and D appropriations have created an entirely new terrain and an entirely new set of problems. It is not merely that the R and D budget has expanded over the years. Of at least equal significance is the fact that so many individual items on that budget are reaching a scale that has a social significance totally independent of and beyond the gross R and D budget or the potential research findings. Even when a strong scientific and social case can be made for a given project, the size of the public works necessary to carry out the project makes it a problem in and of itself because it becomes a significant community variable in and of itself.

It is this conjunction of science and government in large-scale projects that has made science a social problem. We neither began nor completed our inquiry with any antagonism to science or scientists. Quite the contrary. Nevertheless, we felt the logic of the situation forced us to ask whether the scientist has introduced anything more than merely a new industry and a new interest into our system. We had to ask whether his paraphernalia of systematic methodology and complex information technology constituted a new kind of decision-making process. Indeed, given the large potential impact on communities, we had to ask whether the scientist can play at Plato any better than other kinds of decision makers.

We also wanted to ask these questions because even the most tentative of answers would give us some insights into the future of politics in large industrial countries. Will scientists and scientific approaches to decision making lead us to a better political process? Will the policy outcome of such a process be any better than that of their predecessors?

Our work on one major science project constrains us to answer these questions almost entirely negatively. Science, taken as a complex social process, does not offer a One Best Way to anything in particular. The neutrality of science toward the context of its own activities merely makes it capable of serving any master. Its intellectual objectivity enriches it as a discipline; but its policy neutrality helps make it the kind of social problem it has become.

In the case of the accelerator, the scientists got their site. They got a very favorable location for it, and they got it at a very cheap price. No one ever seriously opposed them, and the project will be popular among most of the residents who continue to live in the area.

But it was only after the project and site were settled that the project scientists became seriously concerned with the human and community impact of their presence in the metropolitan fringe. This concern was strong, and it grew, but only after the commitments were made and the size and character of the project had been determined. And their efforts seemed almost totally dedicated to maintaining and enhancing the suburban, upper-middle-class white patterns to which the local authorities and influentials were already overwhelmingly committed.

For instance, plans for collaboration between the accelerator people and the local communities include the development of a new college. This will require the acquisition of new land west of the accelerator, land that had once been defined as impossible to acquire for the accelerator site. Lack of access to this western land had been one of the reasons given for acquisition in the more easterly direction, including Weston. Also, the accelerator plan put the main gate on the west—turned away from the city of Chicago. This symbolizes the relationships the scientists apparently plan to develop in the area.

Completely without legal authority, the accelerator builders have removed every legal reference to Weston. This includes changing the names of all of the village streets and switching the post office relationship from West Chicago to the somewhat more prestigious Batavia. Humane planning for community impact also included a model farm, a Disneyland type of farm replica where nothing is really produced, on a section of site property that was never really needed for science. And on that farm there will be a small herd of buffalo. It will serve to teach the children about the eternal heritage of the American way of life.

The story of Weston—the National Accelerator Laboratory— does not suggest a favorable outlook for a government dominated by science, science projects, and scientists. We say this not because we find ourselves and our political society worse off as a result of science and such science activities as the accelerator. We say it because we find political society no better off.

The problems of government seem to transcend the social types and skills that comprise each governing elite. Styles of politics change. People change. Agendas change, with new problems or with new priorities among the old problems. But in pursuit of those problems there are always the higher-order problems of how that pursuit will advance justice, whether it will introduce significant change, and how much it will keep elites responsible and in circulation. These problems have always been just beyond reach—of the old bourgeois elites, the pluralistic influence brokers, the professionals, the bureaucrats, and the new minority representatives; and they will also be beyond the reach of the new and future scientific elites.

Our inquiries suggest that the real problem is not with people, communities, or scientists but with policy and public institutions. Can we arrange our political and governmental structure in any way to bring out the best in our officials and influentials? Are there ways we can institutionalize a broader view? Is there a way to throw the many parochialisms together into a larger perspective— or at least into a smaller number of broader parochialisms? In brief, can big governments really govern, or are we doomed to see government, even in an age of rationality, submerged, totally without positive moral significance, into the natural environment?

2 **Disorder in the**
Scientific Establishment

Although the United States has had a self-conscious science fraternity since the late eighteenth century, the government-science "establishment" is a mere 30 years old.[1] And only the threat of World War II brought it into being. The traditional pattern of American science had been private autonomy, jealously guarded.

Yet the break with tradition was initiated by the scientists themselves. The establishment, an informal designation for a true, nationwide institution, was designed by science leadership. The construction of the physical and the social structure of the establishment was supervised in almost every detail by science leaders. The scientific establishment is the first "complex" in American national government. It precedes the military-industrial complex by more than a decade. The government-scientific complex was an impressive and, given the goals of scientists, successful achievement.

Nevertheless, it is probable that few scientists were ever altogether happy with science gone public. Although the relationship between them and the government became stable, prosperous, and productive, it was all the same characterized by ambivalence. The pre–World War II fear of government had never entirely disappeared.

This ambivalence is expressed with particular clarity in the formal structure itself, especially in that most sensitive and aristo-cratic of science areas, high-energy physics. The independent com-mission (Atomic Energy Commission) was the chosen device. And, though the hat was doffed in the direction of the problem of military secrecy, the AEC was a comfortable base of operations for scientists in government and scientists working through govern-ment. Physicists in particular were able to enjoy the amenities and the autonomy usually reserved for the university and certain private enterprises while at the same time being amply financed out of public revenues.

Another expression of their ambivalence, resolved in favor of scientists, was the contractor system, a method by which the gov-ernment could extend help and receive help without involving direct absorption into government of a large number of science Ph.D.'s. Scientists protected themselves still further by laboriously developing an elaborate and cumbersome advisory system, whereby committees of scientists determined who among their own com-pany would receive government favor.

The reasons for ambivalence are apparent even to non-scientists. For one thing, the scientists might occasionally have to justify the projects they wished to undertake, and this could come perilously close to telling little white lies or, worse, sincerely play-ing to popular expectations about practicality. There was indeed the possibility of direct government intervention in terms of the kinds of projects that would be approved; there was even the possibility of direct government imposition of certain projects as conditions for government support. But long before such drastic outcomes, and even if such intervention never came to pass, there was always the more general fear about the possibility of *politicization*.

All during more than a decade after the war the scientific establishment, especially the high-energy physics wing, was both dynamic and stable. It was dynamic in the amount of work and the tremendous innovations taking place, yet it was stable in terms of the sources of support, government and community attitudes, and scientific morale. Was it possible that the ambivalent scientists had been unduly pessimistic?

Quite the contrary. The seeds of disorder had in fact been planted from the beginning but had never taken root and sprouted because most of the nutrients for disorder had been temporarily diverted by expansion. When any scientist felt himself, his university, or his region to be inequitably treated, he always had the prospect of some satisfaction, even if not full redress, in the next round of allocations. The history of high-energy physics throughout the postwar decade and beyond was a history of growth, careful balancing of conflicting interests, and restoration of equilibrium.

For some very good reasons, the Midwest scientists finally broke this equilibrium, introduced something of a critical moment in the history of the scientific establishment, and contributed to the realization of most of the old fears about government involvement in the scientific community. The Weston accelerator is as much a product of politicization as it is a product of the logic and dictates of the next step in high-energy physics research. Weston was an effort to restore equilibrium, yet there could never again be complete confidence that any equilibrium could last for very long.

The concerned Midwest scientists had organized themselves into an interest group—one might even say a pressure group in the classic sense. This converted science policy making into an entirely new kind of game.

Whether the new game involves greater irrationalities than the old is a vital question in the future of American politics. The Weston accelerator story is an opening glance into that future. The Midwest scientists did not operate for very long as a pressure group; and they are not the central characters in the larger Weston story. But without their actions the story might otherwise have remained, like many other science policy decisions, the private property of the science establishment.

Background of the Accelerator: Politicization

Herbert Hoover estimated that throughout the nation's history applied research had received $200 million in support, but pure science had received only $10 million *from all sources,* both public and private.[2] Two major reasons seem to account for this situation: first, pure scientists refused government financial support for fear of political entanglements that might have compromised their freedom of scientific inquiry; second, government was uninterested in supporting "unproductive" pure science, especially in the laissez-faire heyday.

Scientists feared potential private support almost as deeply as government "interference." For example, at the turn of the century the near-bankrupt Woods Hole Marine Laboratory refused grants from the Carnegie Corporation and the University of Chicago in order to protect its intellectual integrity. Almost 50 years later this incident was still proudly related to the National Academy of Sciences (NAS) as an example of the properly prudent attitude of scientists fearful of domination.[3]

Unlike the scientists, government was not chary of entanglement—it was simply not interested. During the massive mobilization for World War I, government decided, almost as an afterthought, that perhaps the effort should include one scientist. Thomas Edison, not surprisingly, was the scientist of choice.[4]

However, by the middle of this century an impressive reversal had taken place in the positions of both government and scientists. This reversal was caused by preparation for World War II and was instigated by the scientists. It began in the ranks of what was, at the time, perhaps the least practical of all the sciences, particle physics. The support was warranted, the physicists said, because they would apply their knowledge of pure science to the creation of a new, cataclysmic weapon: the atomic bomb.

The government was, at first, not receptive to the scientists' dream. President Roosevelt created the Briggs Committee to study the proposal, and the committee was hardly enthusiastic. In 1939, it recommended budgeting only $6,000 for 1940 to study the possibility of building an atomic bomb.[5] If left to the Briggs Committee, scientists feared, the necessary applied research would not be carried forward.

Physical scientists continued to press their proposal, and in 1939 Vannevar Bush, a prominent scientific research administrator, convinced Roosevelt to push the project forward. The eagerness the scientists displayed did not imply that they had lost their fears of government domination. On the contrary, Bush sought to allay these fears by requesting of Roosevelt that the government guarantee the scientists both support and autonomy. Roosevelt agreed to create the National Defense Research Committee (NDRC) composed of civilian scientists responsible for developing the atomic bomb, and he allowed them to decide how, where, and by whom funds were to be spent and whether or not it was necessary to spend funds for "pure" research.

From Laissez-Faire to Bureaucratic Energy:
Plus AEC, JCAE

After much postwar congressional and scientific discord, Congress, in 1946, finally established a governmental mechanism to regulate the production and use of atomic energy. The AEC was composed of five members, appointed by the president with the advice and consent of the Senate, and was given responsibility for organizing and supervising the nation's atomic energy program. The AEC also assumed a variety of regulatory and quasi-judicial controls over the private development of atomic energy, which was included under its jurisdiction.

Throughout its history, the AEC has been unique among federal agencies in the extent to which it has depended on various public and private contractors for the performance of its functions. All of its major laboratories, such as Brookhaven and Los Alamos, have been operated on a contractual basis by outside organizations. Probably the most significant factor in the adoption of this policy was the attitudes and experiences of the scientists involved in the early development of nuclear energy and the atomic bomb during the wartime Manhattan Project. The strict secrecy requirements that the army imposed on scientists involved in the Manhattan Project revived and exacerbated the scientists' antagonisms against governmental controls. However, the policy of contracting out operations to private organizations enabled the AEC not only to blur the appearances of government control but also to circumvent the strictures of federal civil service requirements. Thus the AEC ostensibly enabled high-energy physicists to retain their professional autonomy while the taxpayers footed the bill.

After much debate, Congress elected to invest control of the atomic energy program in civilian rather than military hands. But the AEC's enabling legislation reflects the intense military-civilian debate and the eventual compromise: both a General Advisory Committee (GAC), composed of civilian scientists, and a seven-member Military Liaison Committee, composed of representatives of the military services, were provided.

The Military Liaison Committee has played a quiet but important role in the AEC's activities, whereas the GAC has had a more turbulent history. During its first 4 years, when the GAC was composed of several of the nation's most eminent scientists and chaired by physicist J. Robert Oppenheimer, several observers concluded that it actually dominated the AEC's decision making.[6] In 1951, its influence in AEC affairs began to decline, after the AEC's first chairman, David Lilienthal—a strong supporter of the scientists—resigned, and the president rejected the GAC's advice not to proceed immediately with the development of the hydrogen bomb. But during its formative years civilian scientists in large measure determined the formula by which exciting projects could be explored by scientists, who remained virtually autonomous in all ways but financial.

The JCAE: The Institutionalization of Congressional Influence

The second major institutional participant in the development of atomic energy policy has been the Joint Committee for Atomic Energy (JCAE), a unique body. Authorized by the Atomic Energy Act of 1946, the JCAE is one of the few congressional committees established by statute; and it has been the most powerful and influential of the few joint House-Senate committees.[7]

At the outset, the JCAE was interested primarily in the AEC's internal security, and so was constantly at odds with the liberal methods of AEC Chairman Lilienthal. Moreover, the secrecy and complexity of the AEC's work made it difficult for the congressmen to grasp the implications of developments in this field, and the cold war atmosphere of the early 1950s prompted the JCAE to deny itself information about atomic energy that the AEC offered to share with it.[8] As a result, the JCAE initially was not as influential as the GAC in determining AEC policy.

This same cold war atmosphere, however, prompted the JCAE to urge the development of the hydrogen bomb, a position opposed by the GAC but supported by the president. Following this initial success, the GAC fell from grace, whereas the JCAE continued to expand its influence by taking the lead in urging the establishment of a second major weapons laboratory, which was later built at Livermore, California. Since then, the JCAE has taken the lead in urging—and in some instances virtually forcing—upon the AEC such major programs as the development of nuclear-powered submarines and nuclear electric generating plants, the Antarctic reactor program, and the futile but expensive efforts to develop an atomic airplane.[9]

Thanks to JCAE's bold embrace of atomic expansionism, and thanks to Congress's deference to JCAE, AEC has only rarely found itself inhibited by lack of support or funds. It has rarely been restrained in its military programs, and the only significant budgetary restraints placed on its civilian programs have come from the Bureau of the Budget and the president rather than Congress.

Responsibility for the formulation of atomic policy has, through this process, come to be a responsibility shared by the AEC and the JCAE, to a degree probably never matched by any other committee-agency alliance. Their relationship still rests on power, but generally the two agencies have drawn strength from each other. AEC has the statutory responsibility, the public recognition, the expertise, the support of the larger science community, and so on. But JCAE has its own formidable resources. Members of the JCAE tend to attribute their nearly unique role in the policy process to the stability of membership on the committee.

Symbiosis has almost always characterized the relationship between AEC and JCAE. Splits within each and differences between them have never occurred with respect to the important things in their lives. Their relationship can stop scientists, stop presidents, and stump Congress. Their relationship is the context within which almost all matters of science and government can best be understood. But this is especially the case in the field of high-energy physics.

Jockeying for Position: The East-West Cyclotron Cycle

While Congress was debating exactly how the government should support postwar science, General Leslie Groves, military commander of the Manhattan Project, poured leftover war money into basic research, as well as into the weapons program. Scientists and laboratories involved in the Manhattan Project benefited most from his grants, which more than any other single force determined the regional and institutional configurations of high-energy physics for the next two decades.

Four months after Japan surrendered, Ernest O. Lawrence, head of the Berkeley Radiation Laboratory, the prewar pioneer center for particle physics, was pledged $170,000 by General Groves to continue construction of the 184-inch, 200 million electron volt (mev) synchrocyclotron that Lawrence had begun before the war.[10] At the time, it was the world's most powerful accelerator, and it permitted Lawrence and the University of California to dominate this most spectacular branch of physics.

That high-energy physics might become dominated by the West Coast was intolerable to I. I. Rabi, the Nobel laureate from Columbia and the number two man at the M.I.T. Radar Center during the war. The war had already cost Columbia Enrico Fermi, who had been lured to Chicago by Arthur Compton; and with Fermi had gone Columbia's unchallenged prewar preeminence in physics.

Rabi acted quickly to capture some of the dwindling Manhattan Project funds. He organized nine Eastern universities including Harvard, M.I.T., and Princeton into a consortium called Associated Universities, Incorporated (AUI). After some discussion, the AUI decided to locate its cooperative facility, Brookhaven National Laboratory, at the army's abandoned Camp Upton site on Long Island. Here government land was unoccupied, and buildings existed that could be utilized cheaply and quickly. Shortly thereafter, General Groves authorized a grant of $9.4 million for the construction of a 3 billion electron volt (bev) proton accelerator. The "Cosmotron," as it was called, was completed 4 years later, in 1952.[11]

The same friendly but animated coastal competition that had inspired I. I. Rabi to organize the AUI to build Brookhaven continued to exist between Berkeley and Brookhaven. These two laboratories became the mainstays of America's high-energy physics program.

This was the cyclotron cycle. Berkeley and Brookhaven were rewarded with new machines in alternating pattern. First was the Cosmotron, built for Brookhaven by General Groves. Then there was the 6.2-bev "Bevatron" built for Berkeley by the AEC. Next the AEC turned responsibility for the 33-bev machine over to Brookhaven for construction toward the end of the 1950s.

The AEC did not deliberately deprive the Midwest of such

facilities after the war. Argonne Laboratories, one of the Manhattan Project facilities in the Chicago area, had concentrated on the development of reactors for the production of plutonium during the war, and afterward it was designated a National Laboratory by the AEC to continue in its primary mission. The AEC selected the University of Chicago to manage the facility, and Argonne was given $5 million to carry out this useful but scientifically unexciting task.[12] It did not receive pure science research funds. Because the AEC's primary purpose, as set forth in its enabling legislation, was to develop peaceful and military applications for atomic energy, it sought to develop specific uses for the atom rather than foster pure research into its structural components Argonne's assignment achieved a major AEC goal and made construction of another AEC facility in the Midwest unnecessary.

The Midwest's recourse was to follow the Rabi example, with a vengeance. In 1953, a total of 15 Midwestern universities joined together to form a consortium, patterned after Rabi's AUI, with the express purpose of designing and building a particle accelerator in the Midwest.[13] The Midwest version was similar in form only. Ultimately the purpose and result would prove to be very different.

The new consortium, Midwestern Universities Research Association (MURA), was headquartered in Madison, Wisconsin, not in Chicago. The member universities and their physicists had been at loggerheads with the management of Argonne since the war ended. As a *national facility*, Argonne was to provide access to qualified researchers from all over the country, but it was believed that the Argonne management did not equitably allocate machine time between its resident and nonresident users. There were also long-standing nonscientific antagonisms between the University of Chicago and other Midwestern universities. Moreover, the fact that the University of Chicago received $2 million in fees to administer Argonne did not ease tensions or feelings of discrimination at the other universities in the region. Nevertheless, the University of Chicago, with its strong physical sciences programs and outstanding physics faculty, was asked to be one of the original 15 MURA members.

Because the Berkeley and Brookhaven accelerators were designed to maximize energy (that is, the speed at which the particles were accelerated), MURA scientists began work on a design that emphasized intensity (the number of particles accelerated per second) and that had a relatively low energy factor. A year after its founding, the efforts of MURA received support from the National Science Foundation and the AEC for design work. It was expected that when the design problems were resolved the AEC would build the new machine, placing it in Madison, Wisconsin.

It was clear to MURA as of 1955 that the cyclotron cycle had to be broken. American scientists, at the Geneva Conference on the Peaceful Uses of Atomic Energy, learned of a new 10-bev accelerator being constructed at Dubna, USSR. The disturbing reports that Russia would soon have the world's largest accelerator and, with it, the lead in high-energy physics were substantiated when American physicists visited Dubna in 1956. High-energy physics has no known direct utilitarian application, but American scientists were troubled over the imminent loss of their pre-eminent position in a prestigious field. The public might be, too.

To meet the Russian challenge as quickly as possible, AEC first decided to resolve the problems of readiness and supersaturation by authorizing in early 1956 construction of two accelerators. The first, the FFAG, MURA's baby, would be built as soon as MURA designs were ready. The second project was assigned to MURA's Midwest arch-rival, Argonne, "to design a high-energy accelerator which would permit earliest possible construction . . . ." [14] And in its anxiety Congress went along by authorizing $15 million immediately for the Argonne machine.[15]

However, even desperation takes time, and during the passage of that time AEC took a moment to review its response to the accelerator gap. The Dubna machine was not yet in operation, and the Americans weren't really ready to proceed, except for small and quick actions that might give only the semblance of response. Consequently AEC scratched all the Dubna responses, leaving the Midwest holding the atomic bag a while longer. The next round would instead involve a new machine, the Zero Gradient Synchrotron, at a cost of $27 million, to which Congress assented without a murmur.

There were still more unexpected turnabouts before the

Berkeley–New York cycle was broken, for neither the Argonne nor the MURA plans were completed and the ZGS machine was never built. A still bigger $500 million machine would be built instead. It would be designed by Berkeley, supervised by an offshoot of New York, and built in Illinois on top of the unmourned ashes of a defunct MURA.

MURA Breaks the Cycle—And Itself

MURA is the story of the battle that was lost, the war that was won, the little accelerator that was never built, and the big one that was. Thanks to its aborted mission, MURA succeeded in opening the curtain on science and changing the scenario. Without particularly intending to, the MURA scientists and their university lobbyists exposed a tightly knit science oligarchy to the harsh scrutiny of politicians and the public; scientific decision making would never be quite the same again.

MURA was never able to achieve a consensus among physicists for its accelerator design. For a brief moment in 1956 it failed only for lack of readiness, but the tentative approval had been made under heat of apparent Soviet competition, and it was rejected once the desperation level dropped. In 1957, MURA had gone back to the science committees but again failed to obtain scientific support. Among 37 carefully qualified but anonymous brothers, only 16 were confident that the feasibility of the MURA plan was established. Seventeen believed the design principle was dubious; five others thought its technical problems were solvable but unsolved.[16]

This negative appraisal was especially significant because in the same year W. K. H. Panofsky, director of the Stanford High Energy Physics Laboratory, petitioned successfully to build his linear accelerator (SLAC) at Stanford. Panofsky's plan was approved over MURA's despite the fact that it was only an expensive expansion of an already existing machine. And once the machine was approved the entire high-energy physics brotherhood, including the MURA personnel, joined in solidarity to push authorization through Congress. So strong were the mores of high-energy physics politics that MURA made no attempt to break ranks at this juncture; instead, it fought side by side with those who thwarted its efforts to persuade Congress to fund SLAC, its approved if unimaginative rival.

In order to influence Congress, the General Advisory Committee of the Atomic Energy Commission (AEC-GAC) and the President's Science Advisory Committee (PSAC) resorted to their accustomed strategy and jointly appointed a panel to examine the needs of high-energy physics. Typically—especially prior to 1963—the mechanism worked as follows: a committee composed of eminent scientists chosen by other outstanding scientists sat in judgment of proposed scientific projects. When a scientific proposal had no competition, the committee recommended to Congress and the president, via the AEC, funding of the much needed, nay, urgent request. Typically Congress readily complied. If there were competing projects, a committee was chosen to assess the "needs of high-energy physics," it being constantly borne in mind which project could muster the most influential scientific support; then the committee would make its recommendations or priorities public, again via the AEC. Thus the only assessment of the need or worth of a given project came from scientists, either those desiring to utilize it or those appointed to assess it in the very general context of the "needs of high-energy physics."

In 1958 the Piore panel, named for its chairman Emanuel R. Piore, vice-president for research at IBM, concluded that by 1963 it would be necessary annually to support high-energy physics with $125 million. As expected, the panel recommended that Panofsky's SLAC be constructed immediately, "in order to avoid an undue delay in high-energy research." [17] MURA, the panel concluded, should continue to receive design support, despite the inadequacy of its current proposal. In 1960, SLAC was still mired politically, largely because of the recalcitrant JCAE. Thus the Piore panel was reconvened, and it emphasized the importance of "proceeding forthwith" [18] on SLAC.

In a rather oblique statement, the 1960 Piore panel cast doubt on MURA's future by questioning the necessity of a high-intensity proton accelerator, the fundamental parameter emphasized in the MURA design.[19] This was the first *publicly* expressed scientific doubt regarding the necessity of the MURA machine. Prior to this report, MURA leaders believed its project would be funded, if not sooner, then later. The 1958 Piore panel design support recommendation supported this hope. But the 1960 statement cast the first public scientific doubt on MURA's future, and eventually MURA opened Pandora's box by taking its case out of the cloistered, clubbish committees into the arena of the U.S. Congress and the conflict-conscious press.

SLAC received congressional authorization in 1961, which seemingly cleared the field for MURA to request AEC authorization to build its accelerator. But during the protracted SLAC debate Berkeley began designing a 125-bev proton accelerator, a machine emphasizing the energy parameter. Berkeley had not constructed a new accelerator since the 6.2-bev Cosmotron was completed, and that was becoming progressively less useful.

In the 1950s, when money from Congress to science flowed generously, the president might have authorized, and Congress approved, the construction of both machines. However, the attitudes of both Congress and the president regarding government appropriations for pure science had undergone steady change. Congress had become somewhat disillusioned with both the cost and the accomplishments of pure science. Because many Americans believed that scientists provided the nation with unchallenged military superiority after World War II, there seemed to be no limit to what these brilliant men could accomplish if properly equipped and financed. But by the early 1960s congressmen had seen no recent scientific accomplishment as spectacular as the bomb. High-energy physicists had little to show for the millions they had received. It appears that Congress had not understood that the Manhattan Project was applied research directed to a specific tangible objective, whereas the proton accelerators, which it had authorized, were tools of pure research, not designed to create a new technology but to expand the frontiers of man's knowledge.

As Congress's enthusiasm ebbed, the newly inaugurated president, John F. Kennedy, gradually articulated his priorities for science in the 1960s, and they differed from his predecessor's. His goal, to land a man on the moon by the end of the decade, would cost billions of dollars, but Congress could bestow generous funding because the project had captured the public's attention. Consequently, atomic physicists were told by President Kennedy's science advisor, Jerome Weisner, that the Administration was willing to support construction of only one accelerator every 5 years.

Confronted with limited funds and two competing accelerator designs (for MURA and Berkeley were now competitors if the president would finance only one accelerator), the high-energy physics community reconstituted itself once again as an advisory committee to survey the situation. But the situation intensified within the scientific community as the size of the high-energy physics pot decreased and the number of direct competitors doubled; politicization, a dramatic departure from the scientific *modus vivendi,* was required to break open the closed committees, or MURA would simply disappear quietly and without trace.

Assembled to "assess the future needs in the field of high-energy physics," [20] the Ramsey panel, chaired by Professor Norman F. Ramsey of Harvard, gave the final scientific axe to MURA. Appointed jointly by PSAC and the AEC-GAC, the Ramsey panel was composed of distinguished physicists from the NAS, who were geographically representative of the nation.[21] Its recommendations were submitted to the AEC and both "parent" committees (the GAC and the PSAC) for review.

Under the onus of the tight budgetary situation, the Ramsey panel broke with tradition and delineated a priority list for high-energy physics. In the belief that it was more important to use resources to extend energy than intensify, they made three major recommendations:

1. That a 200-bev proton accelerator be constructed by the Lawrence Radiation Laboratory, Berkeley, California.
2. That intensive design studies at Brookhaven National Laboratory on a national accelerator in the range of 600 to 1,000 bev be supported; request for authorization to be anticipated in 5 or 6 years.
3. That the AEC authorize in fiscal year 1965 the construction by MURA of a supercurrent accelerator "without permitting this to delay the steps toward higher energy."

Because of budgetary limitations the AEC was unable to implement all recommendations at once; instead, it worked with the proposals on a year-to-year basis, implementing whatever portion feasible. The AEC, according to Dr. Ramsey, fully committed itself to the panel's goals, which were published in May 1963.[22]

It must be noted that despite the apparent recommendation that the AEC build the supercurrent accelerator the panel really sabotaged MURA. If President Kennedy would authorize construction of only one machine every 5 years, there was no time to build MURA's machine. Five years after the authorization of Berkeley's 200-bev accelerator, Brookhaven's designs for the 600–1,000 bev accelerator would be ready.

Keeping the Rally Alive: MURA Becomes a Pressure Group

MURA understood the implications of the Ramsey Report and felt betrayed. Determined not to be quietly scuttled after 10 years of hard work, it deviated from accepted scientific practice. It attempted to overturn the science establishment's decision by taking its case to Midwestern politicians. For a while this avoided the *coup de grace* implicit in the Ramsey panel recommendations. In the long run, this act of desperation by MURA had more far-reaching consequences in changing the scientific oligarchy than MURA planned or anyone else foresaw.

In desperation MURA in 1963 turned to what had previously been unthinkable to scientists. It retained the services of a lobbyist, Ralph Huitt. Huitt was a very special lobbyist, the ideal sort of lobbyist for academicians. He was a professor of political science at the University of Wisconsin, a scholar of sound reputation, and a leader in the academic study of congressional politics. But he was also a Texan with an ingratiating manner, charming style, and steely clear sense of purpose. Huitt had been an intimate of Lyndon Johnson during all of Johnson's Senate years and was in very large part responsible for the excellent reputation Johnson the senator enjoyed among academicians and journalists. Huitt, in keeping with his academic independence, had also written favorably of the exploits of the more maverick senator William Proxmire. It would have been hard then, or before or since, to find a better bridge for politics between the scientific community and the Washington community.

Huitt and MURA's scientific spokesmen attempted to stress the regional, not the scientific, aspects of the betrayal by the Ramsey panel and other committees. Geography is the most politically relevant value in American politics, and it was pushed accordingly. Huitt attempted to enlist the Midwest congressional delegations to the task of politicking for MURA. He coordinated the efforts of the Midwestern university presidents against regional discrimination and its results in the Ph.D. brain drain. Most surely he reached the president. And his efforts made it increasingly hard to deny the fact that the Ramsey decision was only one in a long series of research projects that the Midwest had been refused. Politicians claimed that the Midwest had been consistently deprived of its fair share of the federal research and development dollar. When the most damaging statistics were cited, the Midwest had a strong case substantiating this discrimination. California, they emphasized, received 34.6 per cent of all research and development money, and Massachusetts received more money than Illinois, Indiana, Michigan, and Minnesota combined.

The arguments in themselves quite openly revealed the "pork barrel" quality of government-science. By the nature of the debate the so-called scientific decisions were undressed for all to see. While East and West Coast politicians unearthed statistics to combat the aroused Midwesterners, the point remained, and MURA's spokesmen reiterated it everywhere: the Midwest was being deprived of beneficial scientific projects and therefore positive economic values. Midwestern congressmen as well as the president were swamped with letters and telegrams.

The corollary to the allegations of discrimination in research and development was the "brain drain" argument, which heightened the controversy. Because the coasts monopolize all the research projects, the argument went, they therefore monopolize the best and largest numbers of "brains" or (in this case) Ph.D.'s. Midwestern universities trained scientists only to lose them to coastal laboratories.

MURA's dramatic entrance into the public political arena expanded the scope of the conflict. No longer were behind-the-scene scientists quietly determining the position the AEC was to defend publicly. And this new political expansion aroused passions beyond the control of the AEC. The AEC had never totally abandoned MURA; instead, it had said in effect, "Yes, we are for MURA as long as we can build the 200-bev accelerator as well." Nevertheless, this meant that unless the president was willing to agree to authorize the inclusion of two atomic accelerators in the budget within a 5-year period the AEC would not defend MURA. This explosive political problem could only be resolved by President Kennedy, and it was still on his desk at the time of the assassination.

Lyndon Johnson was compelled to resolve this situation during his first hectic weeks in office. President Johnson, perhaps unaware of the depth of Midwestern feeling and despite his close personal relationship with Huitt, decided against the high-intensity machine. In a meeting on December 18, 1963, he talked with MURA representatives, Midwestern congressmen, and AEC officials. He gave two reasons for refusing to include MURA's FFAG in the budget: (1) the country could not afford to build both machines, and (2) it was wasteful and unnecessary to begin a new facility at Madison when Argonne was so close.

A New Ballgame?

The most important effects of MURA's widening the scope of political conflict had barely begun. In the wake of MURA's political turmoil there occurred changes in operating and decision-making procedures for the "autonomous" scientists and the AEC; how much autonomy was lost is still unmeasured. And the extent of redistribution of money and talent to the Midwest is unmeasurable because unfinished.

The first inklings that MURA's intervention had been so costly to the scientific establishment came with an AEC press release of January 20, 1964. For that press release announced "no decisions have been made for the construction of either of these large national accelerators [i.e., the 200-bev at Berkeley or the 1,000-bev at Brookhaven] *nor have site locations been selected.*" [23]

Later, in February 1965, in a published review of the past developments and future plans for high-energy physics, the JCAE stated:

> The selection of a site for any major new accelerator facility should
> be based upon careful examination of site parameters and de-
> termination of the greatest overall advantage to the Government
> and high energy physics program. The location of a design study
> group should not determine the site for an accelerator laboratory.[24]

Here was the new ballgame. The old AEC rule of thumb, whereby
the design group proposing a machine sited the machine, had been
abandoned. The oligarchy had been seriously pierced, and Ramsey
panel recommendations had lost their inviolability. In fact, the
august scientific committee, whereby scientists controlled their own
future, had been de-legitimized, and the establishment found itself
adrift, without its hydra-headed helmsman. Although present-day
AEC staff members and the more cautious commissioners are
reluctant to acknowledge the connection, then AEC Chairman
Glenn Seaborg admitted that the "MURA problem" was "in the
back of our minds" when the AEC decided that it would have to
open up its site competition to the country at large.[25] Even that
"admission" grossly understates MURA's impact on the procedures
of all concerned with high-energy physics.

The honeymoon between high-energy physics and government
was over by 1964. The end should have been apparent the minute
MURA "went public" and became a regular interest group. The
entire affair becomes too ironic when one remembers that all
MURA really wanted was a piece of the action, the same kind of
support both Berkeley and Brookhaven enjoyed.

Given the fiscal and, after MURA, the political realities of the
1960s, the AEC would somehow have to make its projects more
generally appealing if they were going to be authorized by Congress. Pursuant to this, the AEC chose to hold an open, national
competition for the site of the coveted 500-bev accelerator. Not
only would this eliminate cries of regional favoritism, it would also
nationalize the lust for the expensive pork barrel, thus heading off
any congressional inclination to turn it down, regardless of where
it eventually went. The AEC was laying the groundwork, according to AEC staff member John Erlewine, to make it impossible for
Congress to ignore the project, if it came to that.[26] Congressional
exasperation with the size and the distribution of research and
development funds was such that [27] the AEC could undermine

the ultimate authorization of the 200-bev accelerator by choosing either Berkeley or Brookhaven as its home. MURA's politicking had made the geographical distribution of scientists and accelerators an especially sensitive issue, but also led to a means to insure the eventual success of the project somewhere.

In April 1965, in a press release entitled "AEC-NAS Enter Agreement on Evaluating Sites for a Proposed New National Accelerator Laboratory," the AEC announced two important departures from the pre-MURA pattern of closed-door decisions. The first departure was the open site competition. Second, the National Academy of Sciences was chosen to review the proposals, evaluate them, and then recommend "to the AEC those sites having the greatest potential." [28]

Inclusion of the distinguished NAS was intended to counter charges that "politics" would dictate the location of this gigantic scientific installation. AEC Chairman Glenn Seaborg attributed the inclusion of the NAS to the desire "to get it above partisan considerations, to stop the in-fighting among the scientific community, to go above the politics of high energy physics." [29] The participation of the NAS also helped to diffuse the pressure involved in a decision of this magnitude. Rather than have the AEC bearing the brunt of the decision alone, the NAS shared. And, finally, NAS review would appear to assure scientists a direct voice in deciding where the accelerator would be located. Although structured differently in the end, it was still scientists who had the most input into the location decision. MURA had caused the decision-making processes among scientists to be restructured but not necessarily to be opened to broader considerations.

Repercussions

The new site selection process had important repercussions in the scientific community. First, by disrupting old procedures, it created tensions among high-energy physicists. As one might have predicted, the physicists from Lawrence and Brookhaven felt their hegemony endangered. The whole system whereby the AEC alternated the accelerators between these two favored laboratories had been challenged, and the future of these two laboratories was no longer secure if new accelerators were to be awarded by open site selection competitions. It was not yet clear to anyone whether the politicization of MURA had significantly altered the balance that had previously prevailed. It could be argued that this new procedure was merely a facade for keeping Congress from cutting the accelerator by emphasizing the *national* need and bringing in a new logrolling member, the Midwest, in a most peaceful war; but in early 1965 the coastal laboratories had no way of gauging the impact of this process on their futures.

In 1965, a MURA representative on the Ramsey panel endorsed the primacy of energy over intensity and signed the report that consigned MURA's designs to oblivion. But Berkeley refused to return the favor by placing the general well-being of the high-energy physics program above the interests of its own laboratory. Berkeley threatened to protest the loss of its dominant position publicly. The AEC and the deans of high-energy physics, aware that another public fracas would endanger congressional authorization, tried to defuse Berkeley's anger.

This led directly to the formation of a national organization to represent high-energy physics' interests. The timing of University Research Association (URA) coincided with the mounting dissension threatening to explode at Berkeley. URA was to be responsible for the management of the new 200-bev hardware on the principle of national scientific access.

The first meeting was held in Washington on January 17, 1965. It was chaired by Frederick Seitz, president of the National Academy, and was attended by 34 university presidents and the AEC officials, including Chairman Seaborg. An auspicious occasion indeed.

The timing of the meeting, a full 3 months before the AEC announced the new site selection procedures, coincided with disturbances at Berkeley over JCAE's report that laboratories responsible for designing an accelerator would not necessarily build the project at home. URA was patently designed to reassure Berkeley at least as to access to management of and participation in the conduct of the 200-bev machine.

In the end, URA played no role in site selection at all. It seems clearly to have been designed only to placate Berkeley. And it gave physics the appearance of a newly united front.

Pacification of unhappy physicists in fact became a major preoccupation at the AEC. Congressional approval rested on it. The future of high-energy physics seemed to depend on it. Special panels, such as Piore and Ramsey, were in constant contact with AEC. In turn, AEC had its own representative at laboratory staff meetings, in addition to holding monthly meetings of all laboratory directors in Washington.

Increased reliance on the National Academy was still another serious gesture by AEC toward the established science interests. It was protection against a spread of participation toward non-scientists. And the special arrangement with NAS for the national site selection competition was a still more pointed effort to help maintain equilibrium among the high energists. One former AEC employee, a prominent physicist himself, suggested to the inter-viewers that the hard-pressed AEC had actually encouraged NAS to make the site decision entirely independently of AEC. NAS, according to our informant, received the request and refused to accept it.

Yet, all such gestures to the contrary notwithstanding, maintenance of the oligarchy was never again easy after MURA. When Edward Lofgren, chief designer of the 200-bev machine, was offered the directorship in Weston, he chose to stay in Berkeley rather than go elsewhere to create and direct the world's largest accelerator. Eventually the job went to an "outsider," Dr. Robert Wilson of Cornell, who had once proposed a smaller alternative to the 200-bev machine. Hard feelings had not dis-appeared 2 and 3 years after Weston had become the "National Accelerator Laboratory." [30]

In this context the decision process improvised to meet the problem of siting the 200-bev accelerator was probably necessary, appropriate, and, from the standpoint of AEC and scientists, successful. Participation was put on a very broad base without seriously weakening scientific control of the vital parts of decisions on hardware or siting. The process was changed but not the actual composition of the science-government decision centers. The rela-tionship between agency and clientele remained so intimate that it was virtually impossible to distinguish the public from the private roles.

But MURA had changed the government-science complex in some permanent way by forcing the improvisation of a new pro-cedure. The manner and extent of this change are another story.

NOTES TO CHAPTER 2

1. Don K. Price, *The Scientific Estate* (Cambridge, Mass.: Harvard-Belknap Press, 1965), p. 97.
2. *Science,* **65**:26–29 (1927).
3. Daniel S. Greenberg, *The Politics of Pure Science* (New York: New American Library, 1967), p. 51.
4. Reported in Daniel Bell, "Notes on the Post-Industrial Society," *The Public Interest,* 28ff (Winter 1967).
5. James P. Baxter, III, *Scientists Against Time* (Boston: Little, Brown, 1946), p. 128.
6. Harold Orlans, *Contracting for Atoms* (Washington, D.C.: Brookings Institution, 1967), pp. 184–186, passim.
7. Harold S. Green and Alan Rosenthal, *Government of the Atom* (New York: Atherton Press, 1963), p. 266.
8. Orlans, op. cit., pp. 155, 155n, 160, passim.
9. Ibid., p. 161.
10. Richard G. Hewlett and Oscar E. Anderson, Jr., *The New World, 1939/1946* (University Park, Pa.: Pennsylvania State University Press, 1962), Chapter 11.
11. Hewlett and Anderson, op. cit., p. 635.
12. Ibid.
13. Ohio State University, University of Michigan, Michigan State University, Indiana University, Notre Dame, Purdue, University of Illinois, Iowa State University, University of Chicago, Northwestern University, University of Wisconsin, University of Minnesota, Washington University of St. Louis, State University of Iowa, and University of Kansas.
14. Atomic Energy Commission Press Release, #785.
15. *AEC Authorizing Legislation, 1958,* p. 194.
16. Greenberg, op. cit., p. 227. Figures not additive in original.
17. Piore Panel Report, 1958, published by the Atomic Energy Commission in *High Energy Physics Program* (1965), p. 149.
18. Piore Panel Report, 1960, published by the Atomic Energy Commission in *High Energy Physics Program* (1965), p. 125.
19. Ibid., p. 127.
20. Ibid., Appendix I, p. 85, quoted from a letter from Paul McDaniel to the Ramsey panel.
21. The members of the Ramsey panel in addition to the chairman were Philip H. Abelson, Carnegie Institution; Owen Chamberlin, University of California; Murray Gell-Mann, California Institute of Technology; E. L. Goldwasser, University of Illinois; T. D. Lee, Columbia University; W. K. H. Panofsky, Stanford University; E. M. Purcell, Harvard University; Frederick Seitz, National Academy of Sciences; and John H. Williams, University of Minnesota.
22. *High Energy Physics Program* (1965), Appendix I, p. 85.

23. AEC Press Release, G 14, January 20, 1964, as cited in Greenberg, op. cit., p. 268. Emphasis added.
24. *High Energy Physics Program* (1965), p. 32.
25. Interview with AEC Chairman Glenn Seaborg, March 25, 1969, at AEC headquarters in Washington, D.C.
26. Interview with AEC staff member John Erlewine, March 24, 1969, at AEC headquarters in Virginia.
27. Interview with Albert Crewe at the University of Chicago, March 21, 1969; corroborated by an interview with Boyd Keenan, University of Illinois, March 15, 1969.
28. Press release by the Atomic Energy Commission, April 28, 1965.
29. Seaborg interview, op. cit.
30. This is mainly true of Berkeley. Information on the Brookhaven group was not available during the period of our story. Brookhaven simply did not speak out, presumably because its 1,000-bev machine was not threatened by Weston. Open animosity in the uncertain world of the late 1960s could hardly help its cause.

CHAPTER 3   Politicization of Science

Science leaders faced a real dilemma after MURA. Intensification of politics meant that new interests and considerations would enter into the competition. Yet the need for the next step in hardware for physics research was so pressing that an expanded base of participation might be worth the risk. If they could accentuate the positive side of participation, perhaps they could gain at least two important benefits: (1) Broader participation was likely to enhance the legitimacy of the final decision. (2) Once the competition was open and public, hundreds of public officials and industrial leaders from all parts of the country would become involved. Their lust for a half-billion-dollar "clean industry" would eliminate any chance that Congress might veto the accelerator proposal.

The story of the decision to build the accelerator and to locate it on top of Weston, Illinois, is complicated, as almost any important public decision is likely to be. Yet even partial justice to reality reveals a number of significant things about the role and behavior of the AEC and its relations with the larger scientific community on the one hand and the larger governmental structure on the other. Our story begins to suggest just what kind of decision process science could develop.

It is quite clear in retrospect that the scientists never lost control of the essential, irreducible issue in the controversy: there was going to be a new accelerator, of a given size and function, and it was going to be located in an area comfortable to scientists and their families. However, competition and expanded participation brought about drastic changes in the procedure used at the center for making the decision.

As the number and variety of participants increased, the scope of the scientists' concerns progressively narrowed itself toward the irreducible element, the hardware. This happened to all the participants in the Weston story, but we feel it is especially significant that it happened to scientists. Competition, although it broadened participation, narrowed the definition of the issue until each participant came to define it as narrowly as he could within his "range of official responsibility." Because no larger perspective was imposed upon them from the outside, the scientists, despite the humanitarian concerns they sincerely expressed *after* the issue was settled, narrowed their predecision demands down and down until they amounted in effect to "Give us the accelerator, but don't tell us how you got it."

The scientists won their site on their own terms because they managed to improvise a new process that would accommodate in their favor to the expanded participation. It was a decision process that arose out of their narrow concerns for hardware and siting; and it was a process that could build upon the narrow and selfish definition of the issue that each contestant brought to the contest.

The decision process they improvised was simple in design, complex in execution, and very probably comfortable to the *modus operandi* of any scientist. Rather than entering outright into the problem, through direct choice or logrolling, or by appealing to higher political authority, the AEC, in joint venture with the National Academy of Sciences, developed a list of "hard criteria" by which the competition could appear to be governing itself, and through which the weaker competitors could appear to be eliminating themselves. As more and more of the stronger competitors had to be eliminated, these criteria for site selection were redefined and strengthened; but in all instances the appearance is that the contestants were eliminated by objective criteria.

This is a special kind of decision process, although not unique.

It is so special that there is no special name for it: Decision making by elimination? Elimination by criteria contrivance? The ratchet effect? By whatever name, the results would smell as sweet. This complicated process of elimination ultimately guaranteed that no choice of site would be contrary to the interests of the high-energy physics community.

By this succession of criteria refinements, carefully described in this chapter, the scientists, through their many site evaluation committees, brought more than 200 original contestants down to six finalists. Because all six of these finalists were acceptable to the potential users, no final choice of one site from the six would matter a great deal. Heads, we win; tails, we don't lose.

By this process it was also possible for the AEC to yield to all sorts of high-level political considerations. The president most surely intruded. So did several Midwestern senators and congressmen, big city mayors, and top businessmen. But by the time these nonscience interests came into play, the field of contestants had been narrowed so systematically that these "irrational" forces could be introduced without serious effect.

Consequently, the scientists were never confronted by fundamental social forces at all. There was never any confrontation among contestants, or between any of them and the AEC. There was never any intermixing or compromising of demands, in any fundamental sense. Representatives of each site competed against each other as bidders compete through sealed bids for a contract. But this only raised the ante, while at the same time it protected the project itself from congressional veto. Broader considerations— political considerations in the best and most comprehensive sense —did not come into play until after the real decisions were made through the criteria. This is certainly a form of disjointed decision making that narrow and selfish perspectives make possible. It is the scientist's variant of logrolling, where no participant is forced seriously to consider the aims of any other participant, or the public.

Background: 200 Billion Electron Volts

No federally funded public work was ever more ardently sought by so many individuals, corporations, groups, and government agencies than the Weston accelerator. In almost every state vast amounts of political and financial resources were invested in influencing the place where the Atomic Energy Commission would finally decide to grant its multibeneficial gift.[1] Congressmen and senators, governors and mayors, professors and executives, community influentials and just plain citizens participated in the making of the AEC decision. By the end at least 200 site proposals were presented by hundreds of individuals through dozens of industrial development agencies from 46 of the 50 states.[2]

This prodigious outpouring was brought on by the AEC's own open invitation to submit site proposals, but it produced an unprecedented and unexpected situation for the agency. As indicated in the previous chapter, the AEC had never before even contemplated the possibility of siting a research machine anywhere other than at a place chosen by its own designers. Most assuredly it had never viewed matters of this nature as issues to be decided in a public arena. This particular route was felt necessary in order to head off a repetition of the MURA affair.[3] The MURA conflict, although bitter, was over an issue tiny in comparison to the 200-bev accelerator. Scientifically the 200-bev machine would be so advanced as to make all predecessors seem like playthings. Economically the 200-bev machine was big enough to have a significant effect on a local area. The economic factor overshadowed the scientific, to the hundreds of nonscientists involved in regional development.

At first, the AEC did not fully recognize the economic, and therefore the political, implications of this facility. They tended to view it as just one more scientific tool.[4] But its significance was not lost on others. This machine was going to be the largest single-purpose federal science research facility ever built, with originally projected construction costs alone in the vicinity of $300 million.[5] In operation it would directly employ an estimated 2,400 individuals, over half of whom would be highly skilled technicians.[6] And once operational it could well be a magnet for accelerated economic development in a large region around the machine. The assumed impact of federal science installations outside Boston, in the San Francisco Bay Area, and around Cape Canaveral had for years been the envy of state and local officials everywhere. Perhaps the biggest surprise of the entire story is the

AEC's surprise as hundreds of applications began to pour in and pressure began to build.[7]

The decision-making process would differ from all previous AEC actions in at least three fundamental ways. First, the atom of science organization was smashed: the AEC split the question of who should operate the machine from the question of where the machine would be located. Hitherto, the location of a machine had been determined by the location of the personnel back of the design, who would then also become the managers. In the case of the 200-bev machine, the two elements were kept far enough apart to prevent the one from having any influence on the other. This was the AEC's way of giving to this immense machine a national character.[8] The magnitude of the project gave them no choice. Second, the prestigious National Academy of Sciences (NAS) assisted the Atomic Energy Commission in organizing the national consortium to operate the machine. Subsequently, NAS organized the process for evaluating the multitude of site contestants. The NAS was brought into the process for the purpose of limiting the political controversy that might develop around the AEC's decisions.[9] It brought to its task an aura of scientific objectivity and neutrality and an image of nonpoliticized technical expertise, which the AEC had not entirely lost for itself during the course of the MURA affair but had certainly compromised. Because of this, AEC looked to NAS as the way to smooth ruffled scientific feathers. When NAS succeeded in this task, it undertook to assist the AEC in the diffusion of the mounting political pressures developing over the question of location.

Third, and by no means of least significance, the process of locating the 200-bev machine was distinguished from any prior effort by the fact that the AEC invited site proposals from any organization or community interested in the machine. This meant competitive bidding among the states. As a result, the agency found itself required to develop a set of detailed standards by which it could publicly judge the various proposed sites. These were called "objective criteria," although they were never discussed or analyzed.[10]

It is in the examination of the intertwining of these latter two developments that the most provocative insights into the character of the policy-making process will be found. For through them the AEC and its constituents in the high-energy physics community were able to continue to exercise very substantial control over the development of the facility as well as the character of its location, in spite of the greatly broadened participation in the policy-making process. Ultimately these two factors insured that the character of the location selected as the site for the accelerator would not be significantly different from what it would have been had there not been any elaborate site selection process at all.

Exploring these issues as they are raised in the Weston case, one ultimately begins to examine the values and norms that scientists invoke in their decision-making activity. This leads inevitably to the question of whether there is anything in the experience of being a scientist that serves to equip one with special expertise in dealing with particular issues of public policy. Or is the scientist simply another political actor with his own values, goals, and prejudices? [11] The case will show how easy it is for scientists to invoke so-called objective and nonpolitical decision making as a strategy for settling quite subjective policy questions. The issue is not that scientists are incompetent or untrustworthy in matters of decision making for science policy. Rather, the final question raised by analysis of this particular decision is simply whether the involvement of scientists in policy is a route to the One Best Way. Our story suggests that scientists improve the average quality of decision-making personnel without necessarily improving on the quality of public policy.

Background: Reconstruction of Science Consensus

Initial planning for the 200-bev machine had actually begun in 1956, when staff at the Lawrence Radiation Laboratory (LRL) had first considered "the concepts and practicality of an accelerator in the 100–300 billion electron volts energy range." [12] In 1962, a proposal was submitted to undertake a design study of such an accelerator. The request was approved and resulted in reports to the AEC by the Berkeley scientists in late 1964 and mid-1965 on the feasibility of such an accelerator.

The decision to go ahead with the facility was for all in-

tents and purposes made in the waning days of 1963, quite independent of any congressional authorization, because approval
of the 200-bev machine had become tied in with veto of MURA's
proposed accelerator for Madison, Wisconsin.[13] In no small part
this was due to the structure of the situation in which the president was then acting. The matter had been brought to Johnson
for decision because the AEC had been committed to building
a facility for the MURA group. The project had become caught
up in the midst of a controversy involving the Bureau of the
Budget and the president's science advisors, who at the time were
contending that the AEC should choose *between* the construction
of the MURA facility and the subsequent construction of the
200-bev machine. However, the largest and most prestigious portion of the AEC's scientific constituency viewed the MURA
project as secondary to the 200-bev facility and had urged the
agency to drop it in order to move ahead on the bigger project.
Given the either-or character of the situation that had developed
as a result of the Bureau of the Budget–AEC disagreement, Johnson, in vetoing the MURA proposal, had appeared to indicate a
willingness to support the 200-bev proposal.[14]

Prospects for the machine were no doubt reinforced by the
fact that virtually all of the other individuals, agencies, and groups
involved in the events leading up to the president's action were
themselves now supporting the construction of the 200-bev accelerator. The scientists had previously put their stamp of support
on the 200-bev proposal through the report of the Ramsey panel.[15]
Traditionally the AEC and Congress, through the Joint Committee on Atomic Energy (JCAE, which on matters of atomic
energy research authoritatively spoke for the Congress), had both
taken actively expansionist postures regarding the development of
high-energy physics research and thus now enthusiastically supported the new accelerator.[16] On top of this, the Bureau of the
Budget and the President's Science Advisory Committee (PSAC)
had both proposed a general guideline of federal support for the
construction of one accelerator every 5 years and had taken the
position that a choice had to be made between the MURA or
the 200-bev projects. Since the last AEC machine (SLAC) had
been authorized in fiscal 1961, they now also joined the ranks of
supporters of the 200-bev machine. Thus with the veto of the

MURA machine the government, without any kind of formal decision-making process or sustained consideration, had more or less committed itself to the authorization of the 200-bev facility.

At least as early as November 1964, a series of high-level but informal discussions between AEC commissioners, led by Commission Chairman Glenn Seaborg, and the National Academy of Science, led by NAS President Frederick Seitz, had commenced. Their primary concern was with the problem of how to organize the operations of the proposed 200-bev accelerator.[17] They were seeking to determine the manner by which it would be possible to achieve the broadest possible consensus in the high-energy physics community over the governance of the facility.[18]

Out of these informal meetings had come an agreement to have Seitz call a meeting of the presidents of the 25 universities across the country that were most actively engaged in high-energy physics research.[19] The purpose of this meeting, which was held in January 1965, was to consider the possibility of establishing for the first time a national organization that would assume the responsibility for governing the proposed 200-bev accelerator.[20] No minutes were kept of the meeting, but a written summary of the conclusions was agreed upon by the participants. This was made public at the request of the joint committee following its March 1965 hearings, and it indicated that eight points of agreement had been reached by the participants.[21] The first and most important point was to create a new association of universities to operate the proposed accelerator. It would be national in scope, but modeled after Associated Universities, Incorporated, the nine-member consortium of Eastern universities that had been responsible for the management of the Brookhaven Laboratory. The meeting participants urged that the new association should be formed as rapidly as possible, and should have an initial membership of about 30 universities, each of which was to be prepared to guarantee a sum of about $100,000 to meet the possible liabilities of the organization.[22]

The Great Bev Chase Begins

In April 1965, the AEC and the NAS jointly published a formal agreement under which the NAS would assist the AEC in the process of selecting a site for the proposed 200-bev accelerator. Unofficial AEC-NAS discussions of this matter date back to the previous year, but it appears that neither party originally anticipated undertaking a joint venture.

On April 28, 1965, the AEC and the NAS jointly released the general procedures and some of the criteria that would guide the site selection process.

> A desirable site would: (1) contain at least 3,000 acres owned by, or reasonably available to, the U.S. Government; (2) have the potential of delivering a firm electric power load of several hundred megawatts and a minimum of 2,000 gallons a minute of high quality water; (3) be reasonably close to communities having adequate housing, cultural and educational facilities for some 2,000 scientific and technical personnel and their families. Also, the site should be close to adequate surface transportation systems and a major airport with frequent service to major U.S. cities.[23]

The release went on to note that the AEC would itself undertake an initial screening of all of the site proposals and then refer "those sites having the greatest potential" to the NAS for detailed study and technical evaluation. In an accompanying attachment, the AEC-NAS further elaborated upon the criteria for site selection and their relative importance:

> It is difficult to establish priorities or weights among the various technical, economic and social criteria that can be described. Some items, of course, are absolutely essential such as acreage requirements, the availability of adequate power, the proximity of adequate transportation, etc. On the other hand, other items such as foundation requirements of deep piles versus shallow piles, one-pass versus recirculating water systems, tunneling versus cutting and filling for shielding the magnet ring, etc., cannot be categorized absolutely and are subject to some compromise in order to maximize the potential of each site.[24]

The attachment went on to indicate that the site should be near adequate transportation facilities and a commercial-industrial center that could provide electronic and precision mechanical equipment as well as personnel skilled in its use. It also added that

> Sufficient housing and community facilities must be available to accommodate the permanent operating and research staff of

several thousand people and the transient staff of several hundred.

Proximity to a cultural center that includes a large university will provide intellectual and cultural opportunities attractive for staff and families.

Regional wage and cost variations as well as labor surplus areas are factors.[25]

It should be noted that the press release and accompanying attachment had already begun to express what subsequently came to be known by those engaged in the selection process as "hard criteria" and "soft criteria." The hard criteria were essentially the technical requirements for constructing the machine—access to certain quantities of water and power at the site, and a particular kind of bedrock base to build upon. The soft criteria involved those particular aspects of a site that made it more or less amenable to the scientists—for example, proximity to a major university, an urban cultural center, or a large airport. As will become evident, it is these soft criteria that are the key to understanding both the character of the selection process and its final results. The particular soft criteria and the manner in which they would be applied could preordain the character of the interests that were ultimately to be served by the final decision.

The first round of the site selection process involved a screening out by the AEC of all sites that were clearly incompatible with its needs. On September 14, 1965, the AEC made public the results of its efforts—148 sites in 43 states were still in the running and would, according to the original plan, be the subject of further evaluative study by NAS site selection teams. Overall, only about a third of the sites, and three states, had been eliminated from contention for the accelerator. Illinois, for example, the ultimate victor, was notified in a letter from the AEC to then Governor Otto Kerner that only one of the eight sites originally proposed had been eliminated.

The news of the AEC's choices brought forth immediate and heated criticism from a variety of political figures. Representative Gerald Ford of Michigan charged that the AEC was succumbing to political pressure in the site selection process.[26] Congressman Craig Hosmer of California, obviously upset that 43 states were still in the running for a project once almost certainly destined for California, complained that the project was becoming a "gigantic pork barrel."[27] He further suggested that the AEC cease its present efforts and begin the task over again.

The critics were further agitated by widespread reports that the AEC had, on the basis of obvious failure to meet the criteria, actually been prepared to reduce the number of sites in contention to below 30, but had backed away in the face of the political pressures being exerted by local interests. In the eyes of its critics, the AEC had abdicated its decision-making responsibility and was attempting to mask this through the use of an extragovernmental agency, the NAS.[28] That the AEC might in fact have shirked duty in the face of strong political pressure is suggested by events that took place in Illinois. A month prior to the AEC announcement (and 3 weeks prior to the first NAS site evaluation visit), Illinois public officials were led to believe that there were to be two Illinois locations among the finalist sites and that there would not be many more than 15 finalist sites when the formal AEC announcement was made.[29]

Scientists and the Site Evaluation Process

The site evaluation committee appointed by NAS President Seitz to aid the AEC in evaluating the remaining 148 sites was the epitome of the kind of blue-ribbon group that had so often been used in the formulation of policies for high-energy physics. Its other members were equally distinguished in government-science circles.[30] The appointment of individuals of such stature to the site evaluation committee tended to work in two ways. First, it would make it rather difficult for the AEC to ignore the recommendations made, even though it was exceedingly unlikely that the AEC would have any difficulty in following the NAS committee's recommendations. Second, it would be difficult for public officials in and out of Congress to ignore the recommendations of such a group. This would be particularly true if the activities of the committee could be cloaked in the rhetoric of objective, nonpartisan decision making based on scientific criteria.

The process by which the committee reached its conclusions is as interesting as the results themselves. Its single most outstanding characteristic was the closeness of the collaboration between the AEC and the NAS site selection committee on both

the determination and refinement of the criteria for selecting the
site and the application of these criteria in the appraisal of the
sites that had been submitted. Indeed, the middle- and top-level
AEC personnel, as well as the NAS president, have indicated
that informal consultation occurred continuously.[31]

In addition to regular informal contact, the AEC and the
NAS team collaborated on a number of formal activities during
the process of reducing the number of sites from 148 to the final
six. It was, for example, not the NAS but rather the AEC that
organized eight inspection teams to visit each of the 148 sites.
These four-man teams, each of which included three AEC staff
members and someone from either a university or from one of
the agency's contract laboratories, obtained detailed information
on many of the proposed sites and then reported back to both
the AEC and the NAS site evaluation committee.[32]

Involvement of the broader national high-energy physics
community in the site selection process was also occurring in a
number of ways, formally and informally. On November 11 and
12, 1965 (10 days prior to a meeting of the NAS evaluation team
with the AEC to develop more site selection criteria), the NAS
convened a panel of 18 of the nation's most prestigious accelerator
scientists for the purpose of reviewing the physical or hard criteria for the future accelerator site. This group was composed of
scientists from all over the country, including such high-energy
luminaries as Edward Lofgren of Berkeley, out of whose laboratory had first come the proposal for the 200-bev accelerator, and
Lewis Rosen, the director of the AEC's Los Alamos laboratory.

Collaboration between AEC and NAS helped maintain peace
through those painful days of weeding out contestants. Each
helped diffuse pressures on the other. The distinguished NAS
committee served to soften political criticism hurled at the AEC
as each contestant was eliminated. But the AEC was in turn
able to insulate the NAS from the more crass forms of lobbying.
For example, when groups such as the very imposing Midwest
Governors' Conference tried to obtain audience with the NAS
committee, they found themselves able, only as a late and final
resort, to meet with some AEC officials.[33] At the same time, and
by the same process, the AEC was taking substantial advantage.
The lobbying kept the AEC informed on political sentiments and

reactions. And the competition between lobbyists pushed up the ante for the site. In the beginning, for example, the AEC had had no requirement of free land. But when it became evident through meetings with local spokesmen that many were ready and willing, free land became for all intents and purposes a requirement.[34]

The Competition Narrows

On March 22, 1966, 11 months after the competition had been announced, the results of the NAS site selection efforts were made public by AEC. The summary of this 44-page report (complete with another 30 pages of appendixes) stated that

> The Committee's principal concerns have included the physical properties of the site, the problems of assembling an outstanding staff, and accessibility for visiting scientists who will conduct about seventy-five percent of the experiments. While none of the recommended sites is ideal, each is excellent in at least one of the most important features and within acceptable limits with respect to others.[35]

On the basis of these criteria, the NAS committee found that six sites were, on balance, clearly superior. Regarding the criteria that guided its decision making, the committee noted in the report that

> the major factors in evaluating sites can be divided into two categories. The first includes the physical features, such as geology, size, configuration, climate, and availability of power, water and industrial support. The second category consists of those less readily measurable factors of environment likely to affect the recruitment of resident staff and the participation of visiting scientists.[36]

The report discussed each of the final six sites in substantial detail, the highlights of which follow:

Ann Arbor, Michigan—Transportation to and from the site was good, with the Detroit Metropolitan Airport only slightly more than 30 minutes away. Immediate proximity to the University of Michigan and the Ann Arbor residential environment as well as general proximity to the Detroit Metropolitan area was an important feature. Other universities, including Michigan State and Wayne State, were in driving distance. The site's major weaknesses were that very deep piles would be necessary to support the accelerator ring and that water might have to be transported to it.[37]

Denver, Colorado—A lovely area, it was physically satisfactory and easily accessible to the Denver airport. Its major drawback was that there was neither significant university strength nor very many user groups in the immediate vicinity. It was the most convenient of the non-California sites for the large number of California users.

Madison, Wisconsin—Physically it was the best site, and was in close proximity to the University of Wisconsin, which was the original home of the MURA group. It was dependent on Milwaukee and Chicago for industrial support. The biggest drawback was the lack of a major airport nearby. Visitors would have to transfer at Chicago-O'Hare Airport for local flights to Madison.

Sierra Foothills—The hard rock surface would have involved extra expenses for blasting and carrying in soil cover for the accelerator. While convenient to the Berkeley-Stanford physicists, for national visitors it would involve transfer at San Francisco Airport to a Sacramento plane and then a 30-minute ride from the Sacramento Airport. The 2-hour drive to the Berkeley campus made the site group dependent on the University of California–Davis campus as the major support facility.

Brookhaven National Laboratory—Located on Long Island about 50 miles out from New York City, the laboratory was the site of the largest existing accelerator in the nation. A wide variety of other scientific activities were also under way there. Construction costs would be a bit higher at this site than others and either a half-hour drive and then a short flight or a 90-minute auto drive would be required in order to reach the nearest national airport.

South Barrington (or Weston), Near Chicago, Illinois [38]— Actually there were two distinct Chicago area sites, both of which were considered satisfactory insofar as the physical or hard criteria were concerned. Water and electrical power potential were adequate in both cases, with the only limitation being that the geology of the Weston site would probably require extra-deep support pilings. Both sites were rated very good with regard to the soft criteria. Proximity to the Argonne Laboratory, several universities (University of Chicago, Northwestern University, Illinois Institute of Technology, and University of Illinois–Chicago Circle—all within 1 hour's drive), and the general Chicago metropolitan area was an important factor. In addition, O'Hare Field, with regular flights to every major city in the country, was within a half-hour's driving time of either site and thus made both particularly attractive. Moreover, the Chicago area was reasonably well centered in relation to many prominent Midwestern universities. The report did not explain why unlike the other sites selected there were in effect two Chicago area alternatives. AEC officials later suggested that this was simply because circumstances produced two sites near Chicago that were equally acceptable, whereas the other areas had only one available site.[39] Although this may be so, it does seem a bit more than coincidental that this should occur only in the one area among the final six in which the AEC already knew that it faced significant local opposition to a proposed site.[40] Alternatively it could be that it was more than mere coincidence, suggesting that the AEC wanted to insure that there would be a Chicago area site among the finalists.

There are at least three reasons why the AEC may have desired to insure the presence of a Chicago site among the finalists. First, it may by this point have been recognized that a site in the general Chicago area provided the best alternative on the basis of the stated criteria. Second, on the basis of the geographic distribution of high-energy users in the Midwest the Chicago area may have been thought the best site. And, finally, there is the possibility that the AEC, with or without the knowledge of the NAS, had already either made, or had been instructed to make, a decision to locate the accelerator in the Chicago area.

On the day following the announcement of the six finalists, the AEC released a copy of a letter of several pages' length written by Emanuel Piore, the chairman of the NAS site evaluation committee, discussing the degree to which the various sites could relate to existing AEC facilities. This letter, particularly in terms of its discussion of sites not included in the final six, further illustrates the relative significance of the hard and soft criteria in the NAS site selection activities. After discussing the various

ways that the Brookhaven, Chicago, Madison, and Sierra Foothills sites could benefit from relations with the existing AEC
facilities at Brookhaven, Argonne, and Berkeley, Piore notes that

> Site proposals associated with other AEC facilities were received
> from Oak Ridge, Hanford, Idaho Falls, and Savannah River. The
> Committee considered these in detail along with the other eighty-
> one proposals referred to them by the AEC. *In evaluating the*
> *proposed sites the Committee, after being assured that a given*
> *site had suitable physical properties, assigned paramount im-*
> *portance to factors which affect the recruiting of personnel for the*
> *laboratory and the participation of the nation's high energy*
> *physicists* . . . . [These] sites either do not have the university
> strength nearby or do not possess the existing design group that
> is considered desirable. Moreover, they are remote from the
> standpoint of users . . . .[41]

The Piore letter is revealing in two respects. In the first
place, it provides further insight into the relative importance of
the two categories of criteria that were used by the decision
makers. It serves once again to illustrate that although the hard
criteria were important it was nevertheless the soft criteria—those
concerned with the cultural, intellectual, and social environment—
that played the most significant role in the selection process. The
Piore letter also serves to illustrate the character of the soft
criteria that were utilized in the decision-making process. They
came down to one consideration: staff amenities, staff comforts.[42]
Consequently, because all six finalists more than satisfied the
soft criteria, scientists no longer had to worry about the political
pressures that might be brought in behalf of one or another
section of the country. No longer could the scientists really lose.
They had found sites in the East, the Midwest, and the Far West
that met their basic needs.

The Final Six: A Balanced Ticket

The six finalist sites that emerged in March 1966 were
logical, probably predictable. Take a historical background in
which Berkeley-Stanford and the "Brookhaven axis" were the
established "centers of excellence," with the Midwest as the determined, persistent, and sometimes enraged challenger; add to

TABLE 3–1   Approximate Location and
Distribution of High-Energy Physics User Groups [43]

AREA	NUMBER OF GROUPS
Northeast	31 to 56
Upstate New York	5 to 8
Maryland–Washington D.C.	3 to 6
South	3 to 6
Chicago Area	7 to 10
Midwest (outside Chicago Area)	17 to 30
San Francisco Bay Area	10 to 20
Southern California	5 to 8
Other	3 to 6

this a knowledge of where high-energy physicists and facilities are located—one more or less comes out with the final six selected sites. Table 3–1 provides information on the general location of the users of such facilities.

As even the layman might have known, the Northeast with its large concentration of prestige universities and the availability of the very advanced Brookhaven facility leads the nation in number of high-energy users groups. Perhaps the most interesting point that the table illustrates, however, is the fact that the San Francisco Bay Area with its much greater research facilities has far fewer user groups than the Midwest. In contrast to the distribution of users, Table 3–2 lists the high-energy accelerator facilities either existent or in construction in 1967.

From Tables 3–1 and 3–2, it is clear that the Midwest (more precisely the Big Ten) was at a clear disadvantage regarding the distribution of these facilities. Using the higher figure for the approximate number of user groups and assuming that the Argonne machine was in fact a Midwestern rather than simply a Chicago area or University of Chicago facility (which it had at least in theory become after the MURA controversy), the ratio of facilities to user groups ranged from 1:5 at Berkeley-Stanford, to 1:40 for the Midwest. Therefore, it is not particularly surprising that of the four locations in the Midwest with more than two high-energy user groups only Champaign-Urbana, the home of the

TABLE 3–2 [44]

LOCATION	NAME	PARTICLE	ENERGY BEV	COMPLETION DATE
Lawrence (Berkeley)	Cyclotron	proton *	1.1	1946 and 1957†
Brookhaven	Cosmotron	proton	3	1952
Princeton	PPA	proton	3	1963
Lawrence (Berkeley)	Bevatron	proton	6.2	1954 and 1963†
Argonne	ZGS	proton	12.5	1963
Brookhaven	AGS	proton	33	1960
Stanford	Mark III	electron	1.2	1950 and 1964†
Cal Tech	Synchrotron	electron	1.5	1952 and 1962†
Cornell	Synchrotron	electron	2.2	1955
Cambridge	CEA	electron	6	1962
Cornell	Synchrotron	electron	10	1968
Stanford	SLAC I	electron	20	1966

   * This facility was originally designed for use at lower levels of energy. Following modifications in 1957, it was capable of accelerating several different kinds of particles, some of them above the 1-bev level.
   † Date of last major improvement project.

University of Illinois, was not among the finalists. The absence of Champaign-Urbana can to some degree be explained by the fact it had fewer user groups than the Chicago area.

   Regarding the presence of the Denver site, it is important to remember that the Sacramento site was the least viable of the six finalists due to a combination of the absence of easily accessible national air transportation and the presence of seismic problems.[45] Thus Denver was the most convenient of the other five sites for daily commuting by the Californians.[46] Moreover, it did not suffer from the disadvantage of being in California, where so much federal money had already gone and which, because of this, had been singled out as a particular villain during the MURA controversy.

   In terms of purely political considerations, the final sites also made rather good sense. Illinois had Richard Daley (at the time thought by many to be the nation's second most powerful Democrat), Everett Dirksen (perhaps then the most influential

Republican in the nation), Paul Douglas (probably the most prestigious liberal politician in the country then actively defending Lyndon Johnson's war policy), Otto Kerner (later to be chosen by Johnson to head up his commission on civil disorders), as well as two members of the JCAE, Melvin Price and John Anderson. All were working hard for any one of three sites in Illinois.

California, with a Democratic governor and with two representatives on the JCAE (including the then Committee Chairman Chet Holifield) pushing one site, could also be considered fairly well represented.

The remainder of the JCAE members, who were primarily from New England, could be presumed to be at least somewhat satisfied by the inclusion of the Brookhaven site.

Decision by Criteria Juggling: How to Hold a Contest Without Actually Holding One

Any analysis of the specific criteria used in judging the potential accelerator sites reveals a great deal about two important dimensions of the decision process: (1) the role of nonscientific factors in science decision making and (2) the extent to which even scientific criteria can nevertheless be used in subjective ways.

It was during the initial round of AEC site visitations that the AEC and the NAS committee jointly initiated efforts to develop the formal criteria by which the sites would be judged and the final selection made. When the AEC-NAS agreement was formulated, in April 1965, the AEC had already established several general standards that a site would have to meet in order to be deemed acceptable.[47] At a formal meeting of the AEC with the site evaluation committee in November 1965—following the September elimination of the first 100 sites—the AEC presented to the committee an 8-page document that elaborated on the initial information which it had prepared. The new document contained eight general categories of criteria to be considered. It was hoped that this extended list of criteria would help bring the list of contestants down from the remaining 148 to some more manageable number:

1. Land suitability.
2. Utility availability.

3. Construction cost.
4. Operation cost.
5. Transportation.
6. Colleges and universities (proximity thereto).
7. Communities (in the site area).
8. Other considerations.[48]

Of particular interest are the specific conditions listed under categories 7 and 8. With regard to category 7, the communities in the vicinity of the site, it was indicated that there must be a minimum population of 50,000 within an hour's commuting distance of the laboratory. Furthermore, it was stated that the "quality and adaptability of public school systems including the growth record and community interest in education are important" and that "churches, entertainment, recreational and other cultural facilities such as museums and libraries should be available." [49]

The inclusion of these criteria in conjunction with the requirement of proximity to fairly substantial university facilities largely predetermined the kind of site that was to be considered. To meet these criteria, a site would have to be in a middle- or upper-middle-class area on the periphery of either a large university town or a metropolitan center. Location in an economically depressed area or a rural community was in fact precluded and the possibility of creating a new town in a largely undeveloped area such as had occurred at the Oak Ridge and Los Alamos facilities was also eliminated.

Under the heading of "Other Considerations," were the following two guidelines:

A. Consideration should be given to the special responsibility of the AEC for its own laboratories and the advantages of effective utilization of present AEC facilities.
B. Consideration to the establishment of a new center of excellence. The impact of the accelerator laboratory on a local university makes possible the transition to a new level of performance. Desirability of broadening the educational base of the nation should be considered.[50]

Both of these were very significant additions to the criteria that were to be considered by the site selection committee, and both were in no small degree a response to the pressures that were continuing to mount regarding the selection of a site. The clear inconsistency of these two guidelines suggests that these pressures were coming from inside the AEC establishment and from scientists as well as politicians.

The inclusion of the first of the two was a relatively straight-forward response to the directors and others connected with existing AEC facilities who sought to have the accelerator located at an already established AEC installation.[51] At least one of the committee members personally advocated the selection of an existing AEC facility in order to make one of the AEC's less attractive facilities more appealing. The remote Hanford and Idaho Falls sites were among his first preferences.[52]

The inclusion of the second guideline served to reassure those who had fought (and lost) the MURA battle. In addition, it provided at least formal compliance with the general policy that President Johnson had outlined in the aftermath of the MURA controversy, when in addition to ordering broader participation in the use of Argonne's facilities he had written to the heads of departments and agencies suggesting that they

> give consideration, where research capability of comparable quality exists, to awarding grants and contracts to [educational] institutions not now heavily engaged in federal research programs . . . [agencies] should use a larger proportion of their research funds in accordance with the intent of the policy.[53]

Yet it was inconsistent with part A and thus seemed to violate one of the sacred AEC laws that preference should always be given to sites at or near exisitng centers of excellence in high-energy physics. Concordance between parts A and B depends on the definition of "center of excellence." It could be defined narrowly to include only Berkeley-Stanford and Brookhaven, where the most avant-garde research at highest energies was being conducted,[54] in which case a new center ought to go to one of these, despite part B. Or it could refer to the conduct of any important physics research, not necessarily at high energies, in which case a center might be new and yet near the University of Chicago or many of the Big Ten universities.[55] This would involve creation of a third center of excellence precisely in high energy.[56] Or, if one disregarded complete inconsistency of part A with AEC's unwritten rule governing high-energy research sites, one could take "center of excellence" in its broadest sense and permit placement of the 200-bev machine near any one of a hundred major universities in the country.

It is impossible to know what the AEC meant by these final criteria. In retrospect, it would appear that it had intended the broader but not the broadest possible definition.[57] But more probably the AEC did not know what it meant. It was grasping for discretion *and* for some automatic formula in the face of the unexpected outpouring of site proposals, and the only way to get both of these inconsistent things was to hide behind a list of guidelines that appeared clear but were not. With each round of elimination, the AEC could clarify its criteria in light of the remaining contestants.

The staging of the elaborate competition was not, as a consequence, a charade. Some agency people insist that the Weston selection process will never be used again, and others believe a similar situation would bring on the same process.[58] But regardless of motives or prospects for the future, the process was probably improvised to cope with the situation, and the improvisation was along lines consistent with the scientific mentality. Moreover, once the procedure was set, its advantages must have been apparent. The broad base of participation guaranteed congressional funding at a time when science budgets were contracting.[59] The competitive bidding among so many contestants helped push up the ante.[60] Following on this, the criteria helped in many ways to do more than merely cope with the numerous, varied, and greedy contestants: Existence of criteria helped legitimize the final decision. Application of the criteria in actual site evaluation, and their extension to meet each new round of elimination, reduced public conflict. Discretion behind the appearance of automatic guidelines left room for political manipulation. And, finally, the widespread though tacit acceptance of the particular criteria guaranteed a white, upper-middle-class, comfortable environment for the project scientists no matter where the project went or who finally decided.

The AEC Chooses a Winner—Itself

The five AEC commissioners considered the six remaining sites from March to December 1966. Finally, just in time to be included in President Johnson's budget for fiscal year 1968 (which began July 1, 1967), the AEC announced its choice. On December 16, 1966, Otto Kerner, then governor of Illinois, received a telegram from the AEC announcing that the village of Weston, Illinois, was to be the site where the 200-bev accelerator would be constructed.

Members of both the JCAE and the AEC have continued to indicate that the decision was made by the AEC solely on the criteria indicated, and that neither political considerations nor elected political officials influenced it.[61] On the other hand, a respectable source in the Johnson administration with an almost unique vantage point from which to view these events has indicated privately that he is certain that the president told the AEC it should do all the research necessary to make the best decision, but to make sure that the facility ended up within 50 miles of Chicago.[62]

No doubt, both interpretations are well founded. The criteria did indeed mean something. Hard criteria alone made some contestants look ridiculously inadequate. Many other contestants could at least be clearly rated accordingly. Moreover, even the soft criteria were seriously adopted and seriously applied. Our criticism is aimed not at the narrow character of these soft criteria but rather at the absence of discussion and weighing of these criteria and at the lack of awareness of the particular social policy biases introduced by these criteria.

On the nonpolitical, AEC side, there is also the undeniable fact that the site for this valuable project was not announced until after the 1966 elections. On the other side, politics is clearly indicated by President Johnson's insistence on a moderate dispersion of AEC research facilities. Politics is indicated by the fact that the Ann Arbor site outranked Weston on the hard criteria and equaled Weston on the soft. The only significant difference was the strength of political forces mobilized on behalf of each. Politics is indicated by the fact that Weston was virtually bootlegged into the contest through its parenthetical inclusion along with the more illustrious Barrington site. Politics is also indicated by President Johnson's assurances to Paul Douglas. Withholding the announcement until after the election turned out to be no act of statesmanship at all but rather a result of the president's conclusion that announcement would do Douglas's faltering campaign no good but might do Pat Brown's uphill reelection fight against Ronald Reagan a lot of harm.

The real point here does not rest on a weighing of the relative significance of politics versus AEC's objectivity and its scientific clientele. The timing of each allowed each in its time to be the dominant consideration. Once the scientists had had a full go with their criteria, it no longer mattered which one of the six finalists was chosen. And as long as some choice was left for politics, the science games would be tolerated. In the end the scientists quite obviously were the big winners. They got everything they had wanted—the new machine in a good environment. The politicians got their chance, but their winnings, albeit hard to measure, were smaller. Republicans won big in most of the big states in 1966, including Illinois, California, New York, and Michigan. And whatever political gains were made in the politicizing of site selections accrued far more to scientists than to politicians.

NOTES TO CHAPTER 3

1. The next chapter covers the activities undertaken on behalf of the various Illinois site proposals. It provides the reader with some better understanding of the enormous efforts that were made on behalf of many of the site proposals. Although the Illinois effort was no doubt among the more elaborate of those made, it is by no means atypical of what occurred in some other states.
2. For a listing of all of the sites proposed to the AEC, see Joint Committee on Atomic Energy (JCAE), AEC Authorizing Legislation, Fiscal Year 1967 (Washington, D.C.: U.S. Government Printing Office, 1966), Part 3, pp. 1627–1630. Four states did not have proposed sites located within their borders. These were Alaska, Hawaii, Vermont, and New Hampshire.
3. The three AEC commissioners who were interviewed readily conceded that the decision to open up the site selection process was directly related to the MURA controversy. Commission Chairman Glenn Seaborg indicated that it was the MURA controversy combined with the fact that the accelerator was to be a national facility that persuaded the AEC to open up the site selection process. AEC Commissioner Gerald Tape, on the other hand, suggested that it was the MURA controversy in combination with the political pressures developing within the agency on behalf of

locating the facility at one of the agency's existing laboratories that was the decisive factor in persuading the commission to handle site selection in the manner that it did. Interviews with AEC Chairman Glenn Seaborg, March 27, 1969, both at AEC offices in Washington, D.C. Regarding the AEC's previous efforts in locating such facilities, see Chapter 2 of this book; Daniel S. Greenberg, *The Politics of Pure Science* (New York: New American Library, 1967); and Harold Orlans, *Contracting for Atoms* (Washington, D.C.: Brookings Institution, 1967).

4. This point was noted by both John A. Erlewine, AEC assistant general manager for operations, and Dr. Paul W. McDaniel, director of the AEC's Division of Research, during the course interviews held at the AEC's general offices in Maryland on March 24, 1969.

5. See "200 BEV Accelerator Design Study, Summary," Lawrence Radiation Laboratory, University of California, June 1965, as reprinted in JCAE, *AEC Authorizing Legislation, Fiscal Year 1967*, op. cit., p. 1591.

6. Ibid., p. 1621.

7. AEC Commissioner Gerald Tape has indicated that he expected at the most about 30 site proposals to be received by the AEC. Interview with Gerald Tape, op. cit. In testimony before the JCAE, Tape has discussed further the great surprise of the AEC at the response to its announcement. See *AEC Authorizing Legislation, Fiscal Year 1967*, op. cit., p. 1308.

8. Interview with Professor Frederick Seitz, then president of the National Academy of Sciences, at the NAS offices in Washington, D.C., March 26, 1969.

9. Interview with Glenn Seaborg, op. cit. Also, on the role of the NAS in science policy making more generally, see Michael A. Reagan, *Science and the Federal Patron* (New York: Oxford University Press, 1969), pp. 82–84; "The National Science Foundation, A General Review of its First Fifteen Years," in The *Politics of Science*, ed. by William Nelson (New York: Oxford University Press, 1968), pp. 139–175; and Greenberg, op. cit., especially Chapters 1 and 8.

10. The character of the criteria utilized in the decision-making process by both the NAS and the AEC was never really held up to public scrutiny or even seriously examined by the JCAE itself. Once, very briefly, during the course of JCAE hearings on the site selection, the issue was mentioned in passing during an exchange between senators Jacob Javits and John Pastore with regard to why the machine was not located at the Brookhaven Laboratory in New York. At that time Senator Javits raised the question of the appropriateness of the criteria on which the decision was made, but then he never pursued the point. This represents virtually the only time during the course of JCAE hearings that extended over

a 4-year period that this issue was ever raised. See JCAE, *AEC Authorizing Legislation, Fiscal Year 1968* (Washington, D.C.: U.S. Government Printing Office, 1967), Part 1, p. 71, for Javits' brief mention of this topic. See also Chapter 5.

On the other hand, a number of instances can be cited in which statements by congressional and agency participants clearly imply that the criteria were essentially the product of expert scientific and objective judgment. For example, JCAE Chairman Holifield has, in speaking about the final judgment, described it as the result of a site selection process that was based upon "expert opinion." *AEC Authorizing Legislation, Fiscal Year 1967*, op. cit., p. 1312. During the course of an interview, JCAE member John Anderson specifically indicated that the decision on behalf of the Weston site was the result of the application by the NAS and AEC of "objective criteria" to the decision-making process. Interview with Congressman John Anderson at his office in the Old House Office Building, March 28, 1969. Likewise, AEC Commissioner James Ramey commented during an interview that the NAS was "scientific and objective in its operations" during the course of the site selection process. Interview with James Ramey at the AEC offices in Washington, D.C., March 26, 1969.

11. This question crops up in almost every case study in the book.
12. Statement of Dr. Edward Lofgren, in JCAE, *High Energy Physics Research* (Washington, D.C.: U.S. Government Printing Office, 1965), p. 62.
13. Interview with Ralph Huitt, at the Brookings Institution, March 24, 1969. See Chapter 2 and Greenberg, op. cit., Chapters 10 and 11, for a detailed examination of the MURA controversy.
14. Subsequent actions taken both by Johnson and by the AEC, probably at the president's direction, in order to pacify the Midwest anger in the face of the veto served to further promote this belief. See Greenberg, op. cit., pp. 267–268, and Orlans, op. cit., p. 56.
15. See U.S. Atomic Energy Commisison, *High Energy Physics Program* (1965), Appendix I, p. 85. See Chapter 2.
16. On the traditional role of the Atomic Energy Commission, see Orlans, op. cit.; on the JCAE, see Harold S. Green and Alan Rosenthal, *Government of the Atom* (New York: Atherton Press, 1963), especially Chapter 7.
17. Interview with Frederick Seitz, op. cit.
18. See letter from Frederick Seitz to Chet Holifield, July 30, 1965, as printed in *AEC Authorizing Legislation, Fiscal Year 1967*, op. cit., pp. 1656–1657.
19. See statement of Leland J. Hayworth in JCAE, *High Energy Physics Research*, op. cit., p. 11.
20. See National Academy of Sciences, Meetings of University Presi-

dents, January 17, 1965, summary of conclusions in *High Energy Physics Research*, op. cit., pp. 8 and 9.

21. Subsequently it was decided that a group of 34 universities would be the founding members of URA. Since that time, membership in URA has been increased to 46 universities. For a general discussion of the administrative and policy implications resulting from the establishment of URA, see Boyd Keenan, "High Energy Administration: Big Science Model for the Future," *Public Administration Review*, 28(3):250–255 (May–June 1969).

22. *High Energy Physics Research*, op. cit., p. 9.

23. See "AEC-NAS Enter Agreement on Evaluating Sites for a Proposed New National Accelerator Laboratory," mimeographed press release by the Atomic Energy Commission, April 28, 1965, p. 1.

24. Ibid.

25. Ibid.

26. *Indianapolis Star*, September 15, 1965 (interview article by Elene Corlett), p. 4.

27. Ibid.

28. One can understand why the AEC may have acted in this manner if one accepts two premises—first, that the agency was more concerned at this point about making certain that the accelerator be built than about where it was to be built; and, second, that it had no doubt that its interests coincided with the interests of the NAS. If both of these conditions were true, then it would be in the interest of the AEC to hand the bulk of the site elimination activity to the NAS, thus avoiding most of the wrath that otherwise would have descended upon the agency. Although this led some to accuse the AEC of shirking its responsibilities, this criticism, vehement as it may have been, was not nearly so great as would have been the wrath of 100 or more spurned congressional suitors. Had the agency assumed the responsibility for a substantial portion of the site elimination at this point it would likely have faced such a fate.

   In addition, it is not unlikely that the AEC could more effectively control the site selection process through the use of its informal relationships with the NAS than if it had used its own authoritative decision-making powers. This premise assumes that in certain respects the NAS, a nongovernmental body, was less susceptible to local political pressure and congressional power politics than the AEC, a governmental body. The fact that the NAS was often taking on tasks of this sort would seem to indicate that, shrouded in its cloak of scientific objectivity, it may very well have been better able to withstand the influences of anxious state and congressional politicians than was a governmental agency such as the AEC.

29. Interview with Kyran McGrath, state of Illinois representative in Washington, D.C., at his home, March 23, 1969.

30. They included Robert Bacher, Provost, California Institute of Technology, and a member of the initial AEC; Harvey Brooks, Dean of Engineering, Harvard University; John W. Gardner (who resigned upon his appointment as HEW secretary and was replaced by Charles Reed, the executive secretary of the NAS); Edwin L. Goldwasser, University of Illinois physicist, who later became assistant director of the 200-bev facility; G. Kenneth Green, Brookhaven National Laboratory; Crawford H. Greenwalt, Chairman of the Board of E. I. duPont de Nemours and Co., Inc.;Val F. Fitch, Princeton University; William B. Fretter, University of California at Berkeley; William F. Frey, University of Wisconsin; and Herbert E. Longenecker, President of Tulane University.

31. Interviews with Tape and Erlewine, op. cit.

32. JCAE, *AEC Authorizing Legislation, Fiscal Year 1967*, Hearings, op. cit., pp. 1309–1310.

33. Frederick Seitz has indicated that the position of the NAS committee was simply to refuse flatly to discuss the matter of site selection with outsiders. Any interested political or business groups that contacted them were referred to the AEC. Senator Henry Jackson has confirmed that this was the response he received upon his attempt to contact the NAS committee on behalf of a location in his home state. As a consequence, he spoke with AEC officials. Interview with Henry Jackson, senator of the state of Washington, at his office in Washington, D.C., March 27, 1968.

34. Interviews with Erlewine and McDaniel, op. cit.

35. Report of the National Academy of Sciences Site Evaluation Committee, *AEC Authorizing Legislation, Fiscal Year 1968*, op. cit., p. 402.

36. Ibid., p. 404.

37. The site descriptions included here are but a very small part of the descriptive material to be found in the report. See ibid., pp. 409–414. An effort has been made to use the phraseology and terms used in the report.

38. This is the heading for these two sites as taken directly from the NAS report.

39. Indeed, when questioned about this subject, the AEC officials indicated that Chicago was by no means the only city that had more than one site within its general vicinity. Interviews with Erlewine and McDaniels, op. cit.

40. When AEC officials had visited the South Barrington site, they were greeted by placard-waving local residents, who were protesting against locating the facility there. See Chapter 4.

41. Correspondence from Emanuel Piore to Frederick Seitz, March

23, 1966, released by the Atomic Energy Commission on that date. Emphasis added.

42. This point had been made in several instances by individuals involved in the site selection process, although in few instances has it been put in such clear-cut fashion. For example, in testimony before the JCAE, Paul McDaniel indicated that what he described as the "cultural criterion" was "one of the main criteria for picking a site." *AEC Authorizing Legislation, Fiscal Year 1967*, op. cit., p. 1325.

43. The data included in Table 3–1 are taken from a map of the United States with the approximate location of user groups indicated, which was prepared and released by the AEC following the public announcement of the decision regarding the six finalist sites.

44. The data in Table 3–2 come from a variety of AEC sources, including "Justification Data for the Physical Research Program," *AEC Authorizing Legislation, Fiscal Year 1968*, op. cit., pp. 615–653, and AEC, *Accelerators* (Oak Ridge, Tenn.: AEC, April 1969), pp. 50–51.

45. Although not stating specifically that the Sacramento site was the least desirable one, AEC Chairman Glenn Seaborg, when interviewed, did indicate that—for the two reasons mentioned above—the Sacramento site was probably one of the less viable contenders of the final six. Interview with Seaborg, op. cit.

46. It was also a pleasant place to visit, both climatically and scenically.

47. Interview with AEC Commissioner James Ramey, op. cit.

48. See *AEC Authorizing Legislation, Fiscal Year 1968*, op. cit., p. 180.

49. Ibid., pp. 181–182.

50. Ibid., p. 182.

51. As we have noted earlier, AEC Commissioner Tape has indicated that the pressure from existing AEC installations was significant enough for it to be an important factor in the decision to open up the site selection process.

52. Ramey interview, op. cit.

53. "Memorandum from the President to the Heads of Departments and Agencies" as quoted in Orlans, op. cit., p. 53.

54. In criticizing the AEC's decision to locate the accelerator at the Weston site, Senator Jacob Javits contended that the AEC had made a serious mistake in not locating the facility at one of the *two* existing centers of excellence, the Bay Area or the Brookhaven Laboratory. See ibid., pp. 72–77.

55. In defending the decision to locate the accelerator at Weston, Illinois, JCAE member John Anderson has suggested that it was a decision to locate at an existing center of excellence. See *AEC*

Authorizing Legislation, Fiscal Year 1968, op. cit., pp. 75–76.
56. During the course of an interview, AEC Chairman Glenn Seaborg indicated that the decision to locate the 200-bev accelerator
at the Weston site would result in the creation of a new center
of excellence. Seaborg interview, op. cit.
57. This is consistent with Glenn Seaborg's comment cited in note 56.
58. AEC administrators Erlewine and McDaniel are on the side of no
repetition. On the other side is former AEC Chairman Glenn
Seaborg, who stated that he would in similar circumstances use
such a process again. Interviews with Erlewine, McDaniel, and
Seaborg, op. cit.
59. Interviews with Erlewine and McDaniel, op. cit.
60. AEC administrator Erlewine indicated one example of this in
noting that at the outset of the site selection process the agency
had no idea of seeking free land. Once the competition grew and
the first offer was made, the agency sought to achieve the maximum amount of free land that it could possibly obtain. Erlewine
interview, op. cit.
61. This point was made by every AEC official interviewed, both
administrators and commissioners, and was repeatedly stated in
hearings by the various AEC commissioners.
62. In addition, there was Paul Douglas, who was, until just prior
to the time that the final decision on the Weston site was made,
the senior senator from Illinois. During the course of an interview he reported how he was flown to the LBJ Ranch on a
presidential plane and told by Johnson that if the Chicago area
sites had no fatal flaw insofar as the hard criteria were concerned,
he, Douglas, could be sure that the accelerator would ultimately
be located at one of them. Interview with Paul Douglas at his
office in Washington, D.C., March 27, 1969. On the other hand,
during the course of interviews for this study, congressmen Hosmer, Price, and Holifield and senators Jackson, Pastore, and
Proxmire have indicated that they did not think the president
himself made the final site decision; however, their opinions are
not based on hard evidence.

CHAPTER **4**   **The Quest for**
the Golden Smasher

Less than 2 weeks after the announcement of a nationwide site competition to be sponsored by the AEC and the NAS, leading interests in Illinois began organizing. The first meeting, an informal one, was taken at the initiative of the University of Chicago, which probably had more at stake in the accelerator than any other single metropolitan institution. The meeting included high-level personnel from the University, the Mayor's Committee on Economic and Cultural Development (Chicago), the Continental Illinois Bank and Trust Company (Chicago's second-largest and the nation's eighth-largest bank), and the Commonwealth Edison Company.[1]

This was a preparing of the way for a full-scale, formal session some 2 months later on May 11, 1965. The first formal meeting was called by Gene Graves, director of the recently created Illinois State Department of Business and Economic Development (DBED), the agency that was to sponsor and coordinate almost all activities on behalf of Illinois' quest for the golden smasher.[2] This was a grand coalition; probably no more impressive a grouping of interests has ever been brought together in Illinois for political purposes.

87

The Grand Coalition

One of the most impressive things about the list is its hetero-geneity. Academicians and government officials were joined by Chicago area business and civic leaders from all points in the metropolis and all sides of political life. Joint ventures among business and political leaders were regular occurrences under the administration of Richard J. Daley.[3] It was through such hand-in-hand arrangements that he had facilitated the great commercial boom in the center city. This had been an essential part of the Daley success formula from the time of his first election in 1955.[4] But never had the formula been applied to so broad a set of interests and to an issue so far from the center of Chicago's own concerns.

All members represented interests that stood directly to gain a great deal from the accelerator. Obviously the academic benefits were most direct. Universities in a very large area, reaching to Urbana, Madison, and Ann Arbor at least, would at last be able to reverse the scientific brain drain and attract physicists from all over the country—indeed, the world.[5]

The tie to other interests was less direct but nevertheless substantial. For Commonwealth Edison, the increase in electric power demands could only be profitable. But the readiness of the company to cut its rates to make the Illinois sites more competitive indicates the scope of their plans for expansion in the region through such increased industrialization.[6] No doubt, it was the development potential of the area, not the site taken by itself, that attracted the giant utility. The growth-generating potential of single sites had been impressively illustrated time and again in the Boston and San Francisco metropolitan areas, where some of the great scientific installations had sparked still greater commercial growth. But perhaps more to the point was O'Hare Airport, which had sparked a tremendous development; yet most of the growth was in no way dependent particularly on the presence of the airport. It had simply been a focal point, and another focal point might spark another development elsewhere in the region.

The state was interested obviously because the site meant net economic growth and political rewards, at almost no cost. Senator Douglas, a well-known and vigorous opponent of "pork barrel" legislation, was at that time contemplating a fourth Senate term.

The accelerator would give him a dramatic answer to the criticism that he had never helped Illinois in the race for federal largesse. Governor Kerner might, as a consequence of successes of this sort, contemplate an unprecedented third term. Moreover, the site would have been the first large step toward full establishment of the new DBED.

The rationale for the city's and Daley's involvement is more ambiguous, until the other city interests are examined. Although all potential Illinois sites were outside the city proper, the city's largest financial and commercial institutions needed all the aggregate regional growth they could get if they were to maintain a healthy universe of operations. Without branch banking, Chicago banks have a more than usual stake in local investment. And many of the largest firms headquartered in the center are locally owned and possess a local commitment for which Midwesterners have perhaps been justly noted since Sinclair Lewis.

The May 11 meeting established the roles and missions that were to guide the Illinois lobbying effort until ultimate success. Corplan Associates, it was agreed, would prepare an Illinois proposal for submission to the AEC. Basic research to back up claims for the region and the particular sites was to be done by each of the participating organizations, and by the State Water Survey Division of the University of Illinois, the State Geological Survey, and the Illinois Department of Labor. This represented a substantial state contribution, but, in addition to that, R and D funds were pledged by the participating corporations.[7]

The role of Commonwealth Edison was going to be of particular importance. Because of its involvement in the region, the utility already had detailed information and maps on area sites with industrial potential. ComEd was indeed its own regional planning agency. It had a staff of specialists skilled in development work, especially site location. Consequently, to the utility went the primary mission of locating and describing the sites that would be proposed to the AEC.[8] ComEd's importance loomed still larger in the person of Murray Joslin, vice-president and nationally known expert on the uses of atomic energy in electric power production. Joslin's connections with AEC had been very close for many years. Upon his retirement from the company, the AEC presented him with an award for his leadership.

Each of the requisites of good lobbying was thus to be provided for by at least one responsible agent: project stature and capacity from the University of Chicago and the remains of MURA; economic stature and economic influence from the top regional industries; site selection and data from state and business agencies already equipped to generate it at a moment's notice; planning and finesse in the public relations for the project from a seasoned and classy professional consulting firm; a superabundance of "political clout," a term invented in Chicago for Chicagoans by the men who had it and would lead it for site competition; and a masterful coordinative role to be played by an ambitious new state agency designed for just such a mission. They started off in high gear.

On May 20, 1965, just 9 days after the charter meeting, the first preliminary information was sent to the AEC by the Illinois Department of Business and Economic Development indicating the state's interest in bidding for the accelerator. The next day, the Illinois congressional delegation was alerted to the fact that the state would submit a proposal.[9] On June 11, 1965, exactly 1 month after the initial formal meeting, Governor Kerner approved for submission to the AEC five copies of an eight-volume research report. With a host of supporting documents, the total package weighed in at 164 pounds.[10] The seven sites suggested in the report included two downstate ones—at Princeton in north-central Illinois and in the southeastern part of the state—plus five Chicago area locations that ringed the central city. Although the report did include the two downstate sites, the major efforts were clearly being directed toward the Chicago area sites. It is likely that the involvement of the Chicago business community, as reflected in the makeup of the planning committee, was influential in this respect. In addition, those involved in the report's preparation had felt that the two downstate sites were likely to fulfill the AEC's already stated site selection criteria.[11]

Meanwhile, the pace was quickening, and the ante was going up. When DBED Assistant Director Charles Schrader delivered Illinois' proposal to Paul McDaniels, Schrader learned that several states, including both Maryland and Indiana, had made offers of free land to the AEC, and that other states planned to make similar offers.[12] Consequently on the following day, with only 2 weeks remaining before the adjournment of the biennial legislative session, the Democratic Party leadership in the Illinois House introduced, at the governor's request, a bill authorizing the DBED to acquire and accept any lands, buildings, or grounds required for construction of the accelerator. The governor also announced plans to call a special session of the legislature to appropriate the necessary monies to purchase property and to turn it over to the AEC if an Illinois site were selected.[13] Within a week the bill was approved without debate by the House and sent to the Senate. There it was passed the following week, again without debate, and sent to the governor.[14]

Solidarity Forever: Midwest on the Move

Site lobbying did not restrict itself to the Illinois charter group. The MURA experience had been a highly instructive one for the Midwest; the pain of that experience had given them wisdom. There was no proof that traditional lobbying tactics are important in influencing government research and project policy, but the MURA experience taught that at least two principles had to be observed if there was to be a chance at all.

The first principle was that political pressure was of little use late in the game, when entered into as a last-ditch effort to head off or reverse a mature decision. Lobbying would have to start early and stay long. This compelling principle, although it sounds obvious enough, had not been observed before.

The second principle MURA had taught was unity, regional unity. Unity was required for influence, of course, but more. It was required as an assurance that the facility would indeed be used efficiently and amicably by everyone. There had been a lot of unity during the MURA controversy, but there had also been a bit too much research independence, most notably on the part of Illinois through the opposition of the Argonne scientists to MURA's Madison project. Even the large Chicago newspapers, more than likely at Argonne's instigation, had opposed the MURA project out of fear that it might impair Argonne's future.[15] At almost all costs, this independence would have to be couched if a facility of 200-bev scale were to be landed.

Consequently on July 10, 1965, the Committee on Economic Development of the Midwest Governors' Conference, led by

Minnesota's Governor Karl Rolvaag, issued a statement in support of the Midwest as the proper home for the new accelerator.[16] This represented the first formal expression of regional solidarity, and from this time forth until the final decision unity was maintained by the Midwest's politicians, who repeatedly indicated that they would all welcome and support any Midwestern location.

During the same period, the serious exertion of political pressure also began. At about this time, David Kennedy, Continental Illinois' chief, who went on to become Nixon's secretary of the treasury, sent a personal letter to Mayor Daley seeking the mayor's direct personal involvement. The letter included a brief description of the nature of an accelerator. It also included the draft of a letter for the mayor to forward to President Johnson urging the selection of a Chicago area site.[17] The letter pointed out that Chicago had not been getting its fair share of federal projects. From this point on, Daley apparently never missed an opportunity to raise this issue with the president, when the president was in Chicago and when Daley visited the White House, where he was frequently an overnight guest.[18] Congressman Dan Rostenkowski, who was present at several such meetings, has indicated that they would begin with Daley noting that it was absolutely imperative that Chicago receive funds that were then pending for a particular public works project and then adding that he would really like to see the area get the accelerator.[19] A similar policy was being followed by Rostenkowski himself, the leader of the city of Chicago's tightly controlled congressional delegation. Also, at this point state officials began what was to become an extremely close working relationship with Congressman Melvin Price on this matter. Price, from the East St. Louis area, was the second-ranking Democrat on the Joint Committee on Atomic Energy (JCAE) and at that time was chairman of its important and relevant Subcommittee on Research and Development.[20]

As the politicians were beginning their concerted assault upon the AEC, the formal site selection process was getting under way. On September 9, the first of many visits to the Illinois sites was made by AEC representatives. Illinois had on hand a massive delegation of state and local officials, led by DBED Director Graves and Commonwealth Edison Vice-President Joslin, to greet the visitors.[21] On this and subsequent visits, the DBED undertook elaborate preparations to host the visitors. The variety of activities ranged from organizing elegant dinners to providing helicopters to assist in the site-viewing process. These efforts contrast sharply with measures taken by many competing states, where such visits were largely matter-of-fact, businesslike affairs.[22]

On September 14, 1965, the AEC's Paul McDaniel notified Governor Kerner that the five Chicago area sites and the Princeton, Illinois, site were among the 148 sites in 43 states still in the running and that these would be the subject of further study by the NAS and its site selection teams.[23] This announcement came as something of a surprise to state officials, who thought, as a result of informal communications from the AEC, that two Illinois sites were to be among a group of not more than 15 finalist sites.[24] It was with these circumstances as a backdrop that Kerner met some days later with over 100 of the Chicago area's top business executives and civic leaders. His purpose was to spread the lobby network and step up the efforts. At a luncheon meeting he explained the project in elaborate detail and generally asked for support of the state's efforts.[25] The roster of those in attendance at the meeting, which was held in the Shareholder's Room of the Continental Illinois Bank, included the board chairmen, presidents, or vice-presidents of most of the Chicago metropolitan area's major industries. Also present were high-ranking executives from several of the nation's largest industries that had strong local ties. The meeting also included top executives from local advertising firms and the city's news media, presidents of most of the area's large universities, financial institutions, and research organizations, and a few leaders of state and local labor groups.[26]

The AEC announcement that Illinois was still very much in the running also produced escalated lobbying action in the entire Midwest, as a further expression of solidarity. Meeting in Michigan in late September, the Midwest Governors' Conference adopted a resolution again urging the location of the accelerator in the Midwest. The resolution restated the basic case being made by both Midwestern physicists and politicians.[27] Shortly thereafter, this was amplified in a detailed report to the AEC that set about documenting the Midwest's failure to receive its "rightful" share of federal projects.[28] Typical of the report was the charge that the 12 Midwestern states, with 24 per cent of the nation's population, supplied 32 per cent of all federal revenue and graduated 34 per cent of the nation's Ph.D.'s, but received only 10 per cent of all federal research and development expenditures.[29]

Once again, while the politicos were politicking, the technicians were cranking up the site selection apparatus. The AEC announced that a team of scientists would inspect the Chicago area sites on November 30. The team members were Dr. John Swartout, Assistant for Research, AEC; Dr. Raymond Fricken, physicist in the Division of Research, AEC; Mr. Jack Bane, engineer, AEC; and Dr. Harold Ticho, physicist, UCLA. The five Chicago area sites were again visited by helicopter while staff and automobiles were stationed nearby should the team desire to travel over the sites by land. Information kits were prepared by Commonwealth Edison and DBED containing maps, details on water, power, and geology, and other pertinent information.[30] Following the visit to the sites, Dr. Swartout, the team spokesman, commented at a press conference that all of the Chicago area sites appeared to be well suited for the AEC's needs. He emphasized the advantage of proximity to O'Hare Airport and pointed out that with this visit Illinois had now become one of only four states to be visited by both AEC and NAS teams.[31]

Unfortunately for Illinois, the first serious problem was about to emerge. Prior to the arrival of the site visitation team, the mayor of the village of South Barrington issued a statement indicating that the village had only recently learned that a site adjacent to it was being considered as a possible location for the accelerator. The village mayor stated that he thought the needs of the accelerator were probably incompatible with the estate residential character of the general area.[32] Disunity was threatening from within.

Trouble on the Homefront: Would You Want a Scientist Living Next Door to You?

On March 22, 1966, the AEC announced the six (or seven) finalist sites, which included Barrington (or Weston), Illinois, and indicated that inspection teams would shortly be visiting each of them. The most significant characteristic shared by the two Illinois sites, apart from the fact that both met the AEC requirements, was the rather high socioeconomic character of the general area in which they were located. The Barrington site was located in proximity to Cook County's wealthiest suburban communities. Indeed, a couple of these communities had zoning ordinances requiring that single-family residential lots be no smaller than five acres in size.

The AEC announcement launched a flurry of activity in Illinois by both supporters and opponents (specifically local property owners) of the two Illinois sites. Individuals near each site began to take a harder look at the implications. Heated controversy began to develop particularly in several of the communities near the Barrington site. In the village of Barrington, for instance, the village president had indicated strong support for locating the accelerator nearby, whereas the remaining members of the village council had voiced their vigorous opposition. In South Barrington, the opposition was almost unanimous. Likewise, the president and other officials of the village of Barrington Hills had publicly indicated strong and unanimous opposition to the plans.[33] All of this was made clear to state and AEC officials, who were the recipients of numerous anguished and outraged letters.[34]

Even in the less affluent Weston area a few rumblings of discontent were beginning to be heard. State officials were, however, able to avoid any direct conflict by acting quickly and decisively in developing a lot of highly vocal support for their efforts there. Immediately after the announcement of the finalists, state officials from the governor's office and DBED contacted local business leaders throughout DuPage County in an effort to gain their assistance in promoting local enthusiasm for locating the project at the Weston site.[35] The purpose of this effort was twofold: to overwhelm any opposition that may have been developing in the area and to attempt to obviate any damage to Illinois' chances that might come from the Barrington controversy. This was the first of at least two state counterpropaganda campaigns.

Having succeeded in generating the efforts necessary to bolster its Weston front, state officials decided to attack the Barrington situation head on by calling a meeting of about 150 community and business leaders from the two proposed sites, including over 50 from Barrington. This April 1 meeting was held at the Argonne Laboratory—which was chosen to illustrate to the dissidents that AEC facilities are physically attractive and that AEC personnel could "fit in" with the local communities.[36] Those attending the meeting heard from several state officials vivid descriptions of the great benefits that Illinois would reap from the accelerator.

In spite of these pleas, the Barrington opposition remained firm. Following a 15-minute caucus, the Barrington group announced that they would continue their opposition. Governor Kerner then brought the 3-hour meeting to a close by walking to the podium and startling those present by stating that

> I have no alternative, I'm sorry to say. Illinois had two sites. I'm speaking in the past tense. I have no alternative but to inform the Atomic Energy Commission that Illinois wishes to withdraw the South Barrington site. I don't know what this does to our chances.[37]

An aide of the governor, who along with the others at the meeting was taken by surprise, later reported that Kerner had come to the conclusion that keeping Barrington on the list despite its opposition would have been more detrimental to the state's chances than complete withdrawal of the site.[38] Although the AEC had informally indicated a preference for the Barrington site, the governor's decision in retrospect was apparently a good one. AEC officials have since indicated to interviewers that they would not have located the accelerator in a community in which there was strong opposition.[39]

Following this disappointing meeting, the state began to direct its efforts toward securing the accelerator for Weston, its most likely site. Officials planned to pull out all stops in welcoming the AEC team that was to visit the state on April 8.[40] Taking a cue from the emphasis that the NAS committee report had placed on the availability of support facilities, state officials sent to Washington statements from the presidents of all the Chicago area universities. Each was carefully worded to indicate a desire to see the machine located somewhere in the "Midwest" generally, and went on to state that the universities would cooperate in any way possible to make the accelerator a reality.[41]

In order to organize a reception for the AEC team and to inform the local community of the state's plans, a public meeting of the area's residents was held in Warrenville, a community neighboring Weston. About 200 people attended the meeting on

April 6, held 2 days prior to the AEC visit. Among those who spoke and expressed their support of the state's efforts were a number of local public officials, including Arthur Theriault, the village president of Weston; other officials from Batavia, West Chicago, the village of Winfield, Aurora, St. Charles, Wheaton, Hinsdale; and the DuPage County Board of Supervisors.[42] Results flowed immediately, beginning the following day when numerous area business and community organizations again issued public statements of support.[43] It was a virtual orchestration.

On the day following, the AEC team arrived, and they were greeted with car caravans, individuals carrying homemade signs (including one preschooler whose sign read "I want an atom smasher"), high school military honor guards, and even a brass band. Adding to the carnival atmosphere was the presence of a host of local officials from such unlikely places as Batavia and West Chicago, as well as the ever-present Otto Kerner, Paul Douglas, and Gene Graves. Illinois experts were present to provide additional information on geology, water, and power. The AEC team, which apparently maintained its composure throughout, included Commission Chairman Seaborg, Gerald Tape, the general manager of the AEC, and several other of the agency's top administrative officers.[44]

No doubt, the climax of the day from the point of view of the state officials came in Warrenville. AEC Chairman Seaborg, after saying a few words to the estimated 1,000 "smasher supporters" on hand to greet the AEC team, asked the assembled multitude if they wanted the accelerator located in the area. The local newspaper reported that the "vigorous and positive response . . . left no doubt about the welcome which would be given to such a decision." [45] It was, as Paul Douglas commented, the state's hope that none of the other five finalists could produce as enthusiastic a welcome to the AEC team.[46]

This was not the last of the state's efforts to persuade the AEC that the accelerator would be received warmly in Illinois. Within a month, the DBED had prepared a booklet for presentation by the governor to Seaborg that provided further information on the water supply in the area and also included even more statements of support from such groups as the Illinois Municipal League and the Naperville Chamber of Commerce.[47]

Meanwhile, the AEC was also pressuring Illinois, and surely other contestants, for information that amounted to bargaining. For example, at its last visit to the Weston site, the AEC had left with state officials a questionnaire regarding the electric power supply and rates for the area. After conferring with state officials, Commonwealth Edison responded to this questionnaire by shipping off a bevy of vice-presidents to Washington to consult with AEC officials regarding the facility's power needs. Chief of this mission was Murray Joslin, whose AEC connections have already been noted.[48] Following the meetings, Commonwealth Edison announced the rate reduction that would make electric power at Weston competitive with power at the other five sites. This actually meant that power costs would be still 8 per cent greater than at Ann Arbor and 16 per cent greater than at Brookhaven, but as much as 30 per cent less than at the other three sites.[49]

Mopping Up

The 200-bev machine had once been dubbed the "Berkeley accelerator" because Berkeley scientists had designed it and, according to established practice, Berkeley scientists had expected to build it somewhere near Berkeley. But by early 1966 the Californians were losing out, and they knew it.[50] California was most vulnerable to the Midwest's charges of inequitable project distribution. The single state of California had received more project support than the whole region of the Midwest and the whole region of the Northeast. Moreover, the Northeast had been generous about spreading this support in turn among the several member states. Brookhaven had as much expertise as California. Brookhaven was a center for a far greater number of participating universities. And Brookhaven had never been involved in access controversies that had broken out occasionally over Berkeley and over Argonne.

This made Brookhaven and the Northeast the most formidable adversary, and it is much to the credit of the Midwest's lobbyists that the Northeast was losing ground, and knew it was losing ground.[51] Given the scientific advantages of the Northeast, there could be only one reason why it was nevertheless losing the battle for the 200-bev machine. It had to be Midwestern unity, and sometimes the only way to beat an enemy is to ape him. In late June 1966, very late in the game, Brookhaven supporters met in order to develop a Midwest-type coalition.

The meeting, to which several hundred executives of the East's largest corporations were invited, was held at the First National City Bank in Manhattan. The organizers—several New York political leaders and some of the bank's own executives—felt that because so much money was involved President Johnson would inevitably exercise the ultimate influence. This meant that the combined efforts of business leaders, civic leaders, and congressional delegations up and down the Eastern Seaboard could still exercise a substantial influence.[52] The meeting produced a flurry of activities, including petitions, Washington lobbying, and further meetings. But, alas, it was too late. In a sense, the Northeast had vanquished itself by confidence and tardiness.

However, the ineffectiveness of this last important competitor did not leave the field free and clear to the Midwest coalition, because there was still opposition from within. Inner dissension had probably always been the chief impediment to Midwestern success. It would not defeat itself or go away voluntarily. It had somehow to be mopped up, swept away, or flanked.

The first of the inner adversaries was greed, the inability of at least a few of the other Midwest site contestants to hold the unity line as they lost their place among the finalists. After the announcement of finalists, Midwest officials, led by Governor Rolvaag despite the fact that all Minnesota's contenders had been eliminated, continued to meet with AEC officials to express full support for any of the remaining three (or four) Midwestern sites.[53] But inevitably the ranks would be broken, for shortly after the release the director of the research council of St. Louis's site team ripped off an extremely critical letter to Chairman Seaborg. He compared, in a less than totally accurate way, the St. Louis site with the six (or seven) finalists, concluding

> It is most unfortunate that the NAS . . . in reporting its site recommendations . . . chose to subordinate your Commission's original criteria of site suitability to its own, subjectively oriented criterion of area capability in high energy physics. Had this been one of your Commission's original site criteria, it would

have automatically ruled out proposals from any but three areas of the nation; the New York and Chicago areas and Southern California.

In view of this, the NAS recommendations easily could be construed to be a wholly unwarranted breach of faith with those communities . . . which spent thousands of man-hours in a precise documentation of their fulfillment of your Commission's criteria of site suitability.

Congress, viewing the NAS site evaluation committee's recommendations as the preconceived preferences of partisan physicists, might take action to delay indefinitely and even doom the prospects of this vitally important research tool.[54]

The St. Louis dissent followed by the formation of the East Coast coalition moved the Midwest leaders to redouble their efforts in a once and final push. Governor Kerner contacted all the Midwest governors personally. He also contacted all of the Chicago business and industrial leaders involved in the case.[55] But, as with any beehive, most of the effective lobbying was being done inside at the center. The major contenders on the Midwest's behalf in these final stages were Mel Price, Dan Rostenkowski, Kyran McGrath, and Paul Douglas.

McGrath, the chief of DBED's Washington office, had one primary function at this time, to keep abreast of the details of the entire proceedings, keeping everyone back home fully in command of all hostile events and potential strategies. For instance, McGrath was first in Illinois to discover that other states were quietly planning to offer free land to AEC. In another instance, he helped avert embarrassment by determining for the Illinois planners that AEC would plan no local support and assistance except for facilities in unsettled areas such as Oak Ridge and Los Alamos.[56] By this means, the Illinois site descriptions could provide additional incentives to the AEC to pick an Illinois location. McGrath continued in that work, especially to provide guidance for the lobbying activities of the others. He worked especially closely with Price, whose efforts, according to McGrath, were the most valuable of all.[57]

Congressman Melvin Price was, as earlier reported, a high-ranking Democratic member of the Joint Committee on Atomic Energy. More to the point, Price was a senior member of the Illinois delegation and was from the St. Louis area, the depressed Illinois side of the river. In keeping with his position on the JCAE,

Price had to remain above the fray,[58] but undoubtedly he earned McGrath's respect by keeping McGrath and the others fully informed of twists and turns in AEC and NAS deliberations. As chairman of the important JCAE Subcommittee on Research and Development, Price could know almost everything about the site selection process. Once the East St. Louis site had been eliminated, Price had no closer ties than to the Chicago area sites.

Congressman Daniel Rostenkowski had a single, simple, but vital mission. As spokesman of the Chicago Democratic delegation in Congress, Rostenkowski was simply to make it known continually that Mayor Daley was interested in the project. His only other task in this was to prevent other members of the delegation from jeopardizing the Illinois case by making too many outlandish claims about the virtues of the site or the risks of retaliation if a Chicago area site were not chosen.[59]

Most of all, however, it was Paul Douglas who in the end became the public leader and spokesman for the state's efforts in Washington. In December 1965, Douglas had a particularly good opportunity to press the state's case at the highest of political levels.[60] While vacationing in Mexico he received a telephone call from Lyndon Johnson, who indicated that he was sending a presidential plane to pick Douglas up and bring him to the LBJ Ranch. When Douglas arrived at the ranch, Johnson indicated that he had simply wanted to find out if there was any way in which the president could help in the impending Illinois election campaign.

Douglas urged Johnson to use his influence to obtain the accelerator for Illinois, and then to help get the Indiana Dunes area established as a national park. The senator detailed at great length the "brain drain arguments" and why Illinois deserved the 200-bev facility. He went on to explain that the selection of an Illinois site would be particularly helpful during his campaign. Johnson's response to this request, Douglas indicated, was that if there was no major technical obstacle to the location of the accelerator in Illinois, the senator could be assured that his efforts on behalf of the state would be successful. Following this meeting, members of Douglas's staff conferred with Johnson aides on several occasions. In retrospect, Douglas has indicated, although he did not get an absolute commitment from Johnson, he had at least gotten a solid promise with something of an escape clause.

The Johnson-Douglas exchange raises several questions of

great significance to this case and all other science policy cases. Obviously the first is to what extent did the president make or influence the making of the final site location decision? Second, why would Johnson commit himself for the maverick Senator Douglas, a man with whom he had never been particularly close in the Senate? Finally, how does this sequence of events fit with the fact that the decision to locate the accelerator in Illinois was not announced until December 16, 1966, more than a month after Douglas had been defeated in his reelection bid by Charles Percy, and several months after the participants at the various sites had expected an announcement?

The precise role of the president in the decision remains unclear and subject to dispute even among major participants. Individuals connected with the AEC are unanimous in their assertion that the commission made the decision, and many have testified to this effect before the JCAE.[61] One AEC commissioner has even contended that the president was notified of the selection of Weston only on the day prior to the public announcement. This interpretation has, however, been disputed by several highly placed administrative officials as well as some officeholders, who have contended that the president alone made the final locational decision. But more significantly, and beyond any matter of interpretation, the president's intervention would not have mattered at all to the scientists or to science control of science decisions. By the time presidential intervention could have occurred, in late 1965 or early 1966, *the scientists already had gotten everything they needed*. Any one of the six (or seven) sites would have been just fine. Everybody won. The president got his credit, surely, for intervening, even if it turns out he made Douglas a promise he had not intended to pursue. Douglas got his wish fulfilled, although too late to help his reelection bid. A grateful Illinois got what it wanted, although at a price it had not figured on. And none of these successes cost the AEC anything.

NOTES TO CHAPTER 4

1. When asked about these discussions, Commonwealth Edison personnel have indicated that George Beadle, then president of the University of Chicago, first initiated them.

2. Interview with Gene Graves, DBED director, April 21, 1969, at his office in Springfield, Illinois. In addition to talking at great length on several occasions in both Springfield and Chicago, Graves was kind enough to share with us a detailed 20-page chronology, developed for internal departmental use, that listed every formal meeting on the accelerator, both public and private, in which DBED personnel had participated. This log included a brief statement of the meeting's purpose, and a list of those who participated in it. On this initial formal meeting, see "Chronology of Events Leading to Illinois Selection as the Site for the Atomic Energy Commission 200 BEV Accelerator," prepared by Raymond Becker, Director of Information, DBED, for Charles Schrader, Assistant Director, DBED, December 18, 1966, p. 1. (Because this compilation of meetings will be referred to in several instances, it will subsequently be listed simply as "DBED Chronology.")

   We are also much indebted to Mr. Ray Becker, DBED press chief during the issue, and to Professor Boyd Keenan of the University of Illinois–Circle Campus.

3. For a wide-ranging examination of several instances that illustrate the character of city–business community involvement in Chicago, see the various case studies in Edward Banfield, *Political Influence* (New York: Press, 1963).

4. For a discussion of the support provided to the Chicago Democratic organization by the city's business community, see Mike Royko, *Boss* (New York: Dutton, 1971), especially pp. 156–159, for the discussion of the 1967 mayoral campaign.

5. The University of Chicago was, as might be expected, the first public beneficiary of the decision to locate the accelerator at the Weston site. When Cornell physicist Robert Wilson accepted an appointment as director of the laboratory he subsequently also accepted an appointment as a professor of physics at the University. Since that time other internationally known physicists have joined the physics department at Chicago.

6. Graves interview, op. cit. As will subsequently be noted, at a meeting in Washington, Commonwealth Edison executives were informed by AEC staff people that one drawback to the Chicago site was the greater cost of electricity. In response, the company indicated a willingness to set its charges at a level that seemed reasonable to the AEC.

7. Graves interview, op. cit.

8. Ibid.

9. "DBED Chronology," op. cit.

10. Interview with DBED Director of Public Information, May 12, 1969, Springfield, Illinois. Also, on the same day the state's report was delivered, the Illinois Science Advisory Council, a gubernatorially appointed citizens' commission, met to discuss

and record its ·public support for an Illinois location for the accelerator. The head of the council, Dr. Frederick Seitz, University of Illinois physicist and then NAS president, did not participate in these deliberations, but his membership could not have gone unnoticed.

11. Becker interview, op. cit.
12. Interview with Kyran McGrath at his home, Washington, D.C., March 23, 1969.
13. At the same time, the governor's staff began to discuss the nature of the legislation needed to facilitate state acquisition of the privately owned land to be used for the accelerator site. It was felt that the legislation needed to facilitate the acquisition, should Illinois win, could best be proposed at a special session. During such a session, the legislation would be the center of attention and as a consequence there was less likelihood of Republican legislative opposition or its entanglement with other legislation. Interview with Chris Vlahopolus, vice-president of the University of Illinois at Chicago Circle, who, during the events described here, was press secretary and chief of staff for Governor Otto Kerner (May 13, 1969, Chicago).
14. See "News," Illinois Information Service (press release), Springfield, Illinois, August 11, 1965 (mimeograph).
15. Cf. Daniel Greenberg, *The Politics of Pure Science* (New York: New American Library, 1967) pp. 255–257.
16. "DBED Chronology," op. cit.
17. Letter from David M. Kennedy to Richard J. Daley, July 16, 1965. Kennedy's importance is underscored by the widely held belief that he had refused a cabinet post in the Johnson administration.
18. Interview with Congressman Daniel Rostenkowski, at his office, Washington, D.C., March 26, 1969.
19. Rostenkowski interview, op. cit.
20. Interview with Congressman Melvin Price, at his office, Washington, D.C., March 26, 1969.
21. See memorandum from Charles H. Schrader, assistant director of the DBED, September 2, 1965, for a detailed discussion of the procedures involved in receiving the AEC visitors.
22. This was the case in Michigan, for example, where the University of Michigan was primarily in charge of that state's efforts. Interview with Geoffrey Norman, vice-president for research, University of Michigan, at his office in Ann Arbor, April 30, 1969.
23. Letter from Paul W. McDaniel to Otto Kerner, September 14, 1965.
24. See Chapter 3. In fact, on August 17, 1965, the DBED sent to the office of the governor a news release it had prepared and had already cleared with the offices of Senator Paul Douglas and Congressman Melvin Price, which stated that they along with the governor were announcing AEC's selection of "two sites in

Illinois that will receive further consideration" from "among the fifteen still in competition." See news release, Raymond Becker, DBED, to Chris Vlahopolus, August 17, 1965.

25. "Remarks of Governor Otto Kerner Prepared for Delivery Before the Business Executive Luncheon," September 17, 1965, Continental Illinois National Bank and Trust Company, typescript.

26. "Invitees for Governor's Luncheon Meeting for Location of Nuclear Accelerator," typescript. This list includes perhaps the 100 wealthiest businessmen in Illinois.

27. "Resolution on the AEC Accelerator" adopted September 21, 1965, by Midwestern Governors' Conference, mimeograph.

28. The material for this document was prepared during 4 days of private and confidential meetings held in Chicago and attended by high-level administrative officials from several of the Midwestern states. See DBED memorandum "Preparation for Meeting," September 23, 1965, typescript.

29. *Midwestern Resources Association Proposal for the Location of the Atomic Energy Commission 200 BEV Accelerator* (undated report), especially Tables I, II, and X. Not only did the report build a case for the Midwest, but also, in a number of its tables and analyses, it specifically singled out the state of California for special note. For example, it reported that in 1964 federal research and development expenditures in education institutions for all 12 Midwestern states amounted to 18.6 per cent of the national total, whereas California educational institutions alone received 29.4 per cent of the national total. See Table XI.

30. At about the same time, an AEC team visited the Princeton, Illinois, site. In this instance, however, DBED did not undertake any extraordinary preparations—no helicopters, no kites, and so on. This is in keeping with the previously stated view that it was not really a viable alternative. See DBED memorandum from Jay Tritelli, November 19, 1965, for a description of the Princeton activities.

31. "Bolster Illinois Hopes to Obtain Huge Atom Smasher" by Ronald Kotulak, *Chicago Tribune*, Sunday, December 5, 1965.

32. "Scientists Tour State for Energy Site" Chicago, UPI, *Illinois State Journal*, Springfield, December 1965. Interestingly, the several accounts of the visits of the scientists to Illinois carried in the Chicago papers do not mention this event.

33. For a more detailed discussion of the opposition that had developed in the Barrington site area, see Chapter 7.

34. DBED files.

35. Becker interview, op. cit.

36. Interview with Paul Douglas, at his office, Washington, D.C., March 27, 1969.

37. As reported in DBED memorandum, undated.

38. Vlahopolus interview, op. cit.

39. Interview with AEC Commissioner Gerald Tape, March 25, 1969, and interview with AEC Chairman Glenn Seaborg, March 27, 1969, both at the AEC offices in Washington, D.C.
40. Graves interview, op. cit.
41. From DBED files.
42. "Memo to City and News Editors" from DBED, and accompanying Agenda for the Atomic Accelerator Meeting Concerning the Weston Site, April 6, 1966.
43. "Weston Site Would Be Ideal for Atom Smasher," editorial, *Beacon News*, Aurora, Illinois, April 7, 1966, as well as a letter from Donald R. Rouser, Aurora Chamber of Commerce, to Paul W. Scott, DBED, listing 13 major activities undertaken in order to generate local support for the location of the accelerator in the area.
44. For a description of the activities undertaken by local residents and state officials in welcoming the AEC team, see Aurora *Beacon News*, April 9, 1966. This includes page-one pictures of Glenn Seaborg, Otto Kerner, and Paul Douglas reviewing the local military academy's honor guard, the local citizenry, and the kid with the atomic poster.
45. Ibid.
46. Douglas interview, op. cit.
47. Supplementary Information of the Atomic Energy Commission, prepared by State of Illinois, DBED.
48. See DBED memorandum, Charles Schrader to Kyran McGrath, April 20, 1966.
49. Joint Commission on Atomic Energy, AEC *Authorizing Legislation, Fiscal Year 1968* (Washington, D.C.: U.S. Government Printing Office, 1967), appendix.
50. Two anonymous but high-ranking AEC officials, one with very close ties to California, have indicated that they shared this impression. In addition, Congressman Craig Hosmer has suggested that this was the case. Interview with Congressman Craig Hosmer, at his office, in Washington, D.C., March 28, 1969.
51. Interview with Arthur Ranandar (who as administrative assistant to the Speaker of the House of the New York State Legislature served as one of the chief organizers of the Northeastern regional efforts) at Madison, Wisconsin, November 20, 1971.
52. For an account of this development, see "Plan 13 State A-Smasher Bloc, Officials in New York Stir Effort to Get AEC Pick," *Chicago Tribune*, June 28, 1966.
53. Rolvaag's efforts in this regard are detailed in a DBED memorandum dated April 20, 1966.
54. Letter from St. Louis Research Council to Glenn T. Seaborg, April 15, 1966.
55. Letters in DBED files.
56. McGrath interview, op. cit.

57. Ibid.
58. Price interview, op. cit.
59. Rostenkowski interview, op. cit.
60. Douglas interview, op. cit.
61. For a more detailed discussion of these matters, see Chapter 3.

CHAPTER **5** **Congress, the Atom, and Civil Rights: A Case Study in Civil Wrongs**

Congress has lost most of its powers of initiative, but Congress has not lost its powers. The power of the legislature in the twentieth century is changing, but it can still be formidable so long as legislators maintain the will to confront the executive and to take seriously the opportunities and options provided by the separation of powers.

The power that still resides in Congress may turn out to be the very thing all large industrial states need most: the institutionalization of second thoughts. A strong individual is nothing without superego. A strong nation needs the functional equivalent of superego. Rationality was the word of industrial governments and their planners in the first half of the twentieth century. Everyone, even the most sincere democratic socialist, depended on using government to maximize the use of resources, to improve relations between means and ends. But looking toward the year 2000, social conscience, not socialism, ecology, not economy, quality, not quantity, and rights, not comforts, are the new criteria. And these require *self*-government more than government. Superego is a psychological phenomenon that does not inhere in institutions. The form it has to take would be some regular exercise of a larger view, a balanced or generalist view that deliberately cuts across the specialized views of the bureaucracies. Modern governments organize their executive branches into bureaucracies primarily to reap the profits of specialization, continuity, expertise, and the rest of the capitalist virtues—that is, rationality. But they pay a mighty price—myopia. Perhaps it is too much to expect agencies to take into account the full consequences of their own actions. But somebody should, and Congress can.

We cannot overemphasize our sympathy with the fact that bureaucracies cannot operate without severe specialization. We grant that bureaucratic agencies cannot be expected to take into account the full consequences of their own actions. But it is precisely this awareness that turns us to Congress as the place where a substantial counterbalance to the bureaucracy is supposed to occur. Congress has the power, and Congress occasionally exercises it. Budgetary review and substantive review, especially by the distinguished Joint Committee on Atomic Energy, provide Congress with frequent and substantial opportunities for the exercise of second thoughts about the general moral context of government action.

Does Congress seize its opportunities? Not very frequently. And its exercise seems to be still less frequent where scientists are involved. Confidence about the capacity of scientists to make good decisions seems to lull Congress into a sense that the job need not be done at all.

There is still another reason why general and substantive review did not take place in our story. We are in the field of public works, historically called the "pork barrel." It does not seem to make any difference whether the decision involves a $500 million project designed and executed by the cream of American culture or a $5 million project designed and executed by local hacks and jaded Army Engineers.

The AEC, the Site, and the Civil Rights Issue

DuPage County is not the land of opportunity for urban people. Median income during the 1960s was fourth among counties in the nation, and, thanks more to biased zoning than blatant bigotry, the black population during that time remained a fraction of 1 per cent. During the time of the Weston acquisition the NAACP estimated that only 589 blacks resided in a county of nearly 400,000 population.[1] It is significant beyond words to us that facts like these played no role in the decision-making process.

At no point did the AEC express any particular sensitivity to the restricted conditions in DuPage County or any serious effort to bring such facts to bear upon the decision. In fact, the evidence is overwhelmingly in the opposite direction.

When interviewed in the spring of 1969, AEC Commissioner James T. Ramey claimed that the AEC and the NAS panel on site selection had considered "improvement possibilities." However, the only solid evidence he could offer was that the AEC tried to review all site candidates rejected by the NAS panel. That is flimsy indeed, considering that the NAS panel had been following AEC selection criteria, and considering that not one of the sites eliminated by the NAS panel was restored to the list by the AEC.

Ramey's claims grow weaker and weaker against evidence suggesting that there might have been an effort to avoid socio-cultural information or to finesse any unfavorable facts pressed upon the commission. Most important in this regard is the original AEC fact—their own site selection criteria. It is quite clear that these criteria stressed the very features that depressed areas lacked and would need most to become developed areas. Some samples of the NAS panel's own interpretation of the AEC requirements dramatically reveal the effort to keep depressed areas out of contention:

> The first category of criteria includes the physical features, such as geology, size, configuration, climate and availability of power, water, and industrial support. The second category consists of those less readily measurable factors of environment likely to affect the recruitment of resident staff and the participation of visiting scientists.
> The site must be so located that management can mobilize and maintain the necessary specialized staff, both resident and non-resident, to accomplish the goals of the research program.[2]

Nearly a year later, after many site visits, and after many sites had been eliminated from the competition, the AEC and the NAS panel seemed even more firmly set on selecting a well-developed, upper-middle-class region:

> This panel was primarily assembled to consider the physical criteria. However, we believe that a prime consideration is the attractiveness of the site and its environment for the permanent staff, and that this consideration should not be subordinated to the physical ones . . . . [A] poor choice of location could result in the assembly of a mediocre staff and consequently a mediocre facility.[3]

Although the AEC claimed that the "civil rights atmosphere" around the potential sites was a constant consideration, no mention was ever made of civil rights when the invitations went out for the site competition. Civil rights was never given as a reason for eliminating a particular site from the competition. The closest the AEC criteria ever came to expressing such concern was a vague and nebulous reference to "the availability of housing" for laboratory staff and the community's "ability of adapting to change." [4]

When under fire in February 1967, nearly 2 months after the announcement of the selection of the Weston site, AEC Chairman Glenn Seaborg could only say that

> the members of the Atomic Energy Commission do care about human rights, about non-discrimination, about open occupancy in housing. We are very concerned about this, and have been from the beginning and continue to be, and we are doing something about it. We believe that we have a positive program.[5]

According to Dr. Edward Goldwasser, a NAS panel member, civil rights was considered by the panel only within the more practical framework of the site's potential for attracting adequate staff. The only active consequence of that consideration was the elimination of all sites located in the Deep South.[6]

The AEC claimed that the civil rights question was brought up regarding the six finalists once these were turned over by the panel to the AEC. But indeed, by spring 1966, the general housing situation in Illinois had been made a national issue by Dr. Martin Luther King and his movement. This awareness was brought directly to bear upon the AEC and the Weston site by Clarence Mitchell, director of the NAACP's Washington bureau, who wrote Dr. Seaborg about housing discrimination in Illinois, comparing the Illinois site unfavorably, for example, with another finalist site near Denver. Mitchell's letter cited Illinois Senator Dirksen's opposition to a national open housing statute as well as the Illinois State Assembly's rejection of state open housing legislation as his evidence for doubt that Illinois could "give assurance that there would be adequate safeguards against persons being deprived of housing solely because of race . . . ." [7]

In responding to the NAACP pressure, Dr. Seaborg revealed that the AEC had sought information from six important agencies of the federal government regarding the discriminatory practices of the six finalists.[8] Dr. Seaborg reported that "none of the agencies advised the AEC to eliminate any of the six sites." In fact, as he reported it, the civil rights records of all six sites were *rated about the same.*

However, this only underscores the absence of serious thought as to the contribution the accelerator might make to the national advancement of civil rights. At no point did Dr. Seaborg indicate any effort on his part, or on the part of the consulted agencies, to add sites with a better civil rights record. It was clear almost from the beginning that potential actions rather than present commitments or past records would determine civil rights considerations. This attitude completely freed the AEC to guide itself entirely by the "soft criteria" it had set for itself at the beginning of the site selection process. And quite clearly these added up to a single set of instructions to the panel: in effect, get us a convenient, attractive, upper-middle-class white community that will give us no social problems; consider our social contribution only as trimming on an already delicious cake.[9]

Stress only on future action produced a lame request for "assurances of non-discrimination and equal opportunity . . . as well as assurances that there would be individual and common effort to prevent or offset discrimination and to deal with it promptly should it occur." [10] As promises are cheap, many assurances of support for these civil rights efforts were sent to the commission. On the basis of this kind of information the commission was able to report an impression of a "progressive attitude in the Weston site area toward equal employment opportunity, efforts to provide equality in suburban public school systems, and a number of community relations councils devoted to eliminating discrimination . . . . [Although there are differing views in the area with respect to nondiscrimination, the commission will expect] that with the leadership of the state and local governments and with the cooperation support of citizens and community organizations in the Chicago area, a broad satisfactory record of non-discrimination and equal opportunity will be achieved." [11] It is impossible to note this kind of optimism without recognizing the actual record of the state of Illinois and the Chicago area counties on open housing ordinances.

Several times the commission sincerely noted its intention to use its presence in the area to improve human relations. During the period of most intense civil rights pressure, the AEC's only black member, Samuel M. Nabrit, announced to Congress that the commission "will endeavor to exert our full leverage of power in promoting betterment in all areas of human relations in the metropolitan area and at state levels as well." [12] But even here, when it came to definite AEC policies, the commission fell back. Primarily, it steadfastly refused to be influenced in its choice of site and its behavior on the site by civil rights considerations. At one time during the hearings, when asked by Rhode Island Senator Pastore "What if you asked the town of Weston to give you an assurance of an ordinance with respect to open housing and they rebuffed you, would you still put it in Weston?" Chairman Seaborg replied lamely, "I would say that I wouldn't want the future of the accelerator to be determined on the basis of one ordinance of that type, where there are other ways of accomplishing the same thing . . . ." [13]

This was the setting for Congress's entry in January 1967.

Congress, the Scientists, and Civil Rights: A Study in Lost Opportunity

The accelerator was the official property of the United States Congress between January and July 1967, when review of the authorization bills for fiscal year 1968 gave Congress its one opportunity to reconsider the project, the site, and the social policies. The AEC bills, introduced on January 24, 1967, requested a total authorization of $2.5 billion. The request included a mere

$10 million for the partial design and construction of the 200-bev accelerator at Weston. The authorization request passed immediately to the Joint Committee on Atomic Energy, which opened its hearings on January 25. Although the accelerator accounted for a tiny portion of the total request, it figured significantly in the JCAE's investigations, partly because the accelerator was considered such an important research tool and partly because three members of the joint committee represented states whose site candidates had been among the six finalists. Because those three members were also joined by three others who were from the Northeastern states rallying to the cause of the Brookhaven (Long Island) site, it was almost inevitable that the JCAE would decide to concentrate "on selected matters that deserve particular attention" rather than to conduct its usual "comprehensive review of the Commission's entire program."

JCAE Chairman Senator John O. Pastore (Democrat of Rhode Island) was one dissident member of the committee who particularly opposed Illinois. But he sought to make an issue of the Weston choice by raising the question of opportunities for minorities and how they could share in the benefits of the new accelerator. Ironically, the problem he and the other anti-Illinois dissidents faced early in the hearings was their uncertainty as to how to bring up the civil rights question and to make it an issue. Congressman Melvin Price of Illinois, JCAE member and chairman of its Subcommittee on Research, Development and Radiation, observed that "as a committee we have not run into this problem before. Although we have located many atomic facilities in the past twenty years this question has not previously been raised." [14] This was a particularly damning observation, but the anti-Illinois faction managed for a brief moment to overcome the lack of precedent for raising moral issues in relation to atomic public works.

The first thing the dissidents did was to engage in their own friendly exchange to set the stage for a general inquiry into the civil rights aspects of this project:

> Chairman Pastore: The point I mean to make, Senator Javits, is that we have a right either to authorize it or not to authorize it. I was going to ask you how far do you think the Congress can go in saying which one of the sites would it be.

Senator Javits: As to picking a site, in my judgment the Congress has no right to pick a site and I don't think the committee has. I think it has an absolute duty to strike down a selection which it considers to be the wrong one because it has an independent authority to authorize or not to authorize. But it has no authority. It would not be wise in my judgment or good policy for the committee to put itself in the place of the AEC and say you pick Weston or you pick Brookhaven.

Chairman Pastore: What guidelines do you think we should follow in this duty to strike it down? How should we superimpose ourselves over the unanimous judgment of the Commission?

Senator Javits: To start with, the most primitive of the guidelines, naturally if the committee found venality, fraud, misrepresentation, anything that would be against ethics, the committee would strike it down unhesitatingly. So we pass that. No one charges that here and the men of the Commission are very distinguished, and I am the first to say that. The other criteria would be these. One, were the selection criteria which the Commission itself chose adequate for the purpose in the judgment of the Congress or should there be any other criteria? For example, would it be proper to have a criterion that it is desirable to establish another national laboratory center in the Middle West? This would be a legitimate question. Congress would then be incurring a new responsibility, developing a new place, as it were, with its eyes open, realizing what it was.

The second criterion would be whether, in applying its own criteria, it omitted any criteria, and if so, whether it would be so material as to require a change in judgment. The third criterion would be whether or not they applied their own criteria in such a way as to require a reversal of judgment because it has so materially affected the decision as to be adverse.

The last criterion would be, does the Congress believe that there are overriding considerations in the national interest which require another selection.[15]

Having established that, JCAE went about its task with its usual seriousness and efficiency. Only occasionally did the parochial interests of committee members interfere with questioning witnesses. Many witnesses invited to testify were representatives from civil rights organizations, who testified almost exclusively on the civil rights question. And from all this one extremely well-documented assertion was that DuPage County ranked among the worst possible places for the accelerator if minority group opportunities were to be increased.

As reported earlier, the AEC commissioners and staff reported on the consideration they gave to civil rights and attempted to defend their decision. However, the most effective witnesses before the committee were the Illinois senators and congressmen themselves. Senator Dirksen reminded the JCAE members of his own record of support for civil rights legislation, claimed that Illinois was making progress toward equal opportunity, and attributed the recent revelations of "untoward things" in Illinois to outside agitators.[16]

Charles Percy, the new junior senator who had only 3 months before defeated the famous Paul Douglas, naively attempted to use earlier federal financial involvement in the Weston houses as evidence that no discrimination existed: "[These homes are] held in title by the Federal Savings and Loan Insurance Corporation. I can't imagine this Government agency being charged with discriminating in the sale or rental of those homes." [17] Senator Percy also cited Argonne National Laboratory as an example of the fine civil rights record of another AEC facility in Illinois. Without giving any specific information, he attempted to claim special knowledge of Argonne on the basis of his membership on the Board of Trustees of the University of Chicago, the parent institution of the Argonne Laboratory. As Senator Percy said, "I have never heard a single case where a scientist, regardless of race, color, or creed—and there are thousands of technical personnel out there—has not found adequate housing . . . . As a Trustee of the University of Chicago I have had a degree of responsibility for that." [18] In his testimony, Senator Percy failed to point out a significant fact. As of January 1967, 225 blacks were employed at Argonne Laboratory, of whom 223 had to commute over 70 miles round trip from their homes in Chicago or Gary.

Ultimately, John N. Erlenborn, congressman from the Weston district, probably got to the crux of the matter. He simply argued that although DuPage County did not have a very good civil rights record *neither did any other place*. However, he was somewhat more devious about another damning fact about DuPage—the DuPage County realtors' attempt to prevent with an injunction the enforcement of Governor Kerner's executive order on open housing. In a remarkable display of eloquent sophistry,

Congressman Erlenborn argued that the realtors' effort was simply an example of their professionalism:

> They have challenged the Governor's order because they believe it to be an illegal extension of the State's licensing power. As legislators, you gentlemen are cognizant of the necessity for watchfulness in this field of executive encroachment. These real estate brokers went to court, not because they are intent on keeping colored people out of DuPage County, but rather because of the principle involved in the Governor's licensing authority.[19]

Undaunted, Pastore pressed on. As chairman, he probed witness after witness on the civil rights question in the Weston area. His were leading questions, aimed at building the case against Weston. For example: Would you say it would be tragic if Congress authorized the accelerator and then found discrimination in the area? Or, what should we do to avoid discrimination? Or, was a state housing ordinance an absolute prerequisite for authorizing the site? Or, should Congress delete the authorization altogether, or forcibly switch sites? Pastore got his answers, especially from the civil rights witnesses, who had a field day.

All this is accepted practice. Pastore was using the prerogatives of his chairmanship to head off a decision, or, failing this, to produce an unfavorable hearings record that might be useful during floor debate. And even if the decision on Weston were not prevented on the floor, this unfavorable record would influence the implementing provisions of the responsible administrative agency, in this case the AEC. Hearings of this serious a nature are an intimate part of what is loosely called the "legislative history" and the "legislative intent."

As expected, Pastore failed to kill the Weston decision in committee. The committee majority voted to authorize the 200-bev accelerator at Weston, and only two other members of the committee joined with Pastore to sponsor a minority report objecting to the Weston authorization altogether.[20] The pressure from this small minority seemed successful to a certain extent, inasmuch as the requested $10 million authorization was knocked down to $7.5 million. However, this was an empty victory. With the authorization coming late in the first year, the accelerator designers considered $7.5 million adequate. Moreover, the majority succeeded in removing from the authorization language a very significant clause: "AEC architect-engineer work only." [21] With that clause, funds would have been limited essentially to the drawing board. Its removal meant that some actual work on the site could begin, and that meant the AEC could irrevocably commit itself to the Weston site.

Pastore, through the minority report and other public channels, continued to press his objections to the authorization at Weston "at this time." He implored his colleagues to consider equal opportunity a "fundamental question of public policy." He persisted in reminding Congress of its independent responsibility to introduce such issues. Then suddenly, as the bill came up for debate on the Senate floor, Senator Pastore and his objections dropped almost out of sight. The senator had tripped over the pork barrel.

O'er the Pork Barrel We Watch: Selective vs. Myopic Legislative Oversight

The House members of the JCAE brought the committee report to the House floor with their unanimous approval. The debate centered mainly on an amendment by a JCAE nonmember, John Conyers (Democrat of Michigan), a black congressman, to delete the Weston item from the authorization bill. During the debate, two JCAE members urged avoiding the civil rights issue altogether. Chet Holifield, a California Democrat and vice-chairman of the JCAE—confirming our own independent impressions—told his colleagues that civil rights had become an issue only late in the selection process of the AEC and had had nothing to do with the actual site selection criteria: "The (original) criteria that were set out had nothing in it in regard to open housing. It was subsequently brought into controversy through speeches by some of the Atomic Energy Commissioners." Another Californian, Craig Hosmer, was still more explicit. He denounced the AEC's handling of the site selection as "lurid, or dismal, or inept, or bungling," and he added that "also, during the process, the AEC allowed the extraneous matter of civil rights to loom large in the site selection criteria." [22]

However, the most effective argument was not the weaknesses of the site selection process or the tardiness with which the AEC included the civil rights question, but rather the threat that application of the civil rights or equal opportunities criterion in this case would create a precedent that could easily apply to all public works projects. In a letter to committee member Holifield, Congressman Erlenborn had pointed out that "If I am to take Chairman Seaborg at his word, then I am to assume that the Atomic Energy Commission will spend no more money in any of the thirty-one states without open occupancy statutes." Representative Holifield took that notion and applied it across the board, or across the barrel, to all federal projects, telling his colleagues in immortal prose, "No occupancy law, no federal funds."

We will probably never know whether the House members were swayed by fear of the precedent that would be set by applying the civil rights question to the selection. But on June 29, 1967, the House rejected the Conyers amendment by vote of 104 to 7 and sent the bill on to the Senate.

In the Senate the debate on the AEC authorization legislation took place almost entirely on one day, July 12, 1967, and, as in the House, the only controversial item in the debate was the authorization for the accelerator. Senator Pastore introduced an amendment to that authorization, in which he was joined by senators Javits (Republican of New York), Hart (Democrat of Michigan), and Brooke (Republican of Massachusetts), the Senate's only black member, as cosponsors.

Although much of the Senate debate was occupied with civil rights questions in Illinois, it was less intense than the committee squabble or the House debate, despite the most recent events in Illinois. First, although the neighboring communities of Wheaton and Joliet had passed open housing ordinances, the Illinois General Assembly had continued to reject pressure for state open housing legislation. Second, the AEC had not yet been successful in securing commitment letters on open housing from a majority of communities in that area. Although the AEC was continuing to claim that its affirmative action program would "advance the cause and benefit of Negroes and other minority groups," the most recent evidence made that claim sound more and more vacuous.

Nevertheless, the Senate debate on civil rights in the site area got thinner and thinner. The clearest sign of this development was Senator Pastore's effort to redefine the issue as narrowly as possible. During the debate he began to emphasize that he was not advocating rejecting Illinois or favoring some other state strictly on the criterion of the presence of open housing laws. He increasingly insisted that Congress should wait to see what happened in Illinois. Departing further and further from the position he had taken as chairman of the JCAE, he more modestly argued that "time has a healing, helping way . . . we should give this good feeling a chance and postpone this project for another year." He was increasingly vague about what he thought would be a sufficient guarantee of equal opportunity in Illinois or in the Weston area, even after the healing passage of time had come to an end. In addition to changing his tune about a year's postponement rather than absolute deletion, Senator Pastore also tried to provide his colleagues with several alternative reasons, rather than just one, for postponement or deletion or both. These reasons included (1) the proposition that the AEC was unsure of the type of machine it really wanted; (2) the proposition that an approaching budget deficit should militate against the projects that are merely "educational gadgets" having "nothing to do with national defense or national security"; (3) the technical question of whether Lake Michigan could legitimately be used as a source of water for the accelerator (although this was never contemplated) and; (4) the original proposition that open housing and equal opportunity for minorities did not exist in the communities near the Illinois site.

Senator Hart, a cosponsor of the amendment and a notable civil rights leader, also tried to soften the issue by narrowing the class of cases to which a precedent set here would apply:

When we are confronted with proposals to correct inequalities which have been the result of geography and history, we are told that so many things have been built up around them that we cannot unscramble them, that it is too bad, time will adjust it, but we cannot do anything very forthright . . . .
. . . [H]ere is a situation where there is nothing but broad acreage and a proposal to put in a massive installation which will soon create a large population. Now is the time to make

up our minds whether we are going to build a ghetto or not. We do have the opportunity this time, without upsetting or unscrambling anything, to practice what we preach around here.

Following that passage in the debate, Senator Pastore came up with still another effort to soften or narrow the meaning of the precedent:

Perhaps we are setting a precedent and the precedent will be that any time a governmental agency brings up the question of . . . fair opportunity . . . they make that a predicate. We have a perfect right to defend that predicate.

It is doubtful whether Senator Pastore fully examined the alternative precedent he was setting here, which would be that social questions could be put on the agenda only by the bureaucracies!

However, these appeals were at least effective on some Illinois civil rights leaders, and they too attempted to soften the application of the civil rights formula. In a letter to Senator Hart, which was entered into the *Congressional Record*, black spokesmen Al Raby and Martin Luther King suggested the following test:

We do not say as Representative Holifield of California has charged that *all* states without fair housing legislation are ineligible for federal projects because of Title VI (of the Civil Rights Act). We do say that in this case and in similar cases, where a job opportunity is so totally dependent upon housing opportunity, Title VI stands against the project being located in Illinois as long as Illinois refuses reasonable cooperation in the creation of those conditions which are absolutely necessary for compliance with the federal law. [Emphasis in original.]

However, these strategies of getting votes by narrowing the application of the implied precedent were lost upon the masterful senior senator from Illinois, Everett Dirksen. As a seasoned member of the House and Senate Dirksen saw right through the Pastore-Hart effort to broaden their appeal for votes against the Weston site. He made quite clear and explicit to his Senate colleagues what he would do in the future if the amendment to delete the Weston authorization were passed in the Senate:

There are twenty states that have open occupancy laws. There are thirty states that have no such laws.

If Congress in its wisdom undertakes at any time to draw that line, then I want to say . . . that line is going to be firmly drawn, and it is going to be equally firmly held.

With respect to any authorization or appropriation bill, an effort will be made to strike every authorization and every appropriation for projects in any State in which this difference between open and non-open occupancy exists. We are going to see if that is going to be the case, that whatever is sauce of the goose is going to be sauce of the gander.

. . . I am going to keep a list handy. Just wait until some of the authorization and appropriation bills come around, and we will spend a lot more time in acting on them if they relate to States that do not have open occupancy laws. If that is to be the requirement, if that is to be the standard, then let us know it now.

To dramatize his intentions, Senator Dirksen arranged for a mock debate that is typical among the senior and more experienced senators. Senator Holland of Florida, acting as Senator Dirksen's straight man, would raise the names of specific federal installations that had been economic windfalls for the areas in which they were located—such installations as the space center at Cape Kennedy, the space center at Houston, Redstone at Huntsville, TVA, and Oak Ridge; Senator Dirksen answered each question with such comments as "We will come down and try to get it away from you"; and "It would not have been put there in the first place if this had been the rule." Few senators believed that Dirksen would actually carry out this threat. But all probably agreed that deletion of the Weston authorization would be an unpleasant precedent, at least as long as Senator Dirksen was around.

The Pastore amendment was defeated by a vote of 47 to 37. Senator Pastore himself attributed the defeat to the efforts of the two Illinois senators, Dirksen and Percy, who were able to get Republicans and Southern Democrats to unite against the amendment by framing it as a civil rights issue. And no doubt this was a consideration for many of the 47 negative votes. But for many others, including most of the 37 who voted for the amendment but did not strongly support it during the debate, it was the more general issue of writing social policy into public works decisions. Many on both sides even doubted whether Congress could legitimately penalize a state for failing to pass open housing laws, which would bend the principle of federalism. Others on both sides of the vote questioned whether the AEC was acting beyond its jurisdiction by raising the civil rights question. But one element overshadowed all the rest: maintaining the flow of public works projects into and out of the pork barrel. Social policy is all right, as long as it knows its place. Its place was definitely not inside, or anywhere near, the pork barrel. Even Senator Pastore began to waffle on this question. He did not reverse his position entirely. He only softened it almost out of existence. Yet, if he had not done that, he would not even have gotten 7 votes, certainly not 37.

Administrative Implementation:
How Not to Reform a Drunkard

Because of the elimination of the clause that would have held the initial authorization to design work, the $7.3 million for fiscal 1968 proved to be enough to commit the AEC irrevocably to the Weston site. Engineering problems could possibly bring about a removal, but this was unlikely because of the excellent technological review of each site made by the NAS panel. Therefore, when Congress approved the authorization, all opportunity to use the Weston site as a leverage for expanding opportunities in DuPage County disappeared, and the only prospect even for marginal influence passed to the local administrators of the newly named National Accelerator Laboratory.

On paper, the administrators revealed an awareness of racial and economic opportunities. In March 1968, the director and deputy director of the National Accelerator Laboratory issued an important "Policy Statement of Human Rights":

> It *will be* the policy of the National Accelerator Laboratory to seek the achievement of its scientific goals within a framework of equal employment opportunity and of a deep dedication to the fundamental tenets of human rights and dignity.
>   . . . [W]e have observed the destiny of our Laboratory to be linked to the long history of neglect of the problems of the

minority groups. We *intend* that the formation of the Laboratory
shall be a positive force in the progress toward open housing
in the vicinity . . . we expect to create conditions for special
opportunity by adopting aggressive employment practices and
by instituting special educational and apprentice training programs.

Prejudice has no place in the pursuit of knowledge . . . in
any conflict between technical expediency and human rights we
shall stand firmly on the side of human rights. However, such
a conflict should never arise. Our support of the rights of members of minority groups in our Laboratory and its environs is
inextricably intertwined with our goal of creating a new center
of technical and scientific excellence . . . .[23]

At least three things stand out in this statement: its utter
sincerity; its enormous ignorance of the social surroundings within
which the NAL was to conduct its hiring practices and locate its
employees; and its complete naivete about the limitations of the
project's influence on community life in the county once the
location of the project was settled. Surely this is a case of
the kindly lady who married the drunkard to reform him. And
the record of the first 4 years of construction and operation seems
to be true to the comparison.

As expected, the directors and planners of the Laboratory
have conducted their own activities and policies in an exemplary
manner. Eventually, the NAL will employ a permanent staff of
2,265, with 111 Ph.D.'s in high-energy physics, 486 B.S. and M.S.
technical personnel and engineers, and around 1,660 other technical and clerical personnel. Experts estimate that about 1.5 other
jobs in service areas will be created for each "basic" accelerator
employee, and during the construction period alone 4,729 construction workers will have been employed. The AEC is of course
obliged, under Executive Order 11246, to include a nondiscrimination clause in all of its construction and employment contracts.
But the NAL has actually taken initiatives in expanding employment beyond the spirit or the letter of the law. After 2 years of
construction and operation, Dr. Goldwasser reported that at least
20 per cent of the NAL's nonprofessional employees were black.
The architectural engineering firm hired by NAL to do the design
and construction work employed 270 people at the end of the

period, and attempts were regularly made to maintain between 10 and 20 per cent minority group composition among its employees.

To insure maintenance and extension of the NAL's own employment practices, several AEC officials were assigned special responsibility for civil rights. Very early in the construction period, a former president of the DuPage County NAACP was hired by the NAL as equal opportunity and community relations officer. He has informed community minority group members of employment opportunities with NAL and NAL contractors and even met with two Chicago street gangs to inform them about opportunities and to recruit among them for specific programs.

The NAL also arranged for preapprenticeship training, run by Local 150 of the Operating Engineers Union, which until then had no black members. Of the 54 blacks enrolled in the program, 52 graduated and secured positions with NAL contractors. NAL staff also recruited over 20 black males from Chicago's ghetto to enroll in a 30-week technician training course at Oak Ridge, with guaranteed jobs, housing, and transportation when they finished. Clerical training programs were set up for minority groups at a neighboring city YWCA; welding training programs were set up at another city nearby; and the NAL also cooperated with the Council for Bio-Medical Careers in assisting minority high school students to develop special training with guaranteed jobs at the end. Minority group contractors were sought out and invited to solicit bids. During the 6 months of late 1968 and early 1969, 40 per cent of the purchase contracts for amounts of $10,000 or less went to minority group contractors.

Although all this creates the impression of NAL sincerity and dedication, it is less than a drop in the DuPage County bucket. All the NAL's efforts merely proved that a substantial influence could have been exercised *only* while the possibility remained of losing the site altogether. Indeed, in the years since the NAL became established, almost every part of Illinois has changed *except* DuPage County. Minority groups have come of age and are exerting pressure. Liberal support has improved in several ways. Before December 1966, only seven Illinois communities had adopted fair housing ordinances, and one was the now-defunct Weston. By spring 1969, a total of 79 communities had passed such ordinances; but only seven of these were in DuPage County, one of the most populous Illinois counties outside Chicago's Cook County. According to the Illinois NAACP, nearly 67 per cent of Illinois' population lived in communities with some kind of open housing law, whereas before 1967 only 40 per cent did. However, only a few of these people lived in DuPage County, which is one of the reasons why nonwhites continued into the 1970s to comprise less than 1 per cent of the DuPage County population.

Weston as Pork Barrel

The failure of this project to pursue larger social goals is not directly attributable to scientists. It only proves that scientists are human and bring nothing but human stuff to the arts of government. The shortcomings of this decision—the steadfast refusal to use the accelerator to pursue larger national goals—ought to be attributed largely to the process of making public works decisions. This is the pork barrel process. Once the bureaucrats proved unwilling or unable to take the larger social context into account, there was nothing in the decision scheme to impose a larger view on them. Quite the contrary, the pork barrel approach is tantamount to a conspiracy to keep the federal government out of social legislation. The committee system in Congress protects the public works agencies in the executive branch. And the lust of individual members of House and Senate for constituency goods militates against the setting of any conditions that might tarnish the goods with risks. Not even the most dedicated liberals in the Senate seemed willing to jeopardize one project for gains in civil rights, because to jeopardize one project put the entire pork barrel process in jeopardy. Senator Dirksen's warning had to be given only once.

NOTES TO CHAPTER 5

1. Press release from Syd Finley, NAACP National Office, quadstate field director, to Lewis Morgan, chairman of the Illinois Atomic Energy Commission, January 19, 1967.
2. "The Report of the National Academy of Sciences' Site Evaluation Committee," March 1966, p. 430.

3. "Report of the Panel of Accelerator Scientists," January 25, 1966. The document is also included in ibid., pp. 424–427, especially p. 424.

4. "Accelerator Siting Factors," November 16, 1965. Also ibid., p. 430.

5. Ibid., p. 157.

6. Interview with Dr. Goldwasser, in Chicago, April 20, 1969, after his appointment as deputy directory of the National Accelerator (Weston) Laboratory.

7. Ibid., p. 400.

8. These were the Equal Employment Opportunity Commission; Community Relations Service; President's Committee on Equal Opportunity in Housing; Commission on Civil Rights; Civil Service Commission; and Office of Federal Contracts Compliance, Department of Labor.

9. For further evidence on the eagerness of the commission to consider only the future and not the present or past, see *AEC Authorizing Legislation 1968*, pp. 159, 160–165, 170–175, passim.

10. Ibid., p. 179.

11. Ibid., p. 179.

12. Ibid., p. 175.

13. Ibid., p. 164.

14. Ibid., p. 139.

15. Ibid., p. 71. Senator Javits was senior senator from New York, whose Brookhaven site was the most likely choice after Weston.

16. Ibid., p. 80.

17. Ibid., p. 83.

18. Ibid., pp. 84–95.

19. Ibid., p. 133.

20. *Report by the Joint Committee on Atomic Energy, Together with Separate Views, Authorizing Appropriations for the Atomic Energy Commission for Fiscal Year 1968*, 90th Congress, 1st Session, House Report No. 369, June 19, 1967. This report with its Separate Views is printed in *House Miscellaneous Reports of Public Bills III*, Vol. 12753-3, House Reports 338-530, with exceptions, 90th Congress, 1st Session, pp. 57–59. Pastore was joined by Senator Jackson (Democrat of Washington) and Senator Aiken (Republican of Vermont).

21. *JCAE Majority Report*, p. 36.

22. Quotations throughout this particular section were all drawn from the *Congressional Record* between June 29, 1967 and July 12, 1967.

23. "Policy Statement of Human Rights," Robert R. Wilson and Edwin L. Goldwasser, March 15, 1968. [Emphasis in original.]

PART II

The Realpolitik
of the Metro

6 **Weston, the Past and the Future**

Twenty-seven miles west of Chicago's Loop lies the scenic Fox River Valley. Bounded on the north and south by railroad lines running west from Chicago, the valley contains cities and towns that are older than Chicago itself. These socially stratified communities are interspersed with open farmland, forming a region that describes itself in a promotional pamphlet as "an area known nationally for the concentration of immaculately kept showplace farms owned by gentleman farmers; it is a community of middle-sized cities, small villages and fine subdivisions." [1]

The forces of urban development have moved outward from Chicago and gradually encroached upon the Fox River Valley, which is divided between Kane and DuPage counties; eastern parts of the valley that lie in western DuPage County have been the most recent areas subject to industrial expansion and suburban development in the Greater Chicago area. Both Kane and DuPage counties have sought to control the regional development and mold it according to their image of a prosperous existence.

When suburban development began to threaten the farms, there was never any doubt, even among county leaders, that the Fox River Valley would yield to Chicago's metropolitan growth and that its rural character would disappear, in time, before urban pressures. The only question concerned the character of change and who would determine it.

Weston: *The Idea Is the Issue*

Matthew Molitor had farmed in the Weston area for over two decades when inheritance taxes, higher taxes on the increasingly valuable land, and the increased production of the larger farms forced his family to give up ownership. It was the first of many farms in the area sold to a land speculator. Mrs. Julia Krafft, an astute businesswoman who had built a homemade chocolates business into a multimillion-dollar fortune, purchased the Molitor farm and land around it in the mid-1950s. Molitor's love for farming this particular land persisted, and he remained as a tenant farmer on the land he had once owned.

By the end of the 1950s, the land was ripe for resale. Plans were under way for a throughway extension from Chicago that would pass near the land, bringing it within easy reach of downtown Chicago and O'Hare International Airport. Already the Chicago and Northwestern and the Burlington line commuter trains were a mere 10-minute drive from Mrs. Krafft's land, and the freight line of the Elgin, Joliet and Eastern Railway (EJ&E) formed a boundary of the farm. In their early 1960s comprehensive plan, the Northeastern Illinois Planning Commission (NIPC) would designate Mrs. Krafft's land as being directly in the main line of development.

In 1958, Mrs. Krafft entered negotiations to sell the fertile Molitor farm to a long-time associate, DeSoto McCabe. Krafft and McCabe had become acquainted through McCabe's housing developments in Florida, where Mrs. Krafft maintained a winter residence. McCabe had concluded that the post–World War II baby boom would create a great demand for low-cost homes in the early 1960s (the demographer's "echo" effect), and he believed that the Molitor farm would be a good location for a housing development. The land was far enough from Chicago to be relatively inexpensive and yet accessible enough to be desirable. The era of Molitor's farming, and indeed farming throughout the area, began to close.

McCabe, a hustling, clever engineer, had spent a lifetime

looking for the right place and the right time to make his fortune. In and out of millions of dollars,[2] this time McCabe believed he had found a golden opportunity. He planned a residential subdivision that would begin on a modest scale with low-cost, low-rent housing, and then rapidly expand into a prosperous middle-class community. McCabe intended to plan, build, and control this community. To carry out this plan, however, McCabe needed financial backing, a need that would eventually cost him control of the community.

McCabe was well known in Chicago's Loop among real estate speculators and lawyers, and he turned to these old acquaintances for financing. In early 1959, one such speculator, Harold Conn, became the promoter of McCabe's project and took a 15 per cent interest. Conn's two partners, the Wolfson brothers, each took another 15 per cent, giving Conn's group 45 per cent of the project. Ten per cent went to the attorney, Sydney Goldstein, and McCabe retained the other 45 per cent. On April 7, 1959, the Wolfson Development Corporation, sharing $1,000 of common stock, was founded in Goldstein's office, and the new corporation arranged to acquire Mrs. Krafft's land.

Mrs. Krafft divided her 420 acres into three parcels, and the corporation agreed to acquire an initial 100 acres at $1,700 an acre.[3] Five acres were purchased for immediate development, and ownership of the remainder would be transferred as it was developed. Mrs. Krafft initiated her own participation in the project by advancing McCabe $13,360 to begin work.

An additional $36,000 in working capital was provided on July 29, 1960, when Commonwealth Edison purchased a 115-foot-wide right-of-way through the property.[4] The electric company paid $1,760 an acre for the land, which it needed for a third high-tension transmission line between Chicago and southern Illinois.

Despite the infusion of additional capital, on May 1, 1961, when the contract stipulated that the first 70 acres were to be acquired and developed, there was no development, and Mrs. Krafft had not been paid for the 70 acres. McCabe's plans for low-cost development were unsatisfactory to the DuPage County government, which had long used strict building and zoning regulations to prohibit lower-income-level people from infiltrating the wealthy county. Indeed, DuPage County building and zoning regulations were such that fewer than half the people living in the county in 1960 could afford to buy a new home. Lot size requirements and land values made sub-$30,000 homes economically irrational. It was rare to find one and by 1961 impossible to build one in DuPage County. Yet, McCabe was planning to develop Mrs. Krafft's land with homes that would sell for half $30,000.

This sleight-of-hand was to be accomplished, in McCabe's plans, by building on lots one third to one half the usual size. County zoning prohibited housing construction on lots of such small size, but McCabe had his two-step strategy all worked out. First, he would get his homes built on lots that conformed to county zoning requirements. He would then fill these homes and incorporate as a legal village. Under Illinois law at this time, any community of 100 people could incorporate, provided that 35 of them were electors. Power over zoning, among other things, passes from the county to the village at the moment of incorporation. This would provide the staging for the second step.

By angling and cornering the homes carefully, it would be possible to divide each set of two lots into three. This would lower land costs and add more home-building capacity, by applying the simple urban principle of intense land use. To carry out this simple plan, McCabe needed to fill only about 35 homes. On that basis, he submitted his plans to the county for the construction of 100.

The county authorities were unhappy with McCabe's proposed development because the second step was not a possibility inconceivable to them. Consequently, the county met his proposal with a series of obstructions that amounted to a 2-year stalling action. The first county reaction was perhaps the most indicative of the power over development possessed by suburban counties, although many other devices followed quickly upon this one. McCabe's plans ostensibly met the county regulations for building and zoning. But the county held that since there was no countywide sewage system, McCabe would have to install central sewerage *and* central water systems, at an estimated cost of $1.5 million.[5] This was a near-mortal blow because the developers had been banking on an oxidation pond already on the land for sewage

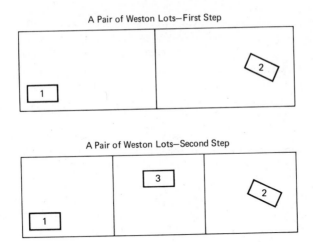

A Pair of Weston Lots—First Step

A Pair of Weston Lots—Second Step

treatment. That was turned down by the county health department, whose approval precedes the issuance of any building permits. Early development funds are extremely difficult for even the most desirable type of project to get, and financing for low-cost suburban housing is particularly scarce. The requirement of an unexpected $1.5 million prior to any construction amounted to absolute prohibition, an eventuality also not inconceivable to the county officials.

As the stalemate was beginning to burn up a second year, it was broken in 1961 by two apparently unrelated developments. First, illegitimate money stepped in where legitimate money had feared to tread. Second, for some mysterious reason, the county government switched to a somewhat more cooperative position on the question of actual construction of a Weston development.

Once promoter Harold Conn had failed in his negotiations with the county, McCabe began looking elsewhere for partners. He called on another Loop attorney, Arthur B. Sachs, with whom he had worked before. Sachs agreed to join and brought in one of his clients, Kenneth Katschke, a man who was to become a key figure in Weston's success and disappearance. Katschke was president of one of the more active suburban financial institutions, the Tinley Park Savings and Loan Association. He agreed to finance a new corporation according to his own practiced methods.

First, Harold Conn was to be excluded.[6] Next, on May 25, 1961, he saw to the formation of the Westfield Construction Company, which was incorporated in the office of Arthur B. Sachs, with McCabe as the sole and controlling stockholder. To this corporation, which was totally independent of Katschke, his federally insured Tinley Park Savings and Loan Association extended $225,-000 in loans to purchase 82.33 acres of that part of the McCabe plat designated for the core of the Weston development. Katschke then persuaded one of his associates, Howard Quinn, president of another suburban group, the Beverly Savings and Loan Association, to share ownership of the 100 lots.[7] Breaking almost completely with the original development group, the new group bought out Goldstein, the Wolfsons, and Conn and forfeited most of the original 420 acres back to Mrs. Krafft.[8] The original Wolfson Development Corporation was now dead, without ever having developed anything but a stalemate.

Katschke's plan was in part predicated upon the fact that he was also vice-president of Gold Star Homes, a manufacturer of prefabricated houses. It helped that he was also an officer in many other companies, real and imaginary ones. Frequently using Sachs as his stand-in, he controlled mortgage companies, builders, decorators, development companies, insurance agencies, heating companies, appraisers' associations, and, most striking, another savings and loan corporation, the Chatham. Although dummy corporations made sense as a tax shelter, the main advantage of these interlocking corporations lay in bankruptcy. Bankrupting a dummy corporation left Katschke and Sachs in control through other corporations while the companies who did the actual work went unpaid or received a few cents on the dollar. The bankruptcies were usually illegal, as was the squeeze on the legitimate contractors.

New financing, before full disclosure of its nature, put the Weston project in a new light. Toward the end of 2 years of stalemate, Arthur B. Sachs managed to convince the county board of supervisors that with or without county cooperation the subdivision would be developed.[9] The county apparently recognized the inevitability of Weston and resorted to secondary control. The supervisors granted a permit for using the oxidation pond. In return,

Sachs had to agree to convey ownership of the pond to the county.[10] Through this ownership, the county would control essential sewage and water service, thereby guaranteeing that the subdivision would always be dependent on the county. Expansion or direction could be controlled as long as the size and use of the pond could be controlled. It would then matter less whether the village became incorporated.

For a while everything seemed to flow easily. Sachs officially became attorney on May 25, 1961, and on July 31 he consumated the trust agreement to convey the oxidation pond to the county. Between August 14 and August 22, 1961, 101 petitions for the construction of prefabricated homes were submitted to the county for approval. Construction of these homes, all to measure 42 by 26 feet with no basement or garage, would then be the first step toward a 400-home subdivision. Building permits were granted in due course, and construction actually began.

Nothing Fails Like Success

By early spring of 1962 the first generation of Weston villagers began to move into homes as they were completed by Westfield Construction Company. In an effort to populate the development quickly (in order to incorporate, subdivide lots, and recover some building costs), the homes were offered at the unusually low rent of $85 per month. The new residents were expected to cooperate with McCabe's plan for incorporation and rezoning. DuPage County's worst fears of a low-income, unstable renting community were being rapidly confirmed.

Arthur Theriault, an offset printer from nearby West Chicago, who moved to the development because of the low rent, quickly agreed to work for the development company when his rent was reduced to only $65 per month. In late July, Theriault circulated a petition for the incorporation of the village, and on August 8, 1962, he filed it with the Illinois secretary of state. The signatures of the required 35 electors came predominantly from company men and their wives. Westfield Construction Company had directed the completion of 35 housing units by Gold Star Homes, and building permits had been issued for another 65. Incorporation petitions had been filed, and soon McCabe would obtain the governmental power to sub-subdivide the lots and to annex available contiguous land for expansion of the project.[11]

However, it was becoming clear that the necessary capital would not be forthcoming. By early 1962, Westfield Construction apparently found itself in financial straits. Subcontractors began to file suits for payment, and the familiar pattern of bankruptcy seemed to be taking form. But this time Sachs and Katschke were so busy plugging leaks elsewhere in their financial dike that they were unable to concentrate on the Westfield project. On the advice of attorney Sachs, Westfield Construction tried to persuade the subcontractors to share in the ownership, for it was increasingly clear that payment was impossible. In August, the Internal Revenue Service issued notice of levies amounting to $121,000 against Westfield Construction's affiliated firm, Katschke's Gold Star Homes.[12] Several other companies also presented accounts for collection. However, Katschke was in no position to provide the needed funds. In the fall of 1962, the two savings and loan associations on which McCabe was dependent could not sustain the economic pressures of tight money and the legal pressures of government investigations. Katschke and Quinn had overextended themselves, and in a wave of legal proceedings against Chicago area savings and loan associations, they were implicated in illegal actions. Bankruptcy of their savings and loan associations—their base of operations, not the dummies—was now imminent.

After 3 years, Weston's progress was stalled once again. Nevertheless, the enterprising McCabe found more money. On October 23, 1962, Tinley Park Savings and Loan Association officially accepted the services of contractor David T. Gorwitz, another McCabe acquaintance, to supervise the completion of the buildings in Weston.[13] Five days later, Arthur B. Sachs and the Westfield Construction Company officially abandoned the project. The savings and loan association still held the property, but the third developer in 4 years now sought to continue the work.

David Gorwitz and his brother Saul founded the Weston Development Corporation on the basis of a claimed investment of $71,000 to make the houses salable, an amount that included $1,900 to furnish a model home and $2,000 "for the formation of the Village of Weston." [14] The Gorwitz brothers offered a few new ideas, but essentially McCabe's plans remained the guide for the project. In addition to the Weston Development Corporation, the Gorwitz brothers founded the Newport Mortgage Company as an instrument for selling the homes that previously were being rented. On February 4, 1963, the Newport Mortgage Company, with Saul and David Gorwitz as the two executive officers, filed petitions at the county seat in Wheaton for the construction of five model homes. The general contractor for the construction was Equity Sales and Construction Corporation, whose headquarters was the residence of John Lowe in Weston. Lowe was brought to Weston by the Gorwitz brothers to reside there and look out for their interests.

On Easter Sunday, April 14, the Weston Development Corporation unveiled its new model homes. The Midwest Skydivers Association entertained people from the area who came to inspect the "Whirlaway Series," samples of the future homes in the project. Publicity was widespread and attendance was reportedly substantial. The new homes were distinctly superior to the modest homes already built by Westfield Construction, which were selling for an inflated price of about $12,995. The new homes were varied in design and promised to break up the dismal homogeneity of the community.[15]

Meanwhile, on March 19 the secretary of state had already reviewed the petition signed by 38 electors resident on the land, and had set May 18 for the vote in the village on incorporation. Seventy-seven votes were cast by the 419 residents Weston claimed,[16] with 65 supporting incorporation, 11 opposing it, and one ballot spoiled. On May 21, 1963, the state of Illinois declared Weston a village.

On June 15, an election of local officials was conducted in the village hall. Samuel LaSusa, the attorney for Newport Mortgage Company who handled the incorporation proceedings, had the wives of the company men nominate their husbands; the company also selected the people who supervised the election. The company slate glided into office. The only opposition came at 5:00 P.M., an hour before the closing of the polls, when Matthew Molitor, the tenant farmer whose land was now a village, initiated a write-in campaign for the village presidency. His disdain for the "machine" character of the election led him to action. Molitor was widely respected by village residents, few of whom were actually associated with the development company, and many ballots were cast during the last hour of voting. However, most of those who wrote in Molitor's name neglected to inscribe the necessary "X" next to it and their ballots were not counted. Thus, John Lowe, the original company man, became the first village president by garnering 35 votes. The first political cleavage in Weston's history occurred almost at its birth, but the company triumphed—for the moment.

During the summer after Weston's incorporation and election the Beverly Savings and Loan Association dissolved in bankruptcy, and in September Tinley Park Savings and Loan also folded. The federal government became the new owner of Weston. Mortgages on the five model homes were foreclosed and the Federal Savings and Loan Insurance Corporation (FSLIC), which took over the assets of the two defunct savings and loan associations, became the newest landlord. FSLIC assumed right and responsibility for the collection of rents in the village and for management of the property.

It was only when the federal government took ownership that the nature and extent of illegal activities within the village were revealed. The crime syndicate had been extensively involved in the village of Weston. The enormous sums of money in which the Gorwitz brothers were dealing seem to have originated with the crime syndicate, and some of the Tinley Park operations suggest similar sources. McCabe's continued presence had aroused the suspicions of the FBI; when the FSLIC entered the village, some of the truth emerged.

Chaos had set in. A variety of arm-twisting rent collectors representing new and old agencies were claiming rent. Some residents found themselves paying the same rent several times; others refused to pay any rent in the confusion. The agents themselves, and other "employees" of the company (with no one quite sure *which* company was really in charge), claimed exception from rent payments. Theriault, Lowe, and Wayne Blankenship, who claimed to represent the Newport Mortgage Company, were all collecting rents. DeSoto McCabe, now a village resident, was also directing who would pay rent and how much.

The situation was moving, however, beyond McCabe's control. When Blankenship started cashing his checks in the bowling alley near the village, the FSLIC was able to trace the goings-on.

Their investigators ultimately would find that some of the rent collectors were stealing money from each other systematically. Blankenship would testify in court that he kept the rents because he was no longer receiving his pay from the company. After the savings and loan associations could no longer provide the illegal funding that had kept the project operating, and with the federal government in pursuit, the Gorwitz brothers fled with around $30,000 to the Bahamas along with one of their crew, Philip Evans.

The Dream Merchant and the Last Revival

William G. Riley was the next developer introduced to Weston by DeSoto McCabe. In the fall of 1963, in the midst of the failures of the savings and loan associations, the Newport Mortgage Company, and Weston Development, McCabe recruited this "boy wonder" [17] of Chicago suburban development, who had earned a reputation for bold and imaginative large-scale construction projects. Riley would submit an altogether new and special plan for Weston. This plan was just right for the Weston dream, and Riley was the dream merchant!

A developer less imaginative than Riley might have considered Weston's situation as desperate rather than ideal for a new development. In September, the Federal Housing Authority refused to insure mortgages on the homes in Weston, and the Veterans Administration followed suit in October. The homes were regarded as an extraordinary risk with inflated mortgages and poor construction, both resulting from the contractor's efforts to squeeze large profits out of each house.

Riley was not troubled by the current financial plight, for he considered the project ideal for his plans to build a new city. The village was already incorporated. All other developers had left. So far, the village board of trustees had cooperated with McCabe's plans, and land for potential annexation was extensive. The absence of federal agencies, he asserted, pleased him, because he wanted the project completely under his control. Finally, he had a source willing to provide the money for his planned development —the crime syndicate. [18] Starting with syndicate seed money, Riley expected to add legitimate financing and raise a total of $550 million.

In January 1964, Riley announced plans to construct what would be the tenth-largest city in the state of Illinois. In his public announcements about the project, which was to be completed in June 1965, Riley boasted that he would use no federal aid in the form of FHA or VA financing.[19] The city would have 73 miles of bridle paths instead of alleys. There would be no traffic lights. The third-largest airport in the state would be integrated into the city, where the largest, most modern high school in Illinois would crown a fully independent school system to educate Weston's children.[20] Homes appealing to all income classes would be included but would be separated into groupings along class lines. Over 11,000 dwelling units housing 50,000 people would cover 4,700 acres. Twenty per cent of the development would be reserved for parks; there would be two golf courses, 11 public swimming pools, five lakes, a 180-store shopping center, 688 acres of industry, a new hospital, and free local bus service connecting with Chicago's rapid transit system.

In order to help finance the new city, Riley reasoned, it would be necessary to increase the cash flow generated by rent payments. More dwellings like the prefabricated homes were unthinkable in the context of Riley's plan, which called for homes of face brick and stone; something temporary but particularly profitable had to be built immediately. Riley and McCabe concurred on the wisdom of what they euphemistically called a "mobile homes court." McCabe, who continued as village engineer and now represented Riley, announced the plan to annex three large tracts reaching within 100 feet of the EJ&E Railroad tracks. The trailer park would be kept at the edge of the city and would cover some 274 acres.[21]

Riley was in financial difficulty. In the autumn, when he was formulating his Weston plans, the syndicate had begun to increase pressure on him for payoffs in his King Arthur Apartments in Northlake. He had reached the point where he was giving the syndicate more money than he was receiving. Previously the Beverly Savings and Loan had been a major source of funds for Riley. Now Beverly and its related financial institutions were falling bankrupt. Riley's traditional sources were gone; there was no money in the village; he could not deal with the government. He took the only course left open—to raise the money himself—and a trailer park was seen as the quickest bet. At the same time, he put great energy into promoting this new town project in the hope of selling shares.

To the people of DuPage County, however, the plan to build a trailer park seemed like one more confirmation of their worst fears about Weston. Weston's unpopularity in DuPage County was already well established. It hardly needed more confirmation. Its average of 4.5 children per household had placed a new and critical strain on already bankrupt school districts. Its low-cost, low-rent structures—which one FSLIC official called "dog houses" —were a blight on the county, attracting what affluent county citizens regarded as low-class people. One official called Weston "hillbilly heaven." Not only were they regarded as lower class, the Weston people also were suspected of likely being Democrats. Many of the 500,000 people of DuPage County may have felt that Weston portended an even more subtle threat: an influx of work-ing-class Democrats might signify that blacks were not far behind. The county previously had stalled Weston's founding for 2 years and now it had no intention of permitting a trailer park that would add little to the tax base but would pour children into the schools and would bring urban problems into the sheltered confines of the white Republican county.[22]

Four days after the January 3 village meeting, a news conference was held at the Sheraton-Chicago Hotel to announce officially the plans for the new city. On display was a 40- by 40-foot scale model, constructed for an estimated $20,000. A special edition of the *Weston Gazette* featured articles about Village President John Lowe, Village Board Member Arthur Theriault, and William G. Riley (Lowe and Theriault were formerly employed by the Newport Mortgage Company; now they worked for Riley). Gover-nor Otto Kerner sent a congratulatory telegram to the press conference hailing Weston's bold leaders, Lowe and Theriault, along with Riley's bold plan.

The news conference was far more impressive than the Easter opening of model homes by the Newport Mortgage Company had been, but the richness of the facade corresponded even more to the lack of substance underneath. For one thing, Riley had serious financial problems with the crime syndicate. Also, the county's irritation over the projected trailer park provoked legal action against the very corporate existence of the village of Weston, the fundamental prerequisite to the success of Riley's plans. Finally, the private sector moved to sever Riley's legitimate financial life-lines by cutting off his access to advertising and capital. His own inadequacies of money and personality, and the attack from the public and private sectors, retarded Riley's plans, dried up investments in the project, and destroyed crucial faith that the project would ever be built.

The DuPage Dragon vs. Sir William

William Riley's optimism was based on a number of question-able assumptions. He wanted more land as well as more people in the belief that the greater the ongoing entity the less vulnerable to public and private attack it would become. This assumption was questionable because the greater the entity the greater the threat to the county. He declared that he owned 85 acres and that he held options on 3,000 more. Actually, the 85 acres by that time belonged to the FSLIC, although much of it was under contract to village residents. The "options" on the other 3,000 acres were, in fact, Riley's assumption that all men had their price and therefore, as long as there were 3,000 undeveloped acres of unincorporated farm-land nearby, it could be had. It was true that the land Harold Conn had purchased in 1961, speculating on the ultimate develop-ment of Weston, was available; in January, while Riley took an option on the 91 acres Conn owned, Conn took an option on 160 acres of the neighboring Herb Anderson farm.[23]

However, the county's hostility was greater than Riley realized. The county, in an effort to crush with finality this latest expansion effort in Weston, employed a weapon rarely used in hostile situa-tions, the *quo warranto* suit, which is normally used amicably to verify in a judicial record the incorporation of a community. The attack was initiated by the three school districts into which Weston had been carved, for the number of children in the area would be increased drastically by a trailer park. On January 22, 1964, a mere 2 weeks after the dramatic Sheraton-Chicago press conference, the DuPage County state's attorney, William Bauer, filed a hostile suit against the village.

Bauer's *quo warranto* suit argued that (1) Weston did not, in fact, have the 419 residents it claimed at the time of incorporation and (2) the petition for incorporation excluded the phrase "village in fact," which was required by the state constitution. The first argument was complicated, for when the petition was filed only 35 homes had been built in Weston, but by the time the village voted on incorporation there were 100 homes, nearly all occupied. The second argument by Bauer was undeniably true, but whether the absence of such a phrase could deny a village's incorporation was questionable.

On January 30 the *Chicago Tribune* noted, "Legal reasoning aside though, a source from the State Attorney's office affirmed that the real purpose of the action is to stop Riley Management." The county's arguments did not have to hold up in court; they had only to be good enough to keep matters bottled up in court, for delays in Riley's plans would endanger the financial backing needed for implementation. To hasten things, Samuel LaSusa, attorney for the village in the suit,[24] attempted to settle matters out of court. He bargained with the county, promising that no trailer park would be built. Arthur Theriault, now chairman of the village zoning commission, in effect the most powerful position in the village, joined Attorney LaSusa in the promise.

Yet further double-dealing overshadowed the promises. On February 12, at a village board meeting, 32 acres belonging to Harold Conn were annexed along the road at the request of Francis Ferris, Riley's attorney. On February 24, 1964, Theriault announced the passage of a zoning ordinance rezoning this annexed land from residential to industrial purposes, a change necessary to permit a trailer park. On February 26, Weston announced plans to annex 50 acres more, and the discrepancies between Riley's ostensible plans and his actions became more evident. In the master plan the land being annexed was to be used for an artificial lake and open space. The oxidation pond in the back corner of the village, the focal point of the sewage and water dispute 4 years before, would be expanded for the creation of the lake. However, Riley ignored the fact that the pond had been deeded to the county. And despite LaSusa's promise, a mobile homes court showed up on the plan, at a considerable distance north of the village.[25]

The enmity grew between the county and the village. The state's attorney was unwilling to bargain with LaSusa, for the county objective was no longer simply preventing a trailer park; now it was annihilating a village, returning to *status quo ante.*

The county did not limit itself to the public *quo warranto* suit. It reportedly also directed financial institutions to freeze the Weston project. DuPage County was committed to stopping a project that had no place in its own plans for development, and all the weapons it could now muster would be used.

Even after the spectacular January 7 press conference at the Sheraton-Chicago, it was clear that there was much hesitation among the Chicago advertising media concerning William Riley. Meeting after the conference, the real estate editors of Chicago's four major dailies decided that the project was not significant enough to be reported and planned to ignore the whole affair. On returning to the *American*, real estate editor Joseph Bolger found to his dismay that the paper was running a front-page article with a seven-column head giving a favorable account of the project. The article had been written on the basis of material submitted by Riley's public relations firm. Bolger complained to managing editor Luke Carroll, who stopped the presses, deleted the whole article, and ran instead an emasculated, tongue-in-cheek treatment of the press conference.

In January, Chicago newspapers carried Riley's advertisements, and on January 30 an article friendly to Riley's plan appeared on the front page of the *Tribune* real estate section. After that day, however, Riley could not buy his way into any Chicago paper. He had been blacklisted by the Better Business Bureau and Chicago's mass media.

The Chicago Better Business Bureau (BBB) is a private organization established to protect the private citizen from unhealthy, devious, illegal, and illegitimate business practices.[26] Actually, the BBB often acts as a powerful consortium enforcing its own political interests and values on the public. In stopping Riley's advertising while other county forces restricted his financial resources, the BBB succeeded in stopping the dream merchant cold in his phantom tracks. Advertising sells real estate and housing projects. Access to the news and advertising columns is crucial to any metropolitan developer.

Chicago newspapers all deny that big real estate advertisers obtain favorable news articles or editorials, a practice that they admit prevails on some newspapers in other cities. Yet Chicago papers do provide elaborate promotions for the real estate industry, such as preparing kits on new development that are mailed to possible advertisers. The involvement of the newspapers in real estate promotion tends to give the papers the same outlook as the real estate industry itself. And, in general, the newspapers often share the view of the news held by the business community.

To check the validity and honesty of ads that are to be published, the papers rely heavily on the Chicago Better Business Bureau, whose creation in 1927 was primarily the result of the efforts of the newspapers themselves. Relations among the BBB, the city's newspapers, and advertising agencies are especially close. The board of directors of the BBB has always included executives from Chicago's newspapers, broadcasters, and advertising agencies, as well as leading local businessmen from all major sectors of the city's economy. The blackball such a group can deliver to any would-be advertiser could be fatal, as William Riley discovered.

On February 11, after conversations with Riley employees, with the director of public works for DuPage County, and with the DuPage representatives of the Illinois district attorney,[27] the BBB sent out a memorandum to all Chicago media, including radio, TV, and newspapers. The memorandum stressed the fact that Chapter 190 of the Illinois revised statutes

> sets out the requirements with respect to the preparation and recording of plats by which an owner of land may subdivide it . . . . The requirements as set forth in Section 1 of this Chapter are quite detailed. *We think residential building lots should be offered from a plat prepared for and approved by the appropriate authorities.* [Emphasis added.]

This memo does not argue that Chapter 190 or any other chapter of the Illinois revised statues requires land to be platted before it is offered for sale to developers. The BBB was only stressing its own preference as to how developers should go about their work. The memo ended on the following note:

> Without a recorded plat specifically identifying lots and blocks by legal description and detailing public areas such as streets, alleys, etc., serious difficulties may well arise relative to accurate identification of the property covered by a sales contract.

The memo does not imply that Riley was violating any state law, but rather that he violated "certain basic guides the Chicago Better Business Bureau follows in analyzing the propriety of advertising offering vacant real estate to the public."

On March 29, the *Chicago Sun-Times* revealed in its Sunday financial page that Riley's development was in trouble. A. B. Johnston, executive vice-president of the Better Business Bureau of Metropolitan Chicago, announced that the bureau had recommended refusal of advertisements from Riley. Such recommendations are religiously heeded by Chicago media. The action was critical, for, by March, Riley's last financial hope was to stimulate investment through advertising.

On April 14, William G. Riley finally got the newspaper space he had been seeking since January 30, but this time he was not an advertiser. In an open letter, he announced that he was abandoning the Weston project because political reaction to the possibilities of a small Democratic community emerging in an intensely Republican county had caused court involvement, an action that froze his funds. In his full-page ad, he wished the people of Weston well, and said he was regretfully departing from the scene.

Riley's Legacy: Dream to Nightmare

William G. Riley was a dream merchant. He was self-confident, and he was convincing. Weston's people believed he really would transform their community. Other attempts had failed, but none had the professional air of Riley's operation. Riley stimulated a dream in the village that lived on long after he was gone.

Riley dreamed himself, for he was somehow naively unaware of the strength of the forces arrayed against him. His advertising agents reported that he seemed to be reaching constantly for new possibilities, new developmental ideas, to sustain the project. He naively believed that he could make his project happen despite the weight of the opposing Chicago business community. Riley's involvement with the syndicate, his personal tactlessness with the landowners of the area, his inability to persuade the press were his own failings. Nevertheless, these failings seem pale in light of the forces that eventually stopped him.

The district court upheld Weston's incorporation in the *quo warranto* suit on May 20, 1964. Judge O'Malley declared that the lack of the phrase "village in fact" was inadequate to deny people their incorporation and their "democratic desires," and Attorney LaSusa proved that the other contention lacked any evidence. But Riley and his dream for the future of Weston were defeated. The court took several months to make its decision, and that was sufficient delay for Riley's option on the land to expire. With that expiration went the last chance to develop the land. After Riley's plans were shattered, he became the state's star witness in the prosecution of Mafia head Sam "Teetz" Battaglia, and then disappeared from public view. Since that time he has remained in protective federal custody.

As Riley's situation weakened, the FSLIC had to play a more active role as the actual owner of the village. In August 1963, when an FSLIC official first sought to establish the rent due FSLIC and the condition of the property, residents forcibly threw him out of the village.[28] Following that embarrassment, FSLIC played something of a waiting game. Between August 1963 and April 1964, the FSLIC operated primarily as an investigatory agency, banking on Riley's salvaging operation to succeed. The FSLIC denies waiting to see how the Riley effort would turn out, but evidence indicates that it was not eager to become a proprietor and would have been delighted if Riley could have bought the land outright. With Riley's failure evident, the agency on April 7, 1964, officially authorized a local realtor to manage the property. Keith Smukler, special projects manager for George Pearce Realtors of Aurora, became responsible for rehabilitating and selling the village.

Smukler took legal action to recover rents and property. On June 12, Philip Evans, Gorwitz's foreman, part-time collection agent, and village trustee, was served with a Forcible Entry and Detainer. Court proceedings were scheduled for June 25, but Evans and his wife failed to appear. Evans abandoned his wife and children and reportedly joined the Gorwitz brothers in the Bahamas, taking with him an estimated $45,000 in stolen rents.

The summer of 1964 was a summer of constant turmoil for the village of Weston. The FSLIC issued eviction notices to those who failed to pay rent, including, therefore, most of the employees of previous development companies. Arthur Theriault, for example, received rent reductions by working for the firms, but he was also employed as an offset printer, so he could afford to remain in the village after the companies were gone. He, however, was an exception. Village President John Lowe had been brought in with the Newport Mortgage Company, as had Blankenship and Evans. Others, such as policemen Stachum and Hoogheem, and Village Trustee Joseph Miller, depended on the development company income. Their financial problems meant political upheaval; in a mere seven months, Weston's future prospects changed from becoming the tenth-largest city in Illinois to being stripped of its leaders and its population.

It was out of this summer chaos that Arthur Theriault emerged as the leading political force in the village. Evans left in June, and other village trustees left during the summer. By fall, the village board was thoroughly disrupted, the FSLIC was in charge, seeking rents and beginning to repair properties, and a second generation of residents were moving into the low-rent homes.

On September 6, the FSLIC served a final eviction notice on Mrs. Evans and her children, put them out, and padlocked the home. On September 18, with Forcible Entry and Detainer proceedings pending, Village President John Lowe, Police and Licensing Commissioner David Stachum, and their families slipped away in the night. According to newspaper accounts and FSLIC reports, moving vans had quickly removed their belongings, although they were being "detained" by the FSLIC. A few nights later, Trustee Terry Biarnesen and his wife evacuated. Trustees Evans and David Schuette had long since gone.

Thus, when the village board of trustees met on September 28,[29] only Clerk Arthur Keir, and Trustees Kenneth Urbanski and Arthur Theriault remained from the original elected officials. The others could no longer afford to stay in the village.

On Ocotber 12, Theriault became president *pro tem.* Urbanski became the clerk *pro tem*, and Theriault appointed DeSoto McCabe as a trustee to fill one of the board vacancies. (McCabe had lingered on in the village, and FSLIC officials had received directives from the FBI to stay away from him, because he was to serve an important purpose for the FBI.) These survivors believed the village dream could be revived.

On November 14, 1964, the village trustees appointed

McCabe chairman of a public relations committee established to upgrade Weston's image, and a respected local attorney from West Chicago became the official village prosecutor. Other steps were taken to revitalize the sinking village. Samuel LaSusa, still acting as village attorney, recommended that the village board invite William Riley to renew his efforts at city building. At first, the village board declined. Then it asked him, and Riley refused (for more reasons than he could at that time divulge).

Meanwhile, the FSLIC authorized George Pearch Realtors to begin selling the Weston homes in an effort to dispose of the burdensome property. Homes were sold on land contract because conventional financing was impossible. Selling prices for the homes, which had been rented for $85 a month, averaged $12,900, with $200 down and monthly payments of $120. This FSLIC sale, which changed Weston from a renter population to a buyer population, profoundly affected the character of the village and its future political involvement.[30]

Weston entered the new year of 1965 with renewed optimism but recurring troubles. The county, in an unprecedented action, appealed the district court's incorporation decision to the state appellate court. On April 10, an attorney representing Winfield Township successfully challenged the bonding of streets in the village, leaving many streets as dead ends or with incomplete paving.

Nevertheless, Weston's second municipal election followed this latest attack by only 10 days. There was a full-scale, non-partisan political campaign pitting former Village Clerk Arthur Keir and a slate of Weston Progressive Party candidates against Arthur Theriault's slate of Weston Citizens' League candidates. In an open struggle for power, Theriault won. But although the election was a victory for democracy, the village lost still more of its dwindling population: shortly after the election virtually all the families of the losing Weston Progressive Party moved out of the village.

With the departure of the Keirs and their electoral slate, all political power in the village became consolidated, and all opposition to DeSoto McCabe apart from a now ineffective but ever-present Matthew Molitor was gone. McCabe appeared to be in a position to renew his development efforts. Then, in late September, like so many others before him, McCabe disappeared from Weston for good.[31]

With McCabe's final exit, Weston gave every appearance of remaining a 100-home subdivision surrounded by open farmland and hostile neighbors. But many of the Weston residents still dreamed of the great city William G. Riley had proposed, and soon the AEC would offer what appeared to them to be an opportunity to realize that dream. But that temporary reprieve would eventually make village death only more painful.

Summing Up

There were many other communities like Weston in the early 1960s, although few with a history quite as colorful. At least two other projects, Westhaven, on the edge of Cook County outside Chicago, and Blackberry Heights, near Aurora in Kane County, were begun at the same time with the same builders, designs, and financial backing. And these projects also encountered financial disaster when the savings and loan institutions went bankrupt. They were all built by Gold Star Homes, and were so much alike that it was possible to take a door from any home in one of them and use it to replace a door in another. All sought incorporation for self-control and expansion. All appealed to the lower middle class. All fell to similar national trends.

The 1968 recession undermined many small developments like Weston, Westhaven, and Blackberry Heights. The period that followed was characterized by young people not marrying at the same early age as the previous generation, so that low-cost housing was built slightly ahead of the demand. For the poorly capitalized developer, the time lag often meant bankruptcy. There was widespread inflation with rapid rises in land values and construction costs, all factors working against low-cost projects. But Weston encountered more county and official opposition than most communities.

Even the syndicate did not anticipate and could not thwart the opposition of DuPage County, when the upper classes declared war against the lower. For once, the crime syndicate was involved as the defender of the poor, whereas legitimate governments and businesses combined to defend the classes one ordinarily thinks need little public defense. Had the Mafia been building mansions, there would probably have been no opposition; their participation in the county's development might never have been discovered. Weston's "hillbillies" had no effective political base against the formidable powers arrayed against them, and without that even the crime syndicate was quicksand.

The involvement of the criminal element was, of course, not a cause but an effect of low-budget development. Nor was crime the cause of Weston's unpopularity; Weston's unpopularity turned legitimate money away from Weston, and that turned Weston toward the illegitimate. Each time the situation worsened, legitimate money became less available, until all respectable interests intervened to stop the development altogether. No low-cost project has ever penetrated DuPage County, and with the absorption of the last large tracts of undeveloped land by the accelerator and by upper-class developments there is not likely to be such a penetration.[32]

Given all the opposition and all the risks, it is difficult to understand why McCabe and his various associates persisted. Profit margins on expensive housing can be great, and planning is usually simpler.[33] There are no political problems or status problems. And McCabe, Riley, and many of the others were not inexperienced with middle- and upper-income housing. Moreover, the charge that it is easier to squeeze the poor must be discounted, if only because of the fact that McCabe resisted illegitimate involvements for 2 years.

There seem to be only three possible explanations. First, McCabe and Riley in particular may have had a sincere dream of building an integrated middle- and lower-class housing complex. Second, the legitimate profit could become as high as 30 per cent from splitting each pair of lots into three. Third, the legitimate profit from a trailer park and a still larger Weston could exceed 100 per cent many times over. The first explanation, although probably true, was quickly rendered implausible by the second and third—even before there was knowledge of the crime element. But the concomitants—transiency, rentals, intense land use, working classes—almost guaranteed failure. These meant urbanism in every black and white sense of the word. In DuPage County, urbanization means war.

NOTES TO CHAPTER 6

1. The information in this chapter and the following one is based on over 100 confidential interviews and original documents furnished by public agencies and private individuals. In many instances we are not at liberty to reveal the specific source of information; in other cases it has been impossible to establish with certainty details related to a given event. We are grateful to those who so kindly gave so much of their time to make these chapters possible; special thanks are due John Will, whose research in 1967 made a major contribution to the product here.

2. It was never possible to interview McCabe, for at the time this research began McCabe was being held in federal protective custody; this information, like other details about him, is based on the confidential testimony of some of his former business associates.

3. The contract called for the sale of some of the land at $1,400 per acre and other land at $1,760 per acre.

4. Commonwealth Edison had owned this right-of-way since the early 1920s. The 1960 purchase expanded the width of the right-of-way for the addition of the power lines.

5. This figure was offered both by county officials and by an associate of McCabe.

6. No clear explanation has been offered for this condition, but it seems that Conn might have been too honest to suit Katschke.

7. According to a 1957 Illinois statute, a savings and loan association is prohibited from engaging directly in construction on its own land. The law was designed to prevent collusion between savings and loan associations and construction firms. Quinn took mortgages on 35 lots so that Katschke could circumvent the law.

8. Conn took options on some contiguous land and might have profited if Weston had survived.

9. Sachs's means of persuasion have never been ascertained; his law partners disclaimed any knowledge of the arrangement (although they frequently signed many of the papers related to the development), and Sachs himself committed suicide when indictment for his involvement with Katschke was pending. The county has been unwilling to discuss the matter; the documentary record offers no explanation. The solution Sachs derived seems too simple after 2 years of bitter political stalemate, but it probably worked through the county's decision to shape rather than prevent development. Attrition may be better than direct confrontation.

10. In 1969 the county filed a petition with the state legislature to install a countywide sewage and water system; the transfer of title in the case of the Weston oxidation pond was the first clear indica-

tion that the county was discovering this new power to recover control over incorporated areas.

11. The original plan called for the purchase and control of much of the surrounding farmland. Harold Conn, the ousted member of the first development company, purchased the Mensing farm with his partner Wilmer Wolfson for $900 per acre. The Mensing farm was on the east side of the Village bordering the EJ&E Railroad and vital to McCabe; Conn planned to sell directly to developers, but his own cash shortage permitted him to secure only 20.75 of the 91.69 acres that he has taken on option. He took a further option on the Herb Anderson farm, a 144.17-acre tract lying south and west of the village site, at $1,200 per acre.

12. When the miniature empire of Sachs and Katschke began to crumble in the closing months of 1961, Sachs sued Paul Pickle, his partner and Gold Star Homes president, in an effort to divert attention from his personal involvement in the operations.

13. Gorwitz claimed his offices were in Michigan City, Indiana; Indiana is frequently chosen by questionable companies for headquarters because there is no legal requirement for the registration of a construction company there and investigation by public and private agencies can thereby be avoided.

14. These figures are taken directly from the Newport Mortgage Company records; the $2,000 was probably for legal fees dealing with incorporation.

15. The Easter opening is one of the more curious events in the Weston history. The purchase of the lots from the Tinley Park Savings and Loan to construct the model homes took place the day *after* the opening; on May 3 release deeds were executed for two of the lots and the first payment was made, but the check was later returned—payment stopped. In the end, only two of the planned homes were actually built; the other three were abandoned. Therefore there is some question as to what was actually displayed that Easter Sunday.

16. As there had never been a census in the village, it was impossible to determine with certainty the population.

17. This was a term employed frequently by the news media in reference to Riley.

18. Riley's relations with the crime syndicate were revealed in his testimony against crime boss Sam "Teetz" Battaglia in 1967.

19. He did not mention that they had refused any association with Weston.

20. This promise was particularly important to the people of Weston, who had already suffered from several confrontations with local school districts and whose children attended schools in three different places.

21. The park appeared on the master plan in a different location, a disparity that was apparently never questioned at the time. The entire meeting invites some dispute: apparently, even television cameras were present, but there was sparse news coverage; the official records were stolen when John Lowe and various other officials fled the following autumn; William Riley's name was carefully excluded from all minutes of the village.

22. The school districts told the story this way, as did partisan DuPage County officials; actually, it seems that Weston's child density was not unusual for the area, nor as high as claimed. See Chapters 10 and 11.

23. McCabe was already double-dealing with Riley, apparently unaware of the depth of Riley's own financial problems, and he induced Conn to option this land.

24. Samuel LaSusa, who had never incorporated a community before, bore the responsibility for the *quo warranto* suit. When Riley took on the Weston project, he refused to deal with LaSusa and insisted that his own attorney, Francis Ferris, become the village attorney. LaSusa had come to Weston through the Gorwitz brothers. He returned to handle the *quo warranto* suit.

25. Despite a rumor that Robert McGary was prepared to sell his land at a mere $10 per acre, Riley never actually optioned this land, and the 50-acre parcel was never annexed.

26. The BBB claims it does not undertake investigations on its own initiative; apparently, DuPage County requested BBB help.

27. The BBB has refused to reveal who initiated these conversations, but it was surely not Riley, and here again the BBB claims it does not initiate such investigations.

28. There were reports, unconfirmed, that Mr. Haren, the official, was greeted by armed villagers and was seriously threatened.

29. The village minutes for this meeting are especially bizarre. They report activity by Philip Evans, who was long since gone; they state that John Lowe, whose departure 10 days before on September 18 is well documented, urged the appointment of DeSoto McCabe as a village trustee, and they report that Lowe submitted his resignation as village president. Matthew Molitor, who was appointed during the summer to fill a board vacancy created by Evans' departure, is reported in the minutes to have opposed Evans' proposal of McCabe's appointment.

30. See Chapters 9, 10, and 12.

31. McCabe's next public appearance was in the trial of crime boss Battaglia; he, like Riley, turned state's witness and went into federal protective custody.

32. In all of DuPage County there are no low-cost, low-rent housing projects by independent developers. The crime syndicate alone undertook to provide such housing, and according to the testimony

of villagers the housing was, contrary to the official view, quite satisfactory. It is difficult, therefore, even to suggest that the crime syndicate was the proximate cause of failure.

33. Upper-class developments usually allocate more open space and therefore require less actual construction.

The Two Histories Collide

During its short and ignoble life, the village of Weston made at least one important public policy decision: to support the Illinois campaign to obtain the accelerator. The village board made the decision, and the community followed along enthusiastically.

In this as in almost everything else, Weston and Barrington were a study in contrast. Barrington, the original Illinois site and one of the wealthiest communities in the state, had greeted the AEC inspection team with nothing but opposition. Barrington saw the accelerator as a threat to the "Barrington way of life," and demanded to be withdrawn from the site competition. No doubt, it was largely in anticipation of this that Weston had become the panhandle candidate.[1] Weston turned out a band and a host of grinning officials to welcome the AEC site visit. What Barrington had seen as a threat, Weston apparently saw as a hope.

In the press and in interviews, Village President Arthur Theriault expressed confidence that Weston support was critical, and he eagerly extended it:

159

> Daley and Douglas and Kerner did much of the outside work, but we, the people of Weston, had to want the project. If we had opposed it like Barrington, Weston wouldn't have been chosen.

Gene Graves, DBED chairman and leader of the Illinois site competition campaign, never sought to deny the point. In an interview he admitted:

> the people of Weston had no positive effect on the decision . . . they could have had a negative effect.

Why would Weston, after having fought so vigorously for survival, so willingly cooperate in its own annihilation?

The explanation rests largely upon the dream created by William Riley. It had persisted, though all reasonable hope for its achievement had long since vanished. Weston believed that the AEC would resurrect that dream despite many indications to the contrary.[2] As late as May 1967, a majority of the people remaining in the village said that the accelerator would improve life in Weston, whereas only a small percentage thought that the accelerator meant the end for the village.[3] The AEC and the state of Illinois had encouraged the Weston dream; consequently, the villagers were rendered as docile as lambs being led to the slaughter.

Weston, Loyal Suburb

When Arthur Theriault heard of the AEC site search, he personally applied on behalf of the village for the accelerator as an especially valuable and large contribution to a more general industrial development. After Weston's troubled beginnings, perhaps he felt that the federal government could be the most reliable developer of all. The political stabilization that the village had been experiencing since the last election, when the opposition departed, permitted the appearance of a united front, and Theriault's enthusiasm created a facade of broad and deep support.

From early in 1966 until the autumn of 1967, Weston was visited by a steady stream of federal officials and scientists, who came to inspect the site, and Illinois leaders, who came to bolster Weston's support for the project. Senator Paul Douglas, for example, visited Theriault twice to solicit his support because the senator believed that solidarity at the local level was a prerequisite for selection.

Despite the encouraging attention of the elite, Weston was thrown once again into turmoil. The Illinois Appellate Court reversed Judge O'Malley's lower court decision upholding Weston's incorporation in the county's hostile *quo warranto* suit: the appellate court insisted that the phrase "village in fact" was essential and that, therefore, Weston was not a legally incorporated village after all.[4] But suddenly Weston did not seem to be the embattled salient.

In March, with Weston moving into the national spotlight, the DuPage County Mayors and Managers Conference responded with surprising sympathy to the appellate court decision:

> We offer our moral support to the people of the Village of Weston who want nothing more than their constitutional rights of self-government.

Evidently they hoped the accelerator would come to Weston to help the development of the area, and they believed that a conflict-free positive image of a prospering village would contribute to the effort.

The state, too, had its motive for this sudden love of an incorporated Weston. In an unincorporated community, the state would have to compensate each resident on a *pro rata* basis for community facilities, including the streets and sidewalks adjacent to each home. In an incorporated village, however, no compensation would have to be paid to individuals for streets and other village properties; under state statute, once fewer than 50 people remained in residence, the incorporation could be dissolved, the common property reverting to the state without compensation.

It is only in this context that the next set of curious events can be understood. On the morning of December 16, 1966, the Illinois Supreme Court upheld the appellate court decision against the incorporation of the village. The basis for the supreme court's decision: as the village had no commerce or schools and had violated the incorporation formula, the village was not a "village in fact." At midday, the AEC announced its selection of Weston as the accelerator site. Then in the late afternoon of the same day the supreme court sent out telegrams withdrawing its decision and announcing a formal reconsideration. In May 1967, it would reverse its own opinion and uphold the incorporation of the village.

The supreme court of Illinois has not always been above political involvement or corruption; indeed, on occasion it has followed not only the election returns, but also the stock market.[5] Thus it could be concluded that by reversing its decision the supreme court had joined the array of forces seeking an easy expropriation of the village. Nevertheless, Weston interpreted the decision as a resounding triumph and a guarantee of a better future.

This left DuPage County itself, whose top elite had not always demonstrated the kind of support for the accelerator the state might have wished. Pursuit of the hostile *quo warranto* suit indicated the uncertainty in the county over the potential site. After all, the site would involve the removal of 6,800 acres from the tax rolls and might add an excessive financial burden on the county. Doubt slowly turned to support as Gene Graves succeeded in laying out for them the compensating economic benefits. The accelerator would mean, he claimed, 3,000 new workers representing $21 million in annual personal income, $17 million per year in bank deposits, and $9 million per year in retail sales for the area. He translated this economic impact into 90 more retail establishments, 9,000 more people, 2,700 more schoolchildren, and 1,900 more people employed in nonmanufacturing jobs. In his sales pitch he failed to mention that all of these people would not necessarily live nearby, that there would be a displacement of jobs, and that more children meant more school district problems. But more and more of the people of DuPage County saw the positive $21 million per year that the accelerator seemed to promise, plus the prospect of finally being rid of Weston.

When the selection of the Weston site was announced on December 16, 1966, one Weston resident said: "I imagine property values will go up a little. Maybe we'll get some schools and a shopping center." Another remarked, "The value of the houses should go up." And another added, "It should boost the economy around here." They, like their DuPage County neighbors, saw only benefit to themselves in the site selection. Most importantly, many assumed the accelerator would be built on the outskirts of the village. Others felt the houses would be picked up and moved to a nearby site. Either way Weston would survive.

When the site was announced, the exact boundaries of the 6,800 acres were still unclear. For the next few months the boundaries would shift around, and the location of the ring on the site would appear to change. It was generally assumed, however, that the village of Weston would adjoin the site, and therefore provided the accelerator with a name.

Weston, Going In and Under

How, then, did Weston come to be included within the boundaries of the site? The official explanation, vigorously promoted by DBED, is that the state for several years had been planning to build a desperately needed highway to run north-south some distance west of the village. If this unbuilt road were used as the western border of the site, then Weston would have to be included in the 6,800-acre site. But this explanation implies that the state would be willing to spend an extra $6 million to acquire the village merely to assure the possibility of one day building a highway in a particular place. Furthermore, the DBED has said natural boundaries were sought in determining the site. The Commonwealth Edison right-of-way, just to the west of the village, originally had been the eastern border of the AEC site, thus excluding the village. Drawing the eastern boundary there would mean the western boundary would extend beyond the highway's proposed route. According to DBED officials, this aroused anger in communities to the west and in Aurora to the southwest, so that the state agreed to look eastward for a boundary.

To the east there are several natural boundaries formed by parallel highways and the EJ&E Railroad. At one point the state projected going all the way to Route 59, several hundred feet east of the EJ&E, but the projected costs of relocating the railroad tracks were far beyond the state's funds.[6] Thus, because of these costs, the DBED says the EJ&E tracks became the eastern boundary, the imaginary highway was saved, and Weston fell within the 6,800 acres of the accelerator site.[7]

A more convincing explanation of how the village came to

be included within the site is simply that the AEC specifically decided it wanted the village. There is much evidence for this explanation in the behavior of the AEC after the site announcement.

Shortly after the AEC settled on the Weston area for the accelerator, the newly appointed director of the accelerator laboratory, Robert Wilson, wrote Governor Kerner expressing the accelerator staff's eagerness to acquire the Weston homes for offices, and asked that the condemnation of the homes be given first priority. The site acquisition committee accepted this request without question.[8]

The AEC gave first priority to the village, yet it has used this property only as office space for the NAL design team. No other use was stipulated in the plans, and it seems clear that the sole purpose for taking this land was to acquire temporary office space. No design requirements of the AEC necessitated the taking of the village, because, at the time of the site negotiations, there was no accelerator design. The Lawrence Radiation Laboratory (LRL) design team, which had proposed and designed a 200-bev machine, refused to adapt the design for the Chicago site. And an accelerator is a unique machine: each is designed individually. At the time that the AEC negotiated the exact boundaries of its 6,800-acre site, it did not have a design team to guide the construction of the accelerator. Thus, it requested the village land only to serve its own, narrow financial and administrative ends: to provide office space. Two other factors support this conclusion.

First, during the "emergency" construction of the H-bomb plant at the Savannah River Project, the AEC felt free to condemn large tracts of land, move the residents out, and use the homes as office space during construction phases. There were other precedents from the Savannah River Emergency Project available for application to the Weston project, such as the use of certain "emergency" powers, including a "quick-take" law condemning the land. This law had been passed as an emergency wartime measure and had not been used in Illinois until the AEC demanded immediate possession of the land at the Weston site. In general, the AEC has used rather freely the extraordinary powers of government usually reserved for times of national emergency.[9]

The second factor was the financial situation of the AEC. By the beginning of 1966, the AEC's request for accelerator funds had been cut 37 per cent by the Bureau of the Budget, and the $3 million previously spent for the Lawrence Radiation Laboratory designs was lost when the LRL team refused to move to Weston from California. The AEC was forced to initiate a new design team and a totally new design. To the AEC, the village represented 83,200 square feet of office and design space, with more than adequate arterial streets, parking, sewage, and water facilities. To reproduce the village facilities would have cost in excess of $2 million, yet the AEC had received a design budget of $7 million, which had to cover construction costs for on-site office space as well as other expenses. With its first-year budget under serious strain, acquisition of Weston would provide an immediate and effective solution to the AEC's financial problems. The village had to be included in the site, and was.

The inclusion of the village actually violated some of the hard criteria of site selection. The original Lawrence Radiation Laboratory site criteria had stated:

> The site should be chosen so that the relocation of railroads, highways, and existing housing is kept to a minimum. Particular attention should be paid to possible conflicts with future developments around the site.[10]

Yet the final site specifically included a railway; an oil pipeline; a butane pipeline; a major high-tension power line tying together the electric generating plants on the periphery of Chicago; three lesser high-tension lines; a village of 106 homes and its various improvements, which included a stretch of four-lane paved highway, sidewalks, a water plant, and a sewage plant for 400 homes. At one time when the site boundary was projected to Route 59, 4 miles of another railroad were included within the site. In its criteria, the AEC had objected to including improvements on sites that would be expensive to move, but these problems disappeared when the state agreed to clear the site without charge to the AEC, and when some present improvements promised to serve the AEC.

Gene Graves has made it clear that there was never any intention of permitting the village to survive. As a hedge, however, on January 15, 1967, the AEC announced that the ring itself, for scientific and geological reasons, would have to be placed on top of the village. This announcement suggested that the village would have to be "removed"; but there is no doubt that the AEC never had any intention of building on top of the village and letting the houses themselves be moved away. To them, removal meant only the people. Its announcement officially defined the village as a public purpose, and that gave sanction to the state to take the village by eminent domain and hand it over to the AEC. Entranced by the accelerator's prospective economic benefits, the metropolitan and suburban press failed to question— or even discuss—the takeover of the village. DuPage's conversion to the 6,800-acre site was now, with the exception of a few site residents, complete.

Throughout this period, Arthur Theriault fashioned his statements and actions on the basis of a profound misreading of what was going on. Even his neighbors were conscious of the threat the accelerator represented to the village and the solidarity that originally had helped influence the AEC began cracking. On December 19, 1966, three days after the site selection announcement, Mayor William Zaininger of neighboring Naperville stated, "Thank the Lord that it is that far away from Naperville." But Theriault could not see it that way. On December 23, he declared:

> We may have to move our homes, and we may not. . . . It would be cheaper for the State to purchase vacant land than it would land with buildings on it. . . . Sometimes it's like being on the launching pad at Cape Kennedy. We've been a fizzle. But now it looks like we are going to get off the pad.[11]

On only one point was Theriault correct: it would have been cheaper for the state to acquire vacant land. Close to one third of the state's acquisition budget would have to be expended to acquire the narrow strip of land east of the Commonwealth Edison lines, a mere fraction of the 6,800 acres.

While Graves guarded his remarks to keep Theriault hopeful, privately he reported:

> Arthur Theriault had a lot of guts. He knew that if the site was selected he would end his political career. . . . He is the Messiah who will lead them into a promised land that won't exist.[12]

But publicly he helped maintain Theriault's illusion. Theriault could thus write directly to the president appealing for model cities money to build a new science city. Theriault envisioned Weston as a testing ground for urban technological advancement and innovation.

The dream William Riley had created didn't just persist, it grew, helped in no small part by Springfield cynicism. At his April 13, 1967, press conference Governor Otto Kerner expressed an interest in the construction of a "Twenty-first Century Village." Theriault assumed he had again set fire to a grand and noble plan. Kerner's remarks were never amplified or clarified. That same week Gene Graves told the authors privately that no new city of any kind would be built:

> Weston will have no part in the building of this new city. . . .
> This is too big and important a project to try to include them. . . .
> Weston will be levelled for many years before the new town is built. I can't and won't move the houses that residents currently live in. We may have to use federal urban renewal provisions, but we can do that.

Kerner's and others' public utterances maintained a useful illusion, the cold remains of the Riley dream.

If discussions between Graves and Theriault had been honest, the discrepancies in their public statements would not have been so great. As Graves' commitment to eliminate the village marched toward implementation, Theriault's efforts became more unrealistic. On August 25, Weston bought its own police car, and Theriault stated:

> This is our first actual step in a direction towards independence, and future expansion. It's an investment in the future.

For Theriault, the future of Weston was very much on his mind.

It did not seem to occur to Theriault that his former enemies now seemed to be his friends. He referred constantly to Graves as a friend and ally, yet Graves was now speaking the same incomprehensible language to Theriault as the county always had. Moreover, Theriault understood no better the language of the federal government. According to several observers, in June 1967

AEC Chairman Glenn Seaborg met with Arthur Theriault and told him explicitly that the village would have to be "removed." However, Theriault interpreted this to mean that although the AEC was most assuredly taking the village's land the homes could be moved elsewhere instead of being left behind. Even words changed their meanings as the various participants sought their advantages.

The Annexation Battle: Theriault's Last Stand

In January 1967, Gene Graves' office announced that the village of Weston would be razed, prompting Arthur Theriault to carry to its logical conclusion his interpretation of the term "removal." In the spring, he proposed that the village of Weston annex land outside the accelerator site and move its buildings there. By moving to previously annexed property, the village would keep its valuable legal status intact and would be able to rezone for the tax-rich commercial and industrial development expected near the accelerator.

The village vigorously pursued this new plan with the flair learned in the Riley days, establishing a zoning commission, a planning commission, and an action committee. It hired a commercial city planning agency to design the new community and hired a lawyer to advise the village on legal questions. It contacted a developer to prepare the new home sites and entered discussions with a house mover who would agree to move all the homes at one time.

Comprehensive plans for relocation were drafted so that, by moving along the railroad tracks and then across, the village could move onto contiguous land and get out from under the ostensible boundary of the accelerator ring. On June 23, 1967, the village filed its annexation petition.

A new plan generated by Weston's own initiative was no more acceptable now than the previous plans. The AEC clearly wanted Weston's buildings, and the state of Illinois initiated actions to stop the Weston move. During the week after the petition was filed, Kenneth Reeling, the chief acquisition officer for the state, wrote to Gene Graves suggesting that the annexation might be illegal because it crossed the EJ&E Railroad right-of-way without the railroad's consent. Reeling contacted railroad officials, told them there was a local objection to the annexation (instigated by Reeling), and convinced them to withdraw their agreement to the annexation of land, which would be necessary if the annexation crossed their right-of-way. On June 29, 1967, Reeling wrote to the DBED director:

> The village officials believe that this annexation provides for the continued existence of Weston as a municipality with the state having the responsibility for relocating the Weston residents and bearing the expense of replacing street improvements, sidewalks, sewer and water systems, and the village hall for a community development on annexed land outside the accelerator site.
>
> I question the legality of these annexations because the petition for annexation of the Elmer Nelson tract included the right-of-way of the Elgin, Joliet and Eastern Railroad although the railroad did not agree to the annexation of its property. I know of no legislation which permits the involuntary annexation of railroad property even though the same individual owns property on both sides of the railroad.
>
> Without the railroad's consent to annexation, it appears that the portion of the Nelson tract east of the railway cannot be annexed legally as it would not be contiguous to local municipal limits thus voiding the Kroning annexation.[13]

The thought that Weston might force the state to bear the costs of saving the village irked Reeling, and he stirred up an old feud to serve his cause by alerting the neighboring community of Warrenville, one of Weston's first and most vociferous foes, of Weston's plans.

Warrenville eyed land alongside the EJ&E tracks for its own industrial development to improve its tax base. Warrenville had existed since 1830 as an unincorporated community whose *status quo* was protected by county ordinances and whose needs were provided by county services; it was not until May 1967, in response to the growing Weston threat and after seven public referenda, that Warrenville incorporated as a city.[14] Incorporation meant that Warrenville could establish a legal buffer zone to limit Weston land annexation and rezoning.

After being contacted by the DBED, Joseph Arado, the EJ&E's vice-president for industrial development, called together representatives of Warrenville and Weston and told them that if they could settle the fate of the property he would accept their decision. If they could not agree, however, he would block the annexation. Arado's diplomatic flourish did not disguise his intention. Warrenville refused to compromise when it saw the potential annihilation of Weston; the railroad then refused to grant the annexation across its right-of-way, and at Warrenville's behest the DuPage County state's attorney instituted still a second *quo warranto* proceeding, this time against Weston's annexation plans. The court action delayed matters long enough to doom the village.

On May 1, 1968, the DuPage County circuit court ruled the annexation illegal, but for none of the obvious reasons. Judge William Guild held that "a right-of-way is not an impediment to annexation," the point upon which the suit had been based. The tract of land that Weston sought to annex lay on both sides of the railroad, but it was all the property of one owner. A 1968 Illinois supreme court ruling concerning the crossing of a right-of-way helped strike down the state's attorney's contention. But, then, Judge Guild turned to a 1965 state statute requiring municipalities to give 10 days' notification to local fire protection districts prior to annexation procedures—and on that basis he invalidated Weston's plans to move.

The DBED also instituted a second tactic of its own to stop the annexation. Generally, in condemnation proceedings the government will sell for salvage prices whatever buildings remain on the condemned land, and the governor had promised the villagers they would be able to buy back their homes. But when the state negotiators came to the village, they refused to sell back homes. If the villagers could not move their homes, their plans for a new Weston could not succeed. Next, to nail down the coffin lid, the state negotiated early with village leaders, who commanded good prices for their homes.[15] Only after their departure did the state agree to sell back some homes. This gratuitous offer recognized that no longer could the village move *en masse* to save itself because most of those who sought this remedy were already gone.[16] Even then, the state pegged its standard salvage price for homes at 6 to 10 per cent. The homes simply could not be moved economically at such high prices. In the end, rather than go to court, the state sold back the homes to the last six persons for salvage prices ranging from 6 to 13 per cent.

After the *quo warranto* suit, the state moved in quickly to oust the residents. Nearly all of the houses were appraised and purchased in the 6 weeks period beginning May 1, 1968. By September 1968, there was no longer a Weston, Illinois. The accelerator staff had moved into the homes and converted them to offices. The villagers, uncertain of when or at what price their homes might be taken (if at all), generally had not painted or kept up property during the previous 18 months.[17] Now the buildings were repainted in bright colors and moved around as if they were on a Monopoly board. The grounds were landscaped, the streets were renamed (with Indian names), and the park, which had been dedicated to a deceased Weston trustee, was obliterated.

Weston's post office service and telephone lines were routed through West Chicago, a nearby lower-middle-class community. But NAL Director Robert Wilson quickly established friendly relations with the nearby upper-class and more prestigious Batavia; he soon changed the accelerator's mailing address and telephone exchange to that village.[18] Moreover, he designed the accelerator site so that it literally turned its back on Chicago; the "ceremonial" entrance to the facility faces west, taking the visitor through an affluent section of Batavia; the truck entrance faces east, Chicago. In a "fact sheet" issued in the spring of 1968, the AEC reported that its new accelerator was located in Batavia. And finally, although the accelerator had long been referred to as the Weston Nuclear Laboratory, Wilson changed its name to the National Accelerator Laboratory, and renamed Weston itself the NAL Village. In the end Weston was to give the accelerator everything but its name.

Donald Goetz, assistant director of the National Accelerator Laboratory, said:

> The whole project had been identified as the Weston accelerator. We are not happy with this. Weston . . . is not a particularly pleasant place to be named after. The local Weston doesn't have a post office, and the village, as far as we are concerned, doesn't exist.

In eradicating every trace of the village of Weston, the Atomic Energy Commission achieved what the upper-middle-class residents of DuPage County had long but vainly sought. These people and the officials of the AEC shared an interest in maintaining the upper-class status of the area.[19] Motorcades now passed through high-status residential areas; luncheons were held at Paul Butler's prestigious Oakbrook Hunt Club and other exclusive sites. The AEC had acquired the office space it needed, and also maintained the status it desired.

NOTES TO CHAPTER 7

1. Cf. Chapter 3.
2. See the discussion concerning a conversation between AEC Chairman Glenn Seaborg and Theriault that follows.
3. See Chapter 10 for a careful analysis of the attitudes of the villagers toward the accelerator.
4. The court insisted that "village in fact" referred to a village as an ongoing enterprise, with schools, and commercial, religious, and industrial facilities. That Weston had none of these meant to the court that Weston was not a village "in fact." In the lower court the judge had addressed himself to this point by being fundamentally concerned with the "democratic desires" of the people.
5. In 1969, two justices, including the chief justice, resigned after being accused of taking bribes on cases. A third justice was implicated. All three were on the court for the Weston case.
6. Actually, the state was not responsible for relocation, and indeed did not help the villagers or the farmers relocate after taking their land. The state did, however, bear relocation costs for Commonwealth Edison, and would have expected to do so for the railroad.
7. Charles Schrader, then the Chicago area director of the DBED, gave in interview an account in which the state and the AEC negotiated over the amount of land and its boundaries well before a site was selected. He suggests that the AEC, anticipating that it might have to bear the relocation costs for the railroad, suggested the tracks as a boundary. Other states had similar negotiations.
8. According to the minutes of the site acquisition committee, when the committee was informed that the village would be first priority in order to provide AEC with office space, the committee did not respond. Later, when the consequences to the village of the pressing condemnation became apparent, the committee maintained its silence. Charles Schrader indicated in an interview that the DBED was trying to work with the AEC and did not criticize or otherwise question its priorities.

9. See Chapter 11.
10. Lawrence Radiation Laboratory, "Site Specifications for the 200 Bev Accelerator," University of California, Berkeley, 1965.
11. *The Beacon News*, Aurora, Illinois, December 23, 1966.
12. Gene Graves, address to seminar on public policy, University of Chicago, Spring, 1967.
13. DBED files.
14. See Chapter 8 concerning Warrenville and the importance of incorporation.
15. See Chapters 10 and 12.
16. Ibid.
17. Properties had been frozen; as no one could move into Weston, there was no one to whom the villagers could sell, and they saw no point in making improvements or landscaping if their ultimate departure was fairly certain.
18. The official name and address as of 1972 are National Accelerator Laboratory, P.O. Box 500, Batavia, Illinois 60510.
19. See Chapters 4 and 5.

CHAPTER 8   County Governments Know How to Plan—And Do

The village of Weston had the misfortune to intrude upon the jurisdiction of a county concerned with its problems, conscious of its resources, engaged in constant political warfare to preserve its way of life, and willing to engage a formidable ensemble of powers against any threat, however large or small. The role of DuPage County in the history of Weston is a good case study in the powers, values, and roles of suburban county government almost everywhere in the United States.

The residents of DuPage County perceive it to be one of the finest residential areas in the nation, offering both convenient road and rail access to Chicago and a great deal of open land devoid of noise, pollution, or congestion. The county includes no major centers of commerce or manufacturing, and its cities and villages are distributed rather evenly throughout the county; the largest, Wheaton, has a population of only some 31,000 in a county whose total population was almost 500,000 in 1970.

DuPage County's citizens are homogeneous upper and upper middle class. The median family income is the highest in the state of Illinois and among the highest in the nation. The county is also highly educated, predominantly Republican, and white (blacks comprise only 0.2 per cent of the population).

175

TABLE 8-1   Median Family Income,
Six-County Chicago Metropolitan Area
(1969) [1]

Cook County	$11,639
DuPage County	$14,457
Kane County	$11,947
Lake County	$12,998
McHenry County	$11,965
Will County	$11,790
Illinois	$10,957
United States	$9,586

Of the county's 463 manufacturing plants in 1962, only 150 were large enough to employ 20 or more persons. The county still contains a considerable amount of farmland. The average value of a DuPage County farm in 1964 was $168,000 as compared with $82,000 in the state as a whole.

A number of circumstances, though, have threatened to destroy the county's idyllic setting. Since the end of World War II, DuPage County has experienced a large and continuous increase in population and housing. Between 1950 and 1960, the county's population increased 102 per cent, from 154,599 to 313,459, with 78 per cent of this increase due to an in-migration. Between 1960 and 1970, the population of DuPage County showed the greatest percentage increase of any Illinois county—another 57 per cent, to almost 492,000.

Old age and high taxes combined to induce increasing numbers of the county's farmers to sell their land to developers and speculators, like Julia Krafft, anxious to provide housing for the newcomers. Thus farmland is gradually being replaced by housing developments, and the county's much-vaunted open space has been threatened by suburban sprawl. Moreover, the constant danger exists that, as in the Weston case, farmers will sell their property to developers interested in constructing subdivisions for lower-income families.

In addition to its population growth, DuPage County's location and resources have attracted increased industrial develop-

T A B L E 8–2 Population, Illinois and Chicago Metropolitan
Area (1940–1960)

	POPULA-TION 1950	CHANGE 1950–1960	POPULA-TION 1960	CHANGE 1960–1970	POPULA-TION 1970
Illinois	8,712,176	15.6%	10,081,158	10.2%	11,109,935
Cook County	4,508,792	13.8%	5,129,725	7.1%	5,488,328
DuPage County	154,599	102.9%	313,459	56.6%	491,882
Kane County	150,388	38.5%	208,246	20.5%	251,005
Lake County	179,097	64.0%	293,656	30.3%	382,638
McHenry County	50,656	66.2%	84,210	-24.5%	104,389
Will County	134,336	42.6%	191,617	29.3%	249,498

ment. Although industry threatens the county's residential
character, its entrance has been encouraged by the county government, anxious for the vital tax revenues it produces. Thus
DuPage County's dilemma—how to maintain its desirable characteristics in spite of inevitable growth and development.

"Planning for Orderly Development": Instruments of Control

To cope with the forces of urbanization, the government
of DuPage County has historically turned to planning. According
to the 1956 DuPage County Comprehensive Plan:

> It is fortunate for its citizens that DuPage County is known
> historically as a pioneer in all that makes for better community
> living: first among all Illinois counties in zoning for orderly
> growth; first to adopt a modern building code; and first, now, in
> regional planning for long-range land use.[2]

The concept of "orderly development" repeated throughout the 1956 plan, and frequently reiterated by former County Board Chairman Paul Ronske,[3] has meant strict control of the types of people and activities permitted to enter the county. The county government realized that rapid population growth through in-migration was inevitable. But it believed the character of the entering population and its housing could be controlled to insure the preservation of the county's essential homogeneity and high property values. Similarly, the character of new industry could be controlled to discourage those industries that would bring noise and pollution and to encourage lighter industrial uses, particularly research and technical centers, on quiet, landscaped lots.

"Orderly development" also implies the orderly placement of industry and population. The creation of large, congested residential or industrial centers was to be avoided in favor of scattered, smaller concentrations of industry. Similarly, orderly development meant

> retention of the rural-suburban character of the county's area, free from such urban hindrances to good living as contaminated air; oppressive noise and congestion; free from all commercialization so far as may be consistent with the holding down of tax rates to reasonable levels.[4]

By carefully controlling population influx, residential construction, and industrial development, DuPage County hoped to maintain its life style in a changing universe.

Illinois law has provided DuPage County with the legal instruments with which to plan for its way of life. Under Illinois statute, counties may

—Tax; borrow money; issue licenses; exercise subdivision control, with regard to the establishment of regulations for the location, width and course of streets and the provision of land for public grounds, schools, parks, etc., and reasonable requirements with respect to water supply, sewage collection and treatment, and street drainage.

—Acquire lands for public grounds and industrial development.

—Prepare a comprehensive plan.

—Establish zoning and setback regulations.

—Provide for and regulate sewage and water facilities and exercise the power of eminent domain to acquire or construct sewage and waterworks systems.

These powers, together with informal powers derived from relations with other government and private agencies, have made it possible for DuPage and other Illinois counties to exercise control over the types of people who may reside within their jurisdictions and the types of activities to be carried on in unincorporated areas therein. Although no county can place guards at the county line to inspect the socioeconomic and racial characterisitcs of newcomers, such powers as zoning and control over subdivision and building codes make the county a highly effective arbiter of the types of structures to be built and, hence, the final arbiter of the types of people who will live in its jurisdiction.

For example, DuPage County enacts a subdivision ordinance requiring a developer to retain a large portion of his prospective subdivision for public facilities such as parks and schools; the county combines this with a zoning ordinance requiring single-family dwellings and a large minimum lot size. This effectively prohibits a developer from profitably building anything but high-cost housing not accessible to lower-income persons.

Stringent county building code standards, requiring expensive building materials and high-quality plumbing, wiring, and heating systems, also serve to increase housing costs. The county's industrial zoning policy restricting heavy industry serves to limit job opportunities for lower-income persons and to prevent a decline in residential property values surrounding an industrial development—which might create housing opportunities for lower-income groups. Moreover, the county's relations with various financial institutions make it difficult for a developer to secure financing for a project not approved by the county. Indeed, because of the obstacles the county is capable of placing in the path of a developer, the county's objection may be sufficient to convince a financial institution that investment in a project would be unwise.

The county's relations with other units of government give it yet another means of influencing the course of residential and industrial development. It is not, for example, an uncommon practice in Illinois for the county forest preserve district to condemn, at the county government's behest, land on which an unwelcome development is planned. Many potential Westons have been eliminated in this manner. And courts have made it a point not to intervene. If the acquisition was for a "public purpose," there is no inclination to examine the underlying motives.

With its self-perpetuating county board and its generally closed politics, DuPage County has been able to exercise its powers of control with an even greater degree of restrictiveness than most other Illinois counties. The DuPage County zoning ordinance, for example, remains the most stringent in Illinois. It is no accident that houses valued under $30,000 have been rare in the county.

Zoning is inherently flexible as an instrument of planning because of the government's power to grant variances and special uses as well as to create floating zones and planned unit developments. This, combined with the strictness and precision of its statutory standards, has over the years enabled DuPage to select all the more carefully and specifically the industrial and residential developments and, consequently, the types of people to be permitted access to the county. Because of these formal and informal powers of control, and in spite of a 102.8 per cent population increase between 1950 and 1960, DuPage County was able to maintain its position as the wealthiest county in the state and as one of the top five in the nation.

The Limits of County Control of Orderly Development: The Politics of Incorporation

One of the primary factors limiting the ability of the county to control its own socioeconomic composition is the shrinking jurisdiction of the county government through town and village incorporation. The incorporation of an area to form a new municipality relieves the county of much of its authority over that area. And new municipalities have been incorporated with growing frequency in recent years.

According to the tenets of democratic ideology, the incorporation of new municipalities is to be viewed as a manifestation of popular desires for independence and self-government in small,

TABLE 8–3   Municipal Incorporations in Six-County Chicago
Metropolitan Area (1940–1967) [5]

	1940–1945	1945–1950	1950–1955	1955–1960	1960–1967	TOTAL 1940–1967
Cook County	1	4	7	12	7	31
DuPage County	0	0	0	5	5	10
Kane County	0	0	0	3	0	3
Lake County	0	0	2	9	10	21
McHenry County	0	0	2	2	1	5
Will County	0	0	1	0	3	4
Total	1	4	12	31	26	74

local units. A belief in the virtues of small, self-governing communities is deeply rooted in American tradition. The vision of a
group of people who live and work in close contact creating their
own democratic institutions, electing their own officials, managing their own affairs, and thereby forming the bulwark of a
democratic society is as much a part of American folklore as the
frontier and the Horatio Alger myth.

Whether this vision of independent self-government closely
approximates historical reality is an open question. In a modern
society the inhabitants of the small community are quite likely
to work and shop elsewhere, maintain their primary ties of friendship elsewhere, worship elsewhere, and derive their values and
culture from mass media produced elsewhere. The political independence of the small modern community is also sharply cur-
tailed. Citizens "managing their own affairs" in a small community
are directly subject to the policies of the nation, state, and county,
as well as a variety of special districts, so that issues ranging from
mosquito abatement to war and peace are beyond their direct,
municipal control. Moreover, the self-governing community is
a creature of state laws of incorporation and is given its legal
standing by the county court.

Nevertheless, incorporation confers important powers upon
an Illinois municipality, powers to govern itself and to defend
itself from outside encroachments. The municipality may tax,

borrow money, exercise the power of eminent domain, issue licenses, regulate the use of its streets, and establish zoning and subdivision ordinances, building codes, health regulations, and the like. For certain important purposes, state and county policies stop at the boundaries of the incorporated municipality. Municipal independence is reinforced by the many federal policies that make use of direct grants-in-aid to municipal governments.

The incorporation of new municipalities severely limits the county's jurisdiction and the effectiveness of the county's "instruments of control" in two important ways. First, the authority of county zoning ordinances and building and subdivision codes generally does not extend into incorporated areas. Second, for certain purposes, the incorporated municipality may extend its own influence beyond its municipal boundaries into unincorporated areas of the county. Villages in Illinois, for example, may acquire land for industrial purposes within 10 miles of their boundaries; may acquire or condemn land for public parks within 4 miles of their boundaries; and may acquire or condemn land for waterworks, sewage, levees, garbage disposal, bridges, drainage, and so on within 10 miles of their boundaries. Moreover, villages exercise subdivision control, zoning, and planning powers over contiguous unincorporated areas within 1½ miles of their boundaries. Under specified conditions, villages may also annex territory contiguous to their boundaries, and an incorporated village can further defend itself from the county and other villages by virtue of the state law providing that it must give its permission before another municipality may either incorporate or annex land within a mile of the village's boundaries. Thus citizens who incorporate a municipality may gain a significant amount of governmental control over their local affairs, and also severely limit the utility of the county's instruments of control.

Yet, despite this and despite the increasing number of incorporations, in the Chicago metropolitan area an increasing number of persons had come to live in unincorporated areas by 1960, as indicated by Table 8–4. One explanation for the preference to remain unincorporated is referred to as the "low tax, low expenditure ideology." [7] Incorporation is likely to produce tax increases to finance capital improvements and services that the residents of an area might prefer to see provided by the county (to

TABLE 8–4   Population of Incorporated Municipalities and
Unincorporated Areas (1940–1960) (reported as total and
per cent of total county population) [6]

	1940	1960
DuPage County		
Incorporated municipalities	72,783 (71%)	386,205 (60%)
Unincorporated areas	30,697 (29%)	122,583 (40%)
Kane County		
Incorporated municipalities	101,185 (78%)	156,327 (76%)
Unincorporated areas	29,021 (22%)	51,919 (24%)
Lake County		
Incorporated municipalities	90,223 (74%)	181,900 (62%)
Unincorporated areas	30,871 (26%)	111,756 (38%)
McHenry County		
Incorporated municipalities	15,515 (42%)	29,991 (39%)
Unincorporated areas	21,796 (58%)	54,219 (61%)
Will County		
Incorporated municipalities	60,233 (53%)	102,430 (53%)
Unincorporated areas	53,977 (47%)	89,187 (47%)

which they must pay taxes anyway), or are willing to forego entirely. Thus Warrenville, in DuPage County, existed as an unincorporated settlement providing no services whatsoever from 1830 to 1967, when, for reasons having largely to do with Weston, as discussed in the previous chapter, its citizens reluctantly incorporated as a municipality.

The second major factor involved in not incorporating is the opposition of the county government and existing incorporated municipalities that have vested interests in determining the kinds of people to live in and the activities to be carried on in their respective jurisdictions. The ethos of government in a county such as DuPage demands that careful controls be exercised over the incorporation of new municipalities lest corporate powers come into the hands of people who might, among other things, permit lower-class persons to enter the county. Because of its continual efforts to block incorporation, DuPage County has shown the greatest percentage increase of persons living in unincorporated areas of all counties in Illinois.

The county government and the various special districts, incorporated municipalities, and residents of unincorporated areas have at their disposal a variety of techniques with which to discourage the incorporation of unwanted new municipalities. For example, the county may encourage a previously incorporated municipality with which it has had good relations to expand by annexation into contiguous territory, thereby preventing that territory from incorporating separately. Similarly, because incorporated municipalities exercise zoning and subdivision powers over unincorporated areas within 1½ miles of their boundaries, they may hamper the creation of developments that might become large enough to threaten to incorporate themselves. The county may also encourage one group of people living in an unincorporated area to incorporate in order to prevent others from so doing. Or, alternatively, the residents of an unincorporated area may incorporate "defensively" to seal off the area from developers they do not approve of and to prevent the incorporation of other municipalities within a mile of their boundaries. The power of eminent domain may be used by existing municipalities or by the various special districts to condemn land on which the creation or expansion of unwanted developments is planned.

In those cases where the efforts of the county and its allies to prevent the incorporation of an undesired municipality have failed, there remains one last, rarely used, legal weapon, the *quo warranto* suit. This suit calls upon the officers of any corporation, including a municipality, to show by what authority they are exercising powers. The burden of proof in such a suit is on the corporation. The officers of a municipality sued in such a manner must prove that the incorporation of their city or village proceeded precisely according to law, or, if a particular action is at issue, that their charter permits it. If the officers are not able to prove that their incorporation was valid, the incorporation of the municipality is dissolved by the court, and the territory is returned to the status of an unincorporated area.

Conscious of its shrinking jurisdiction, DuPage County has been involved in constant political warfare to prevent the expansion of existing municipalities and the incorporation of new ones, especially those not likely to share the county's belief in the values of orderly development. Because so many villages seek incorporation precisely to evade and escape county stringencies, existing interests watch each closely—and fight most.

DuPage County vs. Weston

The reasons behind DuPage County's use of virtually all these powers against Weston are relatively clear. Originally, the county had earmarked the area for "orderly" industrial development and opposed any development of the tract for residential purposes. If, however, residential development was to occur, Weston was precisely the sort of development that DuPage County did not want. Weston's citizens were perceived to be lower class and their homes well below the county's standards. Weston's early development tended to confirm this perception.

The details of DuPage's opposition are provided in previous chapters. Suffice it to say here that DuPage County had to use every possible power to prevent construction on the site and that the exhaustive list of formal powers provided here is almost an inventory of DuPage's actions against the village.

All of this bought an important 2-year delay. Finally the county board, resigned to the fact of Weston, agreed to grant a permit for construction, but only on the condition that title to the oxidation pond, which the developers now proposed to use for sewage treatment, be conveyed to the county. The village might exist but the county assumed that it would be able to use the control it would thus gain over the subdivision's sewage system to prevent any expansion.

Throughout the brief history of the village of Weston, DuPage County authorities refused to cooperate with village authorities in such a relatively routine matter as zoning uniformity. Furthermore, evidence cited in Chapter 6 indicates that the county utilized its informal channels of influence with financial institutions to interfere with the financing of the development of the Weston site, and employed its informal relations with the Chicago Better Business Bureau to block advertisement of the "Riley plan."

These methods of control were informal but nevertheless based on the county's formal position. No financial institution, for example, hoping to remain involved in land development in the lucrative DuPage County market could, in the long run, gain from alienating the county government. Zoning, subdivision, and building codes can be applied by the county in a flexible manner. And the difference between a favorable or unfavorable administrative ruling may involve millions of dollars.

Following each attack on Weston, the county fell back upon still another power appropriate for some later stage of development. Had the county's *quo warranto* suit been successful, the village of Weston would have immediately ceased to exist, and the tract would have reverted to the status of an unincorporated area subject to the authority of the county of DuPage. Given the plans of the speculators for sub-subdivision after incorporation, this formal defeat would have meant death.

The county's unsuccessful appeal of the *quo warranto* suit left it with a generally expensive, but familiar, alternative—the condemnation and acquisition of surrounding farmland to isolate Weston and prevent its expansion.

It was at this point that federal policy entered the picture. The placement of the National Accelerator Laboratory on the Weston site not only isolated the village by removing all the area's farmers but also eliminated the village itself.

The alternative, condemnation and acquisition by the DuPage County Forest Preserve District, had never been so successful or so cheap. Federal and state dollars were providing the county with everything it could want. Federal plans even conformed with the county's long-range notions of orderly development. The accelerator was just the sort of research facility the county desired. According to *DuPage Magazine*:

> The construction of the National Accelerator Laboratory in Weston will have many far-reaching effects on DuPage County, from an impact on real estate values to a position of further prominence in national affairs. It will surely lend credence to our claim to the title "Research County–USA." This huge facility will form literally dozens of other research and technical installations such as Argonne National Laboratories, Armour and Company, and Container Corporation of America. There will be few areas in the country with a more concentrated scientific community.[8]

In place of Weston's lower-class citizens, the accelerator promised to bring highly paid scientists into the county. As *DuPage Magazine* noted, "Perhaps the most important effect, however, will be the people. The scientists and technicians attracted to DuPage County will make an important addition to our population . . . the impact of such fine people is felt in all facets of activity." [9]

The county would lose tax revenues from the 6,800 acres taken by the federal government. But the county had the power to determine future tax burdens. The commercial activity expected to grow up around the accelerator would offer a magnificent source of tax revenues—enough to more than offset the initial revenue loss.

The federal government contributed to the solution of DuPage County's dilemma. But it was the county's own powers and resources that permitted it to make use of the federal funds. The objectives of federal policy were limited to the construction of an accelerator, but federal policy had provided a well-organized local government with additional resources to use in implementing its own objectives. DuPage County's conception of orderly development left no place for housing lower- and lower-middle-class persons or for the heavy industry that might employ such persons. While DuPage County, with the aid of the federal government, pursued a policy of retaining its homogeneity and idyllic residential characteristics, the poor and the black remained locked in the slums of nearby Chicago. DuPage could, if it wished, have planned orderly development toward heterogeneity—but chose otherwise, and had the power to make its choice stick. And the nature of that choice determined the shape of a large piece of the metropolitan future, as it had already determined a large piece of the past.

Orderly Development Needs Outside Help: A Comparison

Other counties of the Chicago metropolitan area—Kane, Lake, Will, McHenry—all faced the same dilemma as DuPage. All wished to maintain their life styles in the face of increasing residential and industrial development and in spite of a shrinking sphere of jurisdiction as new municipalities were being incorporated. These counties were neither as wealthy nor as politically well organized as DuPage. They had the same formal powers as other counties in Illinois but were losing long and bitter fights over the creation of lower-middle-class housing developments. The history of one such development is similar enough to the history of Weston to merit examination.

Late in 1956, L and H Builders, one of at least 14 construction companies owned by Barney Loeb, Quinn Hogan, and their wives, acquired a tract of farmland near Mundelein in Lake County. According to their public statements, Loeb and Hogan planned to use the tract to construct a multimillion-dollar "playground resort," to include a hotel, golf course, supper club, swimming pool, skating rink and "luxury" homes, including two $100,000 homes for Loeb and Hogan themselves.[10]

Residents of surrounding areas welcomed neither the idea of a "playground resort" as a neighbor nor the involvement of Loeb and Hogan, who had developed a reputation for shady dealings. There were local suspicions that the playground· resort would, at some point, become associated with the development of something less than luxury homes. These residents evidently had some in-fluence with the Lake County government, for it soon became clear to Loeb and Hogan that the county could not be persuaded to rezone the area to permit either playground resorts or housing de-velopments. Thus Loeb and Hogan, like McCabe and the Wolf-sons in Weston, hit upon the scheme of incorporating a village on the tract of land they owned in order to capture zoning and sub-division power for themselves. In the space of a few weeks, L and H Builders constructed 24 homes on the tract. These homes, like those in Weston, were on large lots and spaced so that they would conform with the county zoning ordinance and still permit other houses to be built between them as soon as zoning control had been secured. According to Hogan, all of the new homes were occupied by employees, subcontractors, or relatives of Loeb and Hogan. None of the houses was sold, and few of the imported occupants paid rent.

On August 31, 1957, some 30 days after the last house was occupied, Matthew Teolis, an L and H employee and an imported resident, circulated a petition for the incorporation of the village of Vernon Hills, which was purportedly signed by 41 electors (35 were required) and filed with the county court by Frank Opeka, attorney for L and H Builders. The court scheduled a special election on the question of incorporation, but before it could be held a number of residents of the area surrounding the proposed village, represented by Harold Block, a Mundelein attorney, alleged that the persons signing the petition for incorporation were neither electors nor inhabitants of the area, that the proposed village contained fewer than the 100 required inhabitants, and that none of the inhabitants had been in the area long enough to qualify as a village officer. The courts, however, dismissed the case, on grounds that no statutory provision existed for such an intervention.[11]

In July, 1958, the village of Vernon Hills was incorporated, with the village officers being installed in August 1958. Matthew Teolis was elected village president. A number of those neighbors who had opposed the incorporation of Vernon Hills incorporated nearby as the village of Indian Creek in an attempt to protect themselves from whatever plans Loeb and Hogan had for the area. And, before Loeb and Hogan could proceed, a *quo warranto* complaint was filed by the Lake County state's attorney in an attempt to invalidate the incorporation of the village. The suit alleged that fewer than 35 of the signatures on the petition for incorporation were valid; that there were fewer than 100 residents in the area; that fewer than eight of the residents had lived in the area long enough to qualify as village officers (60 days); and that it was contrary to state policy to permit the incorporation of a municipality owned, in effect, by a single corporation, which would be able to use the power and authority of government to further its own ends. Harold Block, who had represented the persons initially opposing the incorporation, was appointed special assistant state's attorney to argue the case for Lake County. After 3 years of legal maneuvering, however, the courts upheld the incorporation of the village of Vernon Hills.[12]

To this point, the history of Vernon Hills is similar to that of Weston. Both were lower-middle-class developments opposed by the county; both were incorporated to evade county zoning and subdivision requirements; in both cases, the county attempted to destroy the village by means of the *quo warranto* suit. Here, however, the similarity ends. By 1970, Vernon Hills was a lower-middle-class community with some 800 inhabitants, whereas Weston had ceased to exist. Lake County was unable with its own instruments of control to prevent the creation and expansion of Vernon Hills, whereas DuPage County, with the aid of federal public policy, was able to destroy Weston. Fortunately for the village of Vernon Hills there were not enough federal projects to enable Lake County to insure its own "orderly development."

Lake County and DuPage are, in powers, identical. The federal decision on the accelerator simply put resources into the hands of DuPage County's government that Lake did not have. Federal resources fueled existing DuPage County machinery, and, in this manner, the federal government killed Weston as surely as if that had been federal policy. Because of the county's powers and the federal government's abnegation of responsibility, federal policy and county policy became one.

How to Plan—And How Not to

The suburban county is a study in effective planning. From the standpoint of the prevailing values of the suburban population, the suburban county is a study in good planning.

These governments have determined upon a certain course of development that is in accord with the preferences of an over-whelming majority of their constituents, and they have doggedly guided all their policies accordingly. No referendum has ever been taken on the master goals; but consensus, so rare in the United States, is usually clear when it does exist, and it needs little explication. Besides, some of the costs of consensus may not stand up to close public scrutiny. First, explicit articulation of these suburban social goals in referendum form would not look good to the general population of the country, and might even be illegal or unconstitutional by national criteria. Second, the economic costs are better borne when not precisely known. The neighboring farmers would suffer in the Weston case as well as the villagers, if there was to be a final solution to the Weston problem. And the removal of 6,800 acres of land from the tax rolls, although another testament to the sincerity of suburbia's commitment to the master goals, would nonetheless be a costly matter better left implicit.

The DuPage master plan, although implicit, can be simply

stated: maintain the suburban way of life as it already exists in the developed areas of the county. Methods and intermediate goals follow. Retain this, exclude that; set standards high on this, be lenient on that; control the development of this, subsidize the development of that. Almost all of the necessary powers exist.

Study of the Weston development and the county's response to it actually reveals two kinds of planning, positive planning and negative planning. Positive planning refers to a process of identifying a desirable state of affairs in a defined future, toward which resources and powers are authoritatively directed. Negative planning refers to a process whereby an existing state of affairs is identified and the resources and prescriptions of government are directed toward their preservation or conservation.

To most professional planners and their clientele, planning actually *means* positive planning. This is the case despite the fact that future states of affairs are extremely difficult to define. It should be equally difficult, therefore, to justify the need to attain these goals, although the rhetoric tends to escalate to a point where the goals seem self-evidently desirable. Costs and benefits of future states of affairs are impossible to assess; the means for reaching any future will remain uncertain as long as the ends remain vague. Consequently, positive planning usually ends up being nothing more than an elaborate rhetoric coupled with a process by which planning activities take place. Certainly there are better and worse ways of making decisions, and all decisions have to look toward a future. But DuPage County shows that there is still another kind of planning. It is negative planning, and under almost any circumstances it is more effective than positive planning.

It should be patently obvious that negative planning can be more specific and concrete about the state of affairs for which a plan is to be made and implemented. A planner could probably quite clearly identify certain features of family life that the community would want to preserve far better than he could identify a future community within which family life might be safer or richer. Similarly, a group of untrained laymen in a vast and complex suburban county can identify a rather large number of existing attributes of their communities that the overwhelming portion of those communities would agree should be preserved. The same was true 20 years ago, and such counties as DuPage are to a large extent the results of negative planning that was undertaken 20 years ago and is being realized in quite concrete form today.

All comparisons with the positive planning of that period come up in favor of negative planning. The waste, the counter-productiveness, and the unanticipated consequences of planning in the cities, done by professionals, seem so often to outweigh the gains. One must wonder, especially after reviewing the recent history of DuPage County, how much better off the cities might have been if their planning had been governed by negative values before and during World War II. What if we had determined at that time that neighborhood integration, community solidarity, and safety were more important than new housing, new transportation systems, and new and more efficient ways of dispensing community services? One might even say that the failure of positive planning a generation ago was greatly responsible for the critical need for a more profound and difficult kind of positive *social planning* today in the cities. If sociologist Jane Jacobs is only 20 per cent correct in her assessment, the contrast between the negative planning of DuPage County and the positive planning of the central city should be given a serious and fundamental reanalysis.[13]

When one looks at DuPage County and looks still further into the kind of negative planning that Southern communities are famous for in racial matters, one is led seriously to ask whether negative planning is a luxury only available to the bad guys.[14] That is not necessarily proven by the fact that the bad guys tend to be so effective with negative planning. The resurgence of ethnic consciousness in the past few years, coupled with a tremendous historical literature on the value of cities, suggests that there are millions of existing urban attributes that negative planning by good guys could maintain, support, foster. Maybe the trouble with good guys is that they are so good. Perhaps they are shamed by the present. Perhaps they are shamed by the prospect of being conservative. Or perhaps they are blinded by some belief that the future is not the future if it possesses elements of the past.

We hope that the experience of DuPage County and how it has used its governmental powers will serve as a lesson to all who have the public interest sincerely at heart. The techniques of government—that is, the instruments of planning—are neutral. They can serve any master. Negative planning is simply a special and concrete way of looking at the future. The techniques are likely to be just as effective in one set of hands as in another.

NOTES TO CHAPTER 8

1. Population and income data based on *U.S. Census* (Washington, D.C.: U.S. Bureau of the Census, 1940, 1950, 1960), and *County and City Data Book* (Washington, D.C.: U.S. Bureau of the Census, 1949, 1952, 1956, 1962, 1967).
2. Carl L. Gardner and Associates, "Comprehensive County Plan for DuPage County, Illinois," prepared for the DuPage County Board of Supervisors, August 15, 1956, p. 143.
3. Interview with Paul Ronske.
4. "Comprehensive Plan for DuPage County," p. 123.
5. Based on calculation from data reported in *Illinois Blue Book* (Springfield, Ill.: Office of the Secretary of State, 1940–1968).
6. Based on calculation from data reported in *Illinois Blue Book,* 1940–1960. Cook County, which includes Chicago, has been omitted.
7. Arthur Vidich and Joseph Bensman. *Small Town in Mass Society* (Garden City, N.Y.: Doubleday, 1968).
8. *DuPage Magazine,* "What's Happening at Weston" (May–June 1968).
9. Ibid.
10. The *Independent-Register,* Mundelein, Illinois, June 4, 1959.
11. 19 Ill. 2d 342 (1960).
12. 20 Ill. 2d. 95 (1961).
13. Jane Jacobs, *The Death and Life of Great American Cities* (New York: Random House, 1961).
14. Richard F. Babcock, *The Zoning Game* (Madison: University of Wisconsin Press, 1966).

9 **The People of**

Weston and the Dilemmas of Understanding

Suburbia is an ideal carried in the heads of suburbanites. It does not exist anywhere in the real world, but the idea is powerful. It operates as a guide to community building, and, although it cannot be articulated in detail, the suburbanite somehow knows when he is in the presence of a threat to that idea, and at that time action is never very far away.

The Weston villagers, by 1967, shared the suburban ideal. Although some were not yet middle class, they had come to share middle-class values, and they chose to live in Weston for essentially suburban reasons. But Weston to the DuPage suburbanite arose out of 1962 realities, and in that it constituted a serious threat to the suburban idea. Weston represented a community model that was, *whatever it was*, not the suburban model; and, not being a suburban model, it was by definition a threat.

Weston was becoming middle class; but that was irrelevant. The image projected by the Weston of 1962 in large part explains Weston's demise after 1967. Weston could not be allowed to exist, even as a tiny core of a much larger service community conveniently near the completed accelerator facility in 1980. Land suitable for the accelerator was plentiful in that area. Weston was not definitely in the original site plan at all—the precise boundaries of the site were not defined until rather late in the process. But the site made sense to the county only with Weston included. No matter that Weston was becoming a suburb. No matter that it was aping its neighbors and making the desirable choice among alternative community models. The hypothesis confirmed itself: the example an unsuburban Weston would set for future development was too serious a matter. The stakes were too high for gambling.

Social Portrait of Weston

The original inhabitants of Weston had arrived in 1961 and 1962. They were low-income transients. Their style of life created an image of Weston the people of DuPage apparently never forgot. In 1967, when asked "Who were the Westonites?" DuPage County could offer an easy answer: "hillbillies." They paid low rent for tiny, basementless, ticky-tacky houses and they lived in the middle of nowhere. Weston was, to DuPage, nothing but a drain on neighboring towns; the village's low-taxed, overpopulated families would require more desks in the schools and more sheriff's deputies on the streets.

Time passed and realities changed. Weston changed fundamentally. But the original image stuck. When the two savings and loan associations that underwrote Weston's development went bankrupt, ownership of the houses was transferred to the Federal Savings and Loan Insurance Corporation. After rehabilitating the houses, the FSLIC's local agent put them up for sale. Resident tenants had first option to buy, but most could not afford to do so, and moved out. A new group—*home buyers*—moved in.

By the time state and county acted to "remove" Weston, taking advantage of the site selection opportunity provided by the Atomic Energy Commission, the community it sought to eliminate had already disappeared. Instead, they removed a community that was a microcosm of the region itself. Wiping out Weston was an action against the nonrebellious children of the county itself. The example of Weston had become more important than the reality.

Who were the Westonites by 1967?

—They were people from the area, who had lived in DuPage County or the Fox River Valley before moving to Weston.

—They were young, but had been married for a while and had children.
—They were steadily employed, in the immediate area.
—They were "suburbanites" in their thinking about the reasons they moved to Weston.
—They were generally skilled workers or lower-level managers, earning good incomes.
—They were discriminating participants in the commercial life of their area.

The discrepancy between DuPage County's view of Weston and this reality is more than merely curious; for Weston, this discrepancy proved to be a plague during life, and the cause of death.

The history of Weston may be divided into four periods, according to the types of occupancy that were possible in the village:

1. Renting, from the original, assorted developers.
2. Renting, from the FSLIC.
3. Buying by former renters, from the FSLIC.
4. Buying by new residents, from the FSLIC.

A few people lived in Weston for more than one of these periods; nevertheless, there were several waves of residents, constituting fairly clear-cut generations.

When we carried out a survey in May 1967, several groups had already passed through Weston.[1] The first group arrived in 1961 and 1962 but no longer lived there in 1967. In many ways, these were the people who provided the county and the region with their image of Weston. There is anecdotal but quite meaningful information about this group in earlier chapters.

The people in the other groups were still around in 1967, and were represented in our study. They can be identified by two variables that partially overlap. First, there were those who moved in when renting was the only possible form of tenancy, and those who moved in later, when purchase was the only possible form of tenancy for new residents. Second, there were those who moved in before Weston was announced as among the final sites in the accelerator competition, and those who moved in later (with hope, or uncertainty, or whatever feeling they might have had). The number of people in our sample who moved in during these various periods is shown in Figure 9–1.

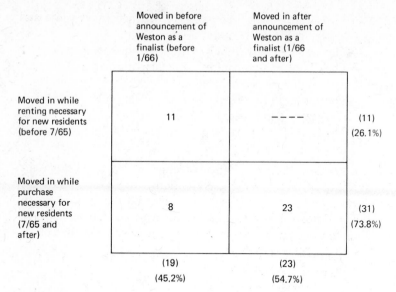

FIGURE 9–1   *Arrival time of Weston residents.*

One of the litany of reasons for exorcising Weston was the presumed source of the villagers, the Appalachian hills. This reason was not an accurate reflection of reality at the time of our survey. Indeed, in our sample, there was no one who had moved directly to Weston from a Southern state or from Appalachia. Rather, if there was a modal "source" for Westonites, it was DuPage County and the Fox River Valley, as shown in Table 9–1.

The simple truth seems to be that after a rather stormy beginning and period of transition the village took its place in the normal cycle of family movement in the metropolis. Social geographer Brian Berry has proposed a grid onto which all towns of a metropolitan area may be mapped.[2] One dimension of the grid is based on the realization that certain towns or neighborhoods seem attractive to families at particular points in their life cycle *as* families. Thus a newly married couple—having limited space needs but specific social needs—might choose to live in an apartment in

TABLE 9-1   Previous Residence of 1967 Weston Families

| COUNTY | TOWN OF PREVIOUS RESIDENCE | NUMBER OF FAMILIES | CUMULATIVE | |
			NUMBER	PER CENT
Kane	Aurora	2		
	St. Charles	1		
	Carpentersville	1	4	9.3
DuPage	West Chicago	8		
	Winfield	1		
	Wheaton	2		
	Glen Ellyn	1		
	Glendale Heights	1		
	Villa Park	2		
	Naperville	4		
	Warrenville	2	25	58.1
Cook	Western Suburbs	4	29	67.4
	Chicago	9	38	88.3
—	Other Illinois	3	41	95.3
—	Other United States	1	42	97.6
—	No Answer	1	43	100.0

a cosmopolitan area. As the couple has children, both its space needs and its social needs change, so the family moves, perhaps to a rented small house. As the number of children increases, and as the children get older, the family moves again, probably buying its own home, with the quality of local schools looming large in its choice of town. As the children grow and leave home, the space and social needs change again, and the couple moves again, perhaps back to an apartment, maybe to a different climate. In this model, there is stability in the function of a specific area or town:

—It tends to remain as a place where families at particular stages in their life reside.

The other dimension on the Berry grid is based on social class status. By examining towns according to their social class ranking, and their attractiveness to people at various points in their family life cycles, and ascribing some numerical weight for each factor,

Berry is able to map the towns on his grid. The pattern followed by any given family may be graphed as a vector of two tendencies:

—Movement through a series of towns as they become suitable at various points in the family life cycle, and movement up (or down) the socioeconomic ladder.

Thus to understand Weston we need to look at more than its social class standing.[3] We need to look at the life cycle position of the Weston families. Did Weston seem to attract families at a particular point in their life cycle? If so, what was this point? We found that

—No one lived in Weston who was not married (excepting the few widowed and divorced persons, and their children).
—Very few couples moved to Weston who were in their first year of marriage.
—Only two couples who lived in Weston were without at least one child (ten families had one child, ten more had two, and another ten had three children).
—Perhaps owing to the small size of the houses, only a few couples had more than three children.

Furthermore, at the time of our study, there was only one couple living in Weston married for less than 2 years. In several cases, Weston provided a house in place of a family's previous apartment.

Weston thus appeared to fit into the Berry grid quite readily as a second-stage residence for couples married 2 or 3 years, with at least one child. These facts, taken together with the DuPage County and Fox River Valley origins of the majority of the families, strongly suggest that the residents of Weston were the grown-up children of the general locale.

Economic Portrait: Employment, Motivations, Income, and Commerce

Among the ways Weston residents were involved in and identified with the life of the DuPage County region was by participating in the area's labor force. Although we did not learn the specific places people worked, we were able to ascertain how far workers had to travel to get to work. And by any accounting the

TABLE 9–2   Distance to Workplace for Weston Residents

DISTANCE TO WORK	NUMBER OF PERSONS *	PER CENT (OF WORKERS)
Up to 5 miles	9	20.4
5 to 10 miles	20	45.4
10 to 20 miles	8	18.1
20 or more miles	7	15.9
Total	44	99.8
No Answer †	29	
Total Responses	73	

* This table is based on individual responses, rather than family data.

† In another question, these 29 persons listed their "work" as "house-wife."

typical worker was employed in the immediate area, as shown in Table 9–2.

By extrapolation and interpretation, it is clear that a substantial majority of the workers in our sample traveled distances (up to 10 miles) that had to be within western DuPage County and Fox River Valley. Several more traveled far enough (up to 20 miles) to reach the western edge of Cook County (18 miles to the east), or north to Cook or Lake County, or south to Will County. And a few traveled so far (20 or more miles), that they might have worked in the western section of Chicago (25 miles away) or even downtown (35 miles east).

Weston was, then, a classic commuter village, but not necessarily a suburb. The "typing" of towns is a subtle and complex affair to be dealt with later in the chapter when more data have been presented. However, in the discussion to follow, Weston is compared to another village, known definitely as a suburb, in terms of the important community attribute of how the villagers looked at their own towns and why they chose to live there.

It seems clear that people do move to a place for rather specific reasons.[4] In Levittown, New Jersey, Gans found that 78 per cent of the residents moved there for reasons related to the low

TABLE 9–3 Reasons for Moving to Weston

REASONS GIVEN FOR MOVING TO WESTON	FAMILIES GIVING THIS REASON WESTON	PERCENTAGE	
		WESTON *	LEVITTOWN †
Money Reasons:			
—Low down payment	8	18.6	7
—Rent was reasonable; cost was low; within our budget	22	51.1	64
—Investment	2	4.6	—
—Chance to buy our own home	8	18.6	—
House Reasons:			
—Home preferable to apartment	5	11.6	—
—Liked the home itself (roomy, good condition)	11	25.5	13
Community or Locale Reasons:			
—Quiet, open county	9	20.9	—
—For the kids' or family's sake (school, play)	13	30.2	1
—To get out of the city	5	11.6	—
—Liked the town itself	11	25.5	2
—Knew people there already	3	6.9	—
Work Reasons:			
—Near work (or college) (own or spouse's)	9	20.9	8
Miscellaneous Reasons:			
—Other	7	16.2	5

* The total is more than 100 per cent because multiple answers were allowed for Weston respondents.

† Taken from Herbert Gans, *The Levittowners* (New York: Pantheon Books, 1967), p. 35.

cost and good value of the house, 13 per cent for features of the house, 3 per cent for reasons related to the community, and the rest for various other reasons.[5]

In Weston, we asked people why they had moved there and

they gave a range of answers not unlike those of the Levittowners; these are shown in Table 9–3. But certain exceptions stand out: Westonites were far more inclined to offer noneconomic reasons for deciding to settle in their town than were the ostensibly more middle-class and "suburban" Levittowners. By the standard measures, Weston perhaps was not yet middle class, but its perspectives were distinctly so.[6]

To deal with the question of social class, we asked each of our respondents to categorize his work, according to a standard occupational scale. Of 73 respondents, 29 called themselves housewives. The remaining 44 described their work in the manner shown in Table 9–4, which shows the range of types of jobs the villagers held.

The most striking feature in Table 9–4 is the large number who described themselves as technical or skilled workers, which seems to conflict with the notion that Weston was a lower-class town. We did not obtain wage information for our sample group, but data for a similar follow-up sample show that although the *jobs* were blue collar the *wages* were high.[7] Such a pattern makes social

T A B L E   9–4   Types of Jobs Held by Weston Workers

CATEGORY	NUMBER OF PERSONS *	PER CENT (OF WORKERS)
Business Proprietor	2	4.5
Salaried Professional	7	15.9
Salaried Manager	5	11.3
Technical, Skilled	19	43.1
Clerical or Sales	6	13.6
Industrial or Manual	4	9.0
Other	1	2.2
Total	44	99.6
Housewives	29	
Total Responses	73	

* This table is based on individual responses, rather than family data.

class descriptions difficult, but skilled workers making high wages cannot necessarily be considered lower class. Taking this finding along with the data regarding the values of its residents, we can fairly say that Weston as a whole was pre–middle class—and on its way. And, of course, some of its residents had already "arrived" at middle-class standing.

Weston also compared to Levittown (in its early days) in that the village had no commercial life of its own; it was totally dependent on outsiders for its economic sustenance. A person could not earn a penny (other than by babysitting or tenant farming) if he did not travel at least a mile from the village. Weston families could choose from a dozen or more places to trade within a short driving distance. Sometimes they changed their choice with each category of items bought. The places where Weston residents shopped are shown in Table 9–5.

There are several interesting features in these shopping patterns. First, Weston families patronized merchants over a wide area of western DuPage County and the Fox River Valley. This meant there was no single town that was the sole recipient of the money spent by Weston's 100 families, although West Chicago and Warrenville were prime beneficiaries of Weston commerce. If there had been a single such town, it might have been counted on to be a friend of Weston in its assorted troubles. Thus the *price* Weston paid for its ability to take its trade anyplace was the lack of at least one town's merchants who would view it as a valued customer. The *benefit* of Weston's independence was its avoidance of a "colonial" or "company town" relationship to its trading centers.

Second, the shopping patterns seem to reflect the interaction of three factors. One of these is *distance*—that is, if the "same" thing was available closer, the families tended to choose the closer location. Another factor is *selection*—except for groceries and drugs, the families tended to go where the selection was wider. Still another factor is *suitability*. It appears that the pattern of commerce reflects two considerations of suitability—price and ethos (whether "our kind of people are welcome there"). For example, Batavia was closer than West Chicago and some believed it had "nicer" food stores, yet Westonites in dramatic numbers preferred to buy food in West Chicago. This was perhaps the result

TABLE 9-5 Location of Commercial Establishments Patronized by Weston Residents

LOCATION	GROCERY STORES	DRUG STORES	BANKS	BARBER (OR BEAUTY) SHOPS	CLOTHING STORES
DuPage County					
Downers Grove	2	—	—	—	—
Elmhurst	1	—	—	—	—
Glen Ellyn	—	—	—	—	1 (1)
Lombard	—	—	1	—	1
Naperville	5 (2)*	—	3 (2)	1 (1)	3 (2)
Oak Brook	—	—	—	—	2
Villa Park	1(1)	—	—	—	3 (1)
Warrenville	—	18 (1)	11 (1)	7	—
West Chicago	19 (6)	15 (5)	21 (5)	19 (4)	1 (1)
Wheaton	—	2	1	—	—
"Various DuPage"	1 (1)	3 (2)	1 (1)	5 (3)	—
Kane County					
Aurora	9	1	—	2	20 (2)
Batavia	—	—	1	—	—
Geneva	3	1	1	1	—
St. Charles	—	—	—	1	—
"Fox Valley"	—	—	—	1 (1)	—
Cook County					
Chicago	—	—	—	—	2 (2)
Hillside	—	—	—	—	1
Other					
"At Home"	—	—	—	1	—
"At Work"	1	—	—	—	—
"All Over"	—	1	—	—	5
No Answer	1	1	3	5	4

* The number in parentheses indicates that the named location is the previous residence for that family.

of an inhospitable atmosphere that some Weston residents said they felt in Batavia.

Third, in many cases people returned to shop in the DuPage/

Fox Valley town where they previously resided, reminding us again of the local origins of many Weston residents.

The profile of Weston that emerged from our survey bears little resemblance to the image of the village widely held in DuPage County. It would seem that the nature of Weston's population had changed; the village had become something other than what the county thought it was. Yet DuPage County failed to perceive these changes. This failure to keep apace of Weston's transitions may have resulted from the antagonism that much of the county felt toward Weston. It is always difficult to see a situation clearly when one is angered or upset. The lag in the county's perceptions also may be a reflection of its difficulties in understanding what kind of place Weston represented, for Weston was a strange creature, neither fish nor fowl, bird nor beast.

Alternative Community Models—The Source of Misunderstanding

It is difficult to understand the sort of place Weston was because the tiny village was quite complex and untypical. To ask "What sort of community was Weston?" is really to ask "What other communities that we know about was Weston like? Have we heard of this kind of place before?" To answer these questions, we will consider some familiar categories of communities to see if Weston was like any of them.

1. Was Weston a suburb? Yes, in part.

It is most tempting to say that Weston was a suburb because of its location, its small population, its commuter pattern, and its relative spaciousness. But was Weston a suburb? What are suburbs, and why do people live there?

Writers have been attempting to explain "the suburbs" almost as long as there have been such places. Nearly 100 years ago, a pamphlet writer attempting to promote interest in "The Highlands of Chicago" (Glencoe to Lake Bluff, on Lake Michigan), gave a succinct explanation:

> The charms of suburban life consist of qualities of which the city is in large degree bereft, namely: its pure air, peacefulness, quietude, and natural scenery.[8]

The residents of Weston offered many of these reasons for moving there. "Suburbs," as we understand the term, developed as soon as it became possible to get to them easily, rapidly, and cheaply. Time, not distance, has been the relevant unit of measurement in metropolitan development. It is clear that suburbs have been outlying residential communities for in-town workers made possible by the development of quick mass transportation. They are communities whose existence presupposes and in some sense is dependent on other, usually larger communities.

Can Weston be regarded as a suburb in this classical sense? If Chicago is used as a referent, Weston clearly was not a suburb because virtually no one went to Chicago, either for work or for shopping. However, if some other city is used as a referent, then Weston may be regarded as a suburb, in some sense. As was shown earlier, Westonites were oriented toward one town for groceries, another for drugs, still another for clothes. And jobs were located in dozens of places in all directions. Therefore, calling Weston a suburb is not entirely false—but it is woefully incomplete and misleading.

2. Was Weston an independent small town? Hardly.

There are essentially two explanations for the origin of a town. The first is that someone settled somewhere and others joined him. This view is not sufficient to explain why some of these places grow and prosper while others do not.

The second explanation tells us that there may be some luck involved, but the reason a particular settlement is established and grows is that it is efficient for people to perform some economic activity there other than agriculture.[9] When the population reaches a sufficient size, it becomes profitable for some people to service the commercial needs of other people. The "economic base" of a town provides employment in the procuring, processing, or transportation of raw materials or final products while other residents assist this economic base by providing various services such as selling food or giving haircuts. Settlements may develop at the source of the raw materials, but the towns most certain to grow and prosper are those located at critical "transfer points" where raw materials or finished products are transferred from one mode of transportation to another.

Was Weston of sufficient size that it could generate its own "service population," or in such an optimal location that it could have become a small town in the economic terms described? Probably not. The village consisted of 100 homes, some of which were never occupied. It had *no* commercial activities or facilities. It may have been large enough to sustain a small grocery store, but apparently no one with capital thought so. A few teenagers made a little money babysitting, and one person worked without pay to raise and lower the flag at the village hall each day. One resident tended a farm, but that was outside the village. Hardly the stuff of which an independent town, let alone a future city, is made.

Weston's location did not have much to offer either. Prior to the opening of the East-West Tollway, the Weston area was not near any major highways; after the opening, it still remained a few miles from one. To the north was West Chicago, long a railroad center with an industrial park. To the west there were several industrial towns along the Fox River—Elgin, St. Charles, Geneva, Aurora. Several miles to the south was the small town/suburb of Naperville, and beyond it the highly industrialized city of Joliet. To the east were occasional clusters of homes on very large lots, small farms, forest preserves, an arboretum, and finally the Chicago suburbs of eastern DuPage County. To the extent that an economically relevant location is an important factor in the development of towns, Weston didn't have it. Weston was a wholly artificial collection of houses placed in the center of the remnants of farmland, encircled at a distance by towns and cities that were established and industrialized, and had good transportation. It might have become a suburb of one of these other places, although by 1967 it had not; and it had nothing to offer anyone that might have transformed it into a small town—unless it had survived the coming of the accelerator.

3. *Was Weston a rural hamlet? A little, outwardly.*

Functionally, the rural hamlet could be seen as a special type of small town. A rural hamlet is a community that either started small and never grew, or once was larger and then declined. The rural hamlet probably has a few facilities for its basic needs: a gas station, a drug store, a small grocery, maybe a post office and a church. For all other services, it depends on some nearby town. It may have a school, but more likely it is a part of a larger district whose schools are several miles away.[10]

Even though there may be a small cluster of buildings or homes that provides the focus for the hamlet, home sites are spread out over several miles. This means, first, that there is a great deal of space between the homes, which produces an illusory sense of privacy. Second, it means that social contacts are not chance or random, but have to be intentional; "visiting" or "just dropping in" is probably inconsistent with the quest for privacy that may have led some people to live there. The people of a rural hamlet are likely to be longtime residents who stay in spite of the basic American movement to the urban centers.

The typical hamlet is found in an agricultural area, although this is not a necessary condition. A hamlet probably serves a cluster of small farmers, providing them with some of their daily necessities. It is not likely to grow, because increase in farm productivity is likely to be the result of mechanization. The large-scale farmer may have his own means of transporting goods to market and will not need to use the hamlet as a terminal or junction point.

Weston was located in the middle of productive farmland, but its existence had nothing to do with farming. Its residents worked in widely scattered places, so Weston did not exist as a service facility for the farmers, or the highway department, or anyone else. It lacked the amenities that even the tiniest of hamlets possess. There were no public transportation links with other towns. The homes were built fairly close together and, by rural norms, the socializing was substantial—hardly a setting for privacy. Most of the people of Weston had lived there a very short time; the few "oldtimers" had lived there only 3 to 6 years.

Weston had certain of the necessary attributes of a hamlet— it was in an agricultural area, and it was small and isolated. But it simply lacked those few features of a purposeful existence that are necessary even for as uncomplex a community as a rural hamlet.

4. Was Weston an urban ghetto? Almost.

In an earlier era, a "ghetto" was an ethnic enclave or settlement to which members of a minority group were restricted.[11]

Currently the idea of a ghetto retains that meaning but also suggests a civic pathology and refers to an area in which very poor minorities are densely packed in deteriorating housing.[12] The locale of the ghetto is usually the oldest part of a city where there are decaying older buildings that have been left behind by the dominant group in the community. There are problems of social disorganization and physical deterioration in the ghetto.[13] Its residents are politically ineffective because they have been defined as an expendable group.

If it develops that the land of the ghetto comes to have renewed economic value to the dominant group, the people, being expendable, can be moved without much trouble. Adequate compensation is rare.[14]

Weston was never pathological, but in its earlier incarnation it did provide housing for a population that was perceived as alien by the surrounding communities. Even though this population changed as renters became purchasers or moved away, the region continued to view the Weston residents as alien, and incapable of changing. DuPage saw the turnover of occupants and mistook it for transiency.

The county, with state and national assistance, treated Weston residents as an expendable population. The village board found itself to be a politically ineffective body in the *quo warranto* and annexation questions. The villagers found that they had been dragged into their own destruction by the two-step maneuver that got the people to believe, first, that Weston would be improved by the accelerator development and, second, that somehow their own sacrifice, when it came to that, was for a higher cause—science, and national defense. Westonites came in some degree to act and feel like ghetto residents for the usual reasons: external social pressures.

Although Weston in some ways was similar to a ghetto, there are certain flaws in the comparison. First, Weston was not poor, even if it was not as wealthy as the rest of the county. Second, its people were not alien—at the end, they were the children of the county, and even the early renters were as lily white as the rest of the county. They also took regular part in the economic life of the region, and identified with that larger region. Third, if they seemed politically ineffective it was because they were fighting a formidable array of enemies—the county, the state, the FSLIC, the AEC, the

Congress, the White House, and the news media—all pursuing objectives that converged into similar actions even when they were not acting in concert. Fourth, unlike in most ghettos, a large portion of the residents were homeowners who, although they may not have been paid a fair price by the state, were not totally uncompensated for their property. And, fifth, Weston was not urban; it was in rural farmland.

Still, Weston could be eliminated when it was perceived to be a threat, because its people were deemed expendable by the larger community. That makes it a ghetto by virtue of its treatment by the external powers. But as a community its true character will remain a mystery because it was becoming something it never was permitted to become. As it stood in the end, Weston was difficult to understand, and its neighbors moved in on it before an effort to understand it was ever really made.

NOTES TO CHAPTER 9

1. Copies of a 7-page questionnaire were delivered to every home in Weston in May 1967. Responses were received from 73 individuals, who were members of 43 families. The information was coded and stored in "individual" and "family" decks, the latter being used where household behavior was more appropriate for analysis than individual behavior. Both types of information are utilized in the present chapter. (For additional commentary on the methodology of the survey, see Chapter 10.)

2. An extended discussion of this mode of community analysis may be found in Brian J. L. Berry and Philip H. Rees, "The Factorial Ecology of Calcutta," *American Journal of Sociology*, 74: No. 5 (March 1969). (Note Figures 14 and 29.) Rees has studied Chicago using this analytical model; see his "The Factorial Ecology of Chicago," in Brian J. L. Berry and Frank E. Horton (eds.), *Geographic Perspectives on Urban Systems* (Englewood Cliffs, N.J.: Prentice-Hall, 1969).

3. We are in any case unable to look at the economic aspects of class in Weston in any systematic way, because we were not able to get income information in the 1967 survey, and the self-descriptions of social class that they gave appear unreliable. Also see notes 9 and 10.

4. For a thorough discussion of the reasons why people choose particular residences and communities, see Carl Werthman, Jerry S. Mandel, and Ted Dienstfrey, *Planning and the Purchase Decision:*

Why People Buy in Planned Communities, Center for Planning and Regional Development Research, Preprint No. 10 (Berkeley: University of California Institute of Urban and Regional Development, July 1965, reissued July 1970). These issues are also discussed in William H. Whyte, Jr., *The Organization Man* (New York: Simon and Schuster, 1956), Chapters 21 ("The Transients") and 22 ("The New Roots").

5. Herbert Gans, *The Levittowners: How People Live and Politic in Suburbia* (New York: Pantheon Books, 1967), p. 35.
6. The question of social class in relation to "suburbanness" has been a problem for many writers. See, for example, William M. Dobriner, *Class in Suburbia* (Englewood Cliffs, N.J.: Prentice-Hall, 1963), particularly Chapter 2 ("Suburbs and the Class Structure"); Bennett M. Berger, *Working-Class Suburb: A Study of Auto Workers in Suburbia* (Berkeley: University of California Press, 1960); and William H. Whyte, Jr., op. cit., Chapter 23 ("Classlessness in Suburbia").
7. Information for 30 Weston families indicated that median family income was $9,950.
8. Quoted in Charles N. Glaab, *The American City: A Documentary History* (Homewood, Ill.: Dorsey Press, 1963), p. 233.
9. This discussion parallels that of Edgar M. Hoover, *The Location of Economic Activity* (New York: McGraw-Hill, 1948), and of Walter Isard, *Location and Space-Economy* (Cambridge, Mass.: M.I.T. Press, 1956).
10. A brief but thorough discussion of one rural hamlet may be found in Alicja Iwanska, *Good Fortune: Second Chance Community*, Institute of Agricultural Sciences Bulletin 589 (Pullman: State College of Washington, 1958). We are grateful to Professor Paul Verdet of Boston University for bringing this booklet to our attention.
11. See, for example, Louis Wirth, *The Ghetto* (Chicago: University of Chicago Press, 1928).
12. See Gerald D. Suttles, *The Social Order of the Slum: Ethnicity and Territory in the Inner City* (Chicago: University of Chicago Press, 1968).
13. See Leonard J. Duhl (ed.), *The Urban Condition: People and Policy in the Metropolis* (New York: Basic Books, 1963).
14. There is an extensive, and increasing, literature on the purposes, implementation, and effects of urban renewal. See, for example, Jewel Bellush and Murray Hausknecht (eds.), *Urban Renewal: People, Politics and Planning* (Garden City, N.Y.: Anchor Books, 1967), especially Part IV ("Execution"); and James Q. Wilson (ed.), *Urban Renewal: The Record and the Controversy* (Cambridge, Mass.: M.I.T. Press, 1966), especially Part III ("Urban Renewal in Practice: Three Cases") and Part IV ("Relocation and Community Life").

PART III

**The Politics
of Conquest**

10 **The Accelerator**
as a Political Issue in Weston

The initial strategy of the state of Illinois toward the residents of the Weston site was simple, subtle, and, until the moment of actual acquisition, effective without the application of direct controls. The strategy was illusion, the illusion that Weston had a future as a village.

This illusion maintained itself rather easily once it was established. State officials simply avoided public denial of Weston's future and then depended on the greed of Weston's leaders to help maintain the idea. Hope for Weston's future remained, despite all contrary indications, until it was too late to organize against the accelerator or toward collective bargaining.

That was enough. The strategy of duplicity had been a success because no organization ever developed in the village. Some organizing efforts were taking place among the farmers just as the condemnations and quick-take procedures were being carried out. None of it came to anything.

Because all the conditions favoring intense and organized community conflict were present in the site area, there has to be some reason why conflict failed to take place at the crucial times. We feel the essential reason is illusion, especially the illusion shared by most of the vocal members of the village, from among whom leadership might have formed. None was prepared to exert leadership because none found anything worthy of the effort.

The way was thus prepared for acquisition. Divide, placate, and conquer—at bargain-basement prices.

Atoms for Peace, Peace for Atoms

As the target for a huge national atomic project, Weston in fact seemed destined for conflict, according to the basic pre-requisites for community strife hypothesized in a noted study by James S. Coleman: [1] The selection of Weston as the site would have a critical impact on the village and the surrounding region. The site would necessarily affect different interests differently; and it was something on which local interests could act to facilitate or prevent.

In addition, this would only have been the latest in a series of issues over which well-organized, locally entrenched, and adamantly competitive groups had formed. The pre-atomic history of Weston was in fact full of internal and external conflicts. Internally, the village had never been without factional dispute and predacious corruption. Externally, Weston had fought recurrent battles with its neighbors in DuPage County. In view of this history, Weston's choice as a finalist site for the accelerator would seem likely to intensify the perennial struggle for village control by increasing the stake for soon, perhaps, control of the village would mean something. During selection, acquisition, and construction almost any observer would have anticipated some manifestations of fierce conflict inside Weston between those who saw the accelerator as a boon and those who regarded it as a menace.

But this is not what happened. The announcement that Weston as the site. Simultaneously, the county's campaign of dep-recation and deprivation against Weston was suddenly stilled. a single organism with a single voice. It mobilized itself to cam-paign for the accelerator, greeting visiting dignitaries with crowds and hoopla and passing unanimously whatever resolutions and ordinances would be most conducive to the ultimate selection of Weston as the site. Simultaneously, the county's campaign of dep-recation and deprivation against Weston was suddenly stilled. The state of Illinois, the county of DuPage, and the village of

Weston became a single team in the competition. This new era of peace and cooperation lasted for a year and a half, until October 1967, when deliberate obstruction of Weston's attempt to survive the atom smasher began.

Having been at odds for years over everything else, why were interests in and around Weston suddenly as one over the atom smasher? A graphic representation of the relationship between the interests and the accelerator can put the matter in dramatic clarity. Until it was too late to make any difference to the outcome, the relations among the interests in the Weston area looked like Figure 10–1. That is, the location in any spot X seems to have been perceived by each interest as beneficial in direct relation to its geographical proximity to site X. Weston was closest, therefore most intensely interested; and so on.

However, there are two alternative possibilities, and even the most superficial reading of the site selection history suggests that either is a more appropriate picture. For example, Figure 10–2,

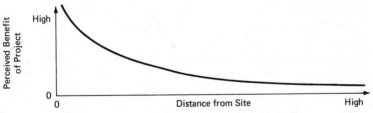

FIGURE 10–1   *National distance–benefit relation.*

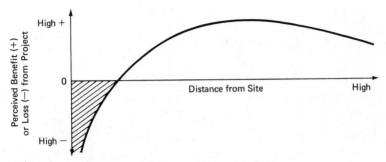

FIGURE 10–2   *Regional distance–benefit relation.*

introduces a reversal of the distance–benefit relationship at extremely small distances, where the prospect of abolition or extreme transformation can reverse attitudes. This model fits Barrington precisely; as soon as there was any prospect of bringing the accelerator to Barrington, important local interests acted vigorously against it. The same was true in nearby Libertyville, whose citizens reacted vigorously and successfully against the building of a Sentinel ABM site in their vicinity.[2]

The third model, Figure 10–3, focuses on the spread of interests rather than their proximity. The first two models assume that each interest can be located in space and that its distance from the site can always be measured. But many important interests were involved rather evenly throughout the entire area, favoring or opposing the site wherever it located. Some of these were the state and regional interests who sought the accelerator for Illinois or the Midwest and were intensely involved no matter where one put the X.

Figure 10–2 or Figure 10–3 captures well all the behaviors, except Weston's. Either figure locates all the interests and clearly anticipates the best hypotheses about roles in and contributions to the accelerator story, except for Weston. Until the end of 1967, a full year after it had been marked with the big X, Weston and all interests therein operated as an integral part of the state and

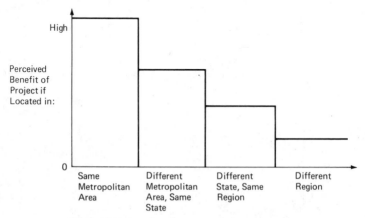

FIGURE 10–3 *National territory–benefit relations.*

regional teams, as though Figure 10–1 were the truth of the matter. In late 1967, Weston began to behave according to Figure 10–2, the representation of a community conflict model.

Gallantry, Gullibility, or Gaggery?

Weston's cooperativeness, in violation of the reasonable expectations based on Figure 10–2, is both interesting and important. It is important theoretically because the pattern goes contrary to expectations. It is important practically because it probably saved Illinois millions in land costs, court costs, and political costs.

Three possible explanations come to mind. First, the entire Weston citizenry may have been willing to sacrifice their village for the accelerator out of a belief that such a sacrifice served national, state, Chicago, and University of Chicago interests. A second, more selfish explanation would hold that the people of Weston may all have been convinced by federal, state, and local officials, or by their personal optimism, that the village would not be destroyed by the accelerator and indeed might instead be greatly enlarged and enhanced. Or, third, the people of Weston may have been truly divided over the issue, but somehow the opposition was kept silent while only the pro-accelerator faction expressed its views.

There is some plausibility in all three explanations. In the first case, it is reasonable to suppose that Weston residents believed in making sacrifices for their county and their state, especially for "science" and more especially for "atomic energy," with its aura of national defense. In addition, although it is true that DuPage County had unceasingly attempted to destroy Weston, the people of Weston were, after all, largely children of DuPage County and the Fox River Valley. Having moved to Weston from elsewhere in the area, and having maintained working, shopping, entertainment, and social contacts in a variety of surrounding communities, the Westonites might well have felt willing and (unlike the surrounding farmers) able to move nearby again without fear of being uprooted from what they considered home. Because of their continual struggle against the hostile county, and the negative identity that the county attempted to give them, the residents of Weston might even have half-welcomed this opportunity to vacate the village and lose this identity without the appearance of capitulation.

It would be just as reasonable, however, to believe the second explanation. It was not made clear to Weston that the village would be eliminated until about a year and a half after it became officially one of the six site finalists, because different government officials had given different impressions to Weston, and the same sources gave different information at different times. For a long time, room was left for the belief that Weston either would be outside the site boundaries or would be able to move its dwellings to land beyond the site limits and continue to exist. A village that had fought for life in the face of seemingly hopeless obstacles and won could be expected now to believe in its own charmed existence, even if the federal government (previously represented in Weston by the friendly FSLIC) should join the anti-village ranks.

The third explanation, that of silent or silenced opposition, seems less plausible. Although local elites often systematically suppress dissent openly expressed, dissent had come to the fore over issues far less consequential than the life-or-death question of the accelerator. In any event, the chronology of events does not record any early opposition to the accelerator within the village, so that the history of the Weston site thus agrees with only the first two explanations for Weston's support of the project.

The chronology of events, however, does not tell the whole story, for what was seemingly the least plausible explanation does in fact contain the most truth: opposition to the accelerator was extensive in Weston; it simply was not vocal. In the midst of a period of peace and cooperation, when nation, state, county, and village seemed at one, a probe was inserted below the seemingly placid surface of Weston. The probe was a self-administered questionnaire, left with all adult villagers one day in May 1967, and picked up a few days later. To our surprise, it recorded eddies of uncertainty, and, beneath these, it found an entire stream of opposition, almost as extensive as the topmost layer of support that had formed the only visible manifestation of Weston public opinion.

What, then, were the form and the magnitude of the anti-accelerator feeling in Weston? How was it so successfully hidden from public view for so long? And why did it not produce conflict?

The opinions of the villagers must be examined in three

stages. First, were there differences of opinion, and what aspects of the accelerator, if any, engendered differences of opinion? Second, what were the relationships among these various opinions; that is, did some opinions cluster, as a syndrome, whereas others did not? And, third, how did these opinions relate to other attributes of the Weston citizens; that is, what kinds of people were on each side of the issues? With this information it might be possible to find reasons why one important segment of village opinion, the opposition to the accelerator, remained invisible.

1. Judging from the responses to our questionnaire, every aspect of the accelerator issue evoked a deep split in the village of Weston. The villagers differed from each other in their understandings of what the accelerator would do to Weston, in the ways they would react to a displacement of the village, and in how they would feel about the accelerator in their midst. For example, when asked to assess the effect construction of the accelerator would have on Weston, 33 respondents believed that if this actually happened the village would move to a new site. On the other hand, 33 predicted that if plans to build the accelerator there were fulfilled "Weston will no longer exist." The responses to this question, shown in Table 10–1, reveal that it was already clear to all the villagers by May 1967 that the accelerator would "remove" the village, but there was no agreement on what was meant by that word.

A similar split appeared in the villagers' anticipated reactions to the accelerator. When asked what they would do if Weston were relocated, 28 loyal villagers reported they would go where Weston went, but 33 declared that they would leave the village entirely, as is shown in Table 10–2.

Similarly, the villagers were by no means unanimous in their feelings about the plans for an atom smasher in Weston. Considering the united front Weston presented to the public, universal elation is what one might have expected, but, as Table 10–3 shows, 40 per cent of our respondents said they would feel indifferent or worse if the plans went through. Thus it seems clear that negative feeling toward the accelerator was widespread in Weston months before public events showed that any villagers were hesitant at all.

2. These anti-accelerator responses, moreover, were not unthinking or inconsistent. There were strong intercorrelations among

TABLE 10-1   "Suppose the Accelerator Is Built in Weston. What Will Happen to Weston?"

RESPONSE	NUMBER CHOOSING THIS RESPONSE
"Nothing will change."	0
"Weston will remain where it is and will become a better place to live in."	0
"Weston will stay where it is and will become a worse place to live in."	0
"Weston will be moved to another piece of land but will not change much."	5
"Weston will move to another piece of land and will become a better place to live in."	27
"Weston will move to another piece of land and will become a worse place to live in."	1
"Weston will no longer exist."	33
Write-in or no response	7
Total	73

TABLE 10-2   "If Weston Is Moved When the Accelerator Is Built, What Will You Do?"

RESPONSE	NUMBER CHOOSING THIS RESPONSE
"Move along with Weston and stay with the new Weston."	28
"Move somewhere else."	33
"It won't matter, since we're planning to move before that time anyway."	4
Write-in or no response	8
Total	73

TABLE 10-3 "Let's Suppose the Accelerator Is Built in Weston. All in All, How Will You Feel About It?"

RESPONSE	NUMBER CHOOSING THIS RESPONSE
"Wonderful"	13
"Very good"	12
"Good"	14
"Indifferent"	15
"Not very good"	11
"Terrible"	4
Write-in or no response	4
Total	73

the answers to all questions about the accelerator and other issues attendant to it. In other words, the attitudes occurred in sets, or syndromes, to such an extent that we were often able to predict a respondent's answer to a series of questions by knowing his answer to only one question. Positive and optimistic responses on all of these questions tended to come from the same people, and negative or pessimistic responses all from other people. For example, people who tended to feel the accelerator would leave Weston free to move and improve also planned to move with Weston, to feel good about the prospect of the accelerator, to attribute the same good feelings to their neighbors, and to believe that the people of Weston had been instrumental in getting their village selected as the site. The same set of linkages existed in the negative.

To facilitate analysis, let us focus on those who exhibited these two syndromes most purely. Let us define the first group as those who felt "good" or better about the accelerator, believed that all or most of their fellow Westonites would feel good about it, anticipated that Weston would move to a new piece of land and become a better place to live in if the accelerator came, and thought that the villagers' support had been important in the site decision. Nineteen respondents fell into this pattern, which we shall call the

TABLE 10–4   "If Weston Is Moved When the Accelerator Is Built, What Will You Do?"

RESPONSE	PRO SYNDROME	ANTI SYNDROME
Move along with Weston	15	4
Move somewhere else	3	11
Moving before then anyway	1	1
Write-in or no response	0	3
Total	19	19

"pro syndrome." On the other side, 19 respondents fell into what we shall call the "anti syndrome," consisting of those who gave more pessimistic answers to at least three of these four questions just described.[3]

3.   We are now in a position to perform the third stage of our analysis by relating these syndromically organized opinions to the other characteristics of the populace. Who were the 19 pro-syndromic and the 19 anti-syndromic respondents? First, the pro syndromics tended to be older residents of Weston. As is shown in

TABLE 10–5   Year Moved to Weston

YEAR	PRO SYNDROME	ANTI SYNDROME
1961	2	0
1962	4	1
1963	1	0
1964	3	2
1965	5	3
1966	4	12
1967	0	0
No response	0	1
Total	19	19

Table 10–5, 15 out of the 19 pro syndromics had moved to Weston before 1966, while only a third of the 18 anti syndromics for whom we have this information had done so. Similarly, the pro syndromics more often felt themselves at home in Weston: 14 of the pro syndromics but only nine of the anti syndromics said of Weston that they felt they "belong here" and that "this is my home." In response to a series of five standard alienation items naming "Weston" and "village officials" as the alienating elements, only two of the pro syndromics expressed agreement with the majority of the items—demonstrating feelings of alienation—whereas eight of the anti syndromics did so.

Pro syndromics were also more active in the organized life of the community or in organizations and public affairs in general. Thirteen of them had been members of organizations since their arrival in Weston, versus seven of the anti syndromics. Twelve of the pro syndromics claimed to vote occasionally or frequently in local elections or referenda, versus only five of the anti syndromics.[4] After ranking the issues that they considered most important, 13 of the pro syndromics replied that they discussed these issues "a lot," whereas only seven anti syndromics gave this response, as is shown in Table 10–6.

The most outstanding characteristic of the pro syndromics was their familiarity with their neighbors and with Weston officials. Eleven of the pro syndromics and only four of the anti syndromics claimed to know more than 10 Weston families by name. And though 12 of the pro syndromics said they were well acquainted

T A B L E 10–6 **Frequency of Discussion of Issues with Friends and Neighbors**

FREQUENCY	PRO SYNDROME	ANTI SYNDROME
"A lot"	13	7
"Some"	6	8
"Seldom"	0	1
"Just about never"	0	2
Write-in or no response	0	1
Total	19	19

TABLE 10–7   Number of Village Officials Respondent
Fairly Well Acquainted With

NUMBER OF OFFICIALS	PRO SYNDROME	ANTI SYNDROME
0	3	7
1	2	3
2	1	3
3	1	0
4	0	2
5	0	0
6	1	0
7	1	0
8	0	0
9	0	0
More than 9	10	1
Write-in or no response	0	3
Total	19	19

with more than five Weston officials, Table 10–7 shows that a mere
one anti syndromic claimed to know this many. On the issue of
open housing, the anti syndromics were more likely to oppose it
(11) than the pro syndromics (5), a position that put the anti
syndromics in opposition to official village policy. These data, and
the figures mentioned earlier on alienation, make sense when we
see that seven of the pro syndromics, as opposed to two of the
anti syndromics, were village officials themselves.

The syndromes defined here apparently are part of wider syndromes, which include not only attitudes but also demographic
and political characteristics. The population seems to have divided
itself into an old and a new group. The old residents, who generally
supported the accelerator, were more involved in the community.
They largely constituted the village government, and they identified themselves more strongly than did the new residents with the
village of Weston itself. Thus the village leadership—the group
most capable of opposing the accelerator—was also the group most
sanguine about it and hence least inclined to oppose it.

From Model Three to Model Farm

Two questions clearly remain to be answered. First, why was the anti-accelerator view in Weston so hushed, even though it was apparently so strongly held? Second, why did the two groups come to feel the way they did about the accelerator in the first place? Given the distribution of opinion, one might well have expected the anti syndromics to protest. After all, they had the example of Barrington to follow. Westonites too might ward off the accelerator by simply raising their voices; farmers near Weston had already begun to complain. Furthermore, the anti syndromics knew (by definition) that their neighbors were not all delighted at the prospect of the accelerator, and this fact was fairly well established in the minds of the rest of the villagers as well. Although only 15 of our villagers thought that everyone would feel the same way about the accelerator, 52 respondents anticipated a split in opinion among their neighbors, as Table 10–8 shows. Why did the anti syndromics keep quiet until *we* asked them to speak, even though they lived in a village noted for its factional conflict and they knew there were others who agreed with them? Their reticence can be understood in the light of three possible contributing causes. First, perhaps the villagers were never asked what they thought. Second, perhaps the anti syndromics felt it did not

TABLE 10–8 "How Do You Think Most People in Weston Will Feel About the Accelerator If It Is Built in Weston?"

RESPONSE	NUMBER CHOOSING THIS RESPONSE
"Just about everybody will feel good."	11
"Most people will feel good, but some will feel bad."	38
"Most will feel bad, but some will feel good."	14
"Just about everyone will feel bad."	4
Write-in or no response	6
Total	73

matter. Third, perhaps they felt powerless to make their voice heeded.

Because there was so much commotion surrounding the news of a possible accelerator in Weston, it is easy to forget that those responsible for the site selection never really asked the people of Weston what they thought about the idea. The acceptability of the accelerator in the site community was one of the informal criteria for selecting the site, yet at no time did any federal official go beyond or behind the mayor of Weston to ask the feelings of the village population or of the residents of the surrounding farms. There was no referendum, no informal poll, no public meeting to field questions or objections. Nor, if they were ever asked by the press how they felt, were the villagers' answers ever reported.

It is hardly likely that the anti syndromics would have had nothing to say had they been asked. Because they believed the accelerator would spell the end of the village, they undoubtedly would have demanded a confirmation or denial of this opinion. At the time of our questionnaire, however, only three of the anti syndromics named "the atomic accelerator" as the issue most important to them, and many of them claimed that they would be "indifferent" to the construction of the accelerator. Perhaps, then, they were silent because they were indifferent.

Alternatively, however, these may really be symptoms of the third suggested cause: powerlessness. The atomic accelerator may have seemed unimportant as an issue precisely because it looked like a *fait accompli*. The selection of Weston as the site had indeed already been announced by the federal government. Even if the anti syndromics had been against making Weston the final site before the decision was announced, they were mostly non-office-holding newcomers and thus (in contrast to the situation in Barrington) without knowledge of how to intervene or the ability to be accepted as village spokesmen by the outside world. In addition, the anti syndromics (again by definition) took little stock in the ability of the village to affect the outcome anyway.

In other words, although the village was quite divided over the question of how much influence it had had over the site selection (see Table 10–9), those who (properly) had confidence in their ability to affect the outcome were largely pro-accelerator, and those who opposed the project felt helpless to prevent it.[5]

TABLE 10-9 "How Important Was the Activity of the People of Weston in Getting Washington to Decide to Recommend the Accelerator for Weston?"

RESPONSE	NUMBER CHOOSING THIS RESPONSE
"The people of Weston had very little to do with it."	26
"Our support did not help, but our opposition could have killed it."	8
"Our support definitely helped bring the accelerator here."	32
Write-in or no response	7
Total	73

The Origin of the Specious

This speculation about the reasons for the invisibility of the opposition leaves one question still unanswered: what were the reasons for the fervent campaign waged by the pro syndromics for the accelerator? If the village leaders were highly attached to Weston as a community (as they should have been after fighting so hard for its survival), why did they openly invite a visitor that might gobble up the village without leaving a trace? In parallel with the case of the anti syndromics, and as partly suggested earlier, we can speculate as to three likely reasons. The first is that they were never told. The second is that they did not care. And the third is that they felt the lure of power.

In the first place, just as no one ever asked the anti syndromics how they felt about the accelerator, so no one ever told the pro syndromics that the accelerator would mean the obliteration of Weston, as has been noted in earlier chapters. Perhaps the village leaders honestly hoped, until it was far too late, that Weston could be spared.

But perhaps, alternatively, they really did not care. Farfetched though it may seem, it is possible that the old guard in Weston had fought so hard for their Weston that they would be willing to see the village turned into a mile-wide ring if only this meta-morphosis would enshrine the name "Weston" in perpetual national glory.[6] They may have been assessing the accelerator not in terms of its effects on them personally, and perhaps not even in terms of its effects on Weston as a village, but rather as a prize for which "Weston" had competed against other communities across the nation. Sufficient identification with "Weston" could, para-doxically, bring satisfaction with its victory, even if the price of the prize was Weston's corporate and corporeal existence. Thus Figure 10–2, which we referred to at the outset, may represent only tangible benefits, whereas Figure 10–1 represents symbolic gratifica-tion, even down to the target site, where it may be so intense that it counter-balances (and perhaps obscures) the tangible deprivations that are likely to result.

A third possible reason for the quest by Weston's leaders for the accelerator is the attraction of power. They may have felt powerful enough by virtue of their local offices to proceed without consulting the whole village population. Also, they may have felt powerful as a village against their environment. Punch drunk after so long a fight, they may have felt able to use the accelerator in their battle against the county (just as the county was secretly planning to use the accelerator to KO Weston). And the village leaders may have felt the taste of the political power that would be theirs when they became the political leaders of a shiny new "science city" that would sprout out of their village. Whether Weston remained or moved,[7] the coming of the accelerator could only enhance the size and importance of Weston and could be expected to provide opportunities for self-enhancement to those in control of village affairs. When viewed against their background as a group struggling to save Weston from legal and financial ruin, the potential increase in status appears considerable.

All three of these reasons may help explain the behavior of the Weston officials. A fourth force, however, unlike those that might explain the silence of the anti syndromics, must be con-sidered in the case of the village officials. This is the leadership that one man, Mayor Arthur Theriault, exercised over the village government and residents. We do not know whether Theriault was influenced by a belief that Weston would not have to move, or by a willingness to let the village be sacrificed in victory, or by a quest for the increased power and status that might be his if Weston became a scientific center. We do know that he was regarded as ambitious by at least one colleague, and that he himself told an interviewer of his interest in higher public office. Formerly a printer and clerical worker, in 1968 he was given a position as a "methods analyst" by the Continental Illinois Bank and Trust Company of Chicago, one of the primary supporters of the Weston site, after he was fired from his previous job for spending too much company time working for the accelerator. We also know that he had built up great trust among many of those in the village. And, finally, we know that Theriault initiated support for and commitment to the accelerator, in part by writing directly to the AEC, when the possibility of a Weston site was first revealed, before anyone even requested his aid.

Back of the mayor was a local elite who had faith in the mayor and his commitment to the site competition. It so happened that the grand illusion was held by this group and their community following rather than by the newly arrived outsiders in Weston.[8]

It might be going too far to conclude that the mayor and other village leaders groundlessly deluded themselves into courting communal destruction. We have presented some evidence suggesting deliberate misrepresentation of the probable consequences of the project for the village by knowledgeable officials. This, plus the absence of reliable information about the frequently changing plans and the vague boundaries of the site, made it reasonable to believe almost anything. Thus it would be wrong to say that the pro syndromics, in their battle for "Weston," were led only by illusions to betray Weston; it would also be wrong to ascribe illusions to the anti syndromics who refused to believe the bright predictions their local officials proclaimed. *Both* groups had bases for their beliefs.

Thus, although the influence of illusion was strong, its strength can be exaggerated. It is more accurate and meaningful to put the matter this way: illusion made a pro-accelerator position possible. Other, supportive attitudes made it reasonable. And the consistent organization of these attitudes into syndromes probably explains the persistence of the position despite all later information to the contrary.

The internally self-reinforcing position of the pro's also helps explain the persistent yet invisible existence of the anti's. The attitude structure of the anti's was almost as internally consistent as that of the pro's, and thus it, too, persisted in the midst of a confusion of communications. But in addition to that the anti's experienced two other things. First, they faced the enthusiasm of the pro's, illusory as it might have been. Second, they were all too aware of their own lack of commitment, lack of efficacy, and lack of prospects in face of the undoubted dominance by the pro's of the tiny elite structure of the village. On their side it was a pure case of quiet alienation, the self-fulfilling prophecy that because Weston had no future there was no use objecting to it. This was an opposition that defeated itself, in incipience.

As a consequence, there was no community conflict, despite the objective conditions that almost always give rise to it. Instead, there was a vigorous mobilization of the village government for an end that was not only opposed by many but that even the local elite itself had reason to doubt was in their own interest. All of this pacified Weston's relations to other groups and principalities at a time when they should have been stormy, and this paved the way for the final solution of the Weston problem for DuPage, for Illinois, and for the AEC.

In the process we also may witness an example of the absence of two elements inherent in most democratic political theories: The first is profit-maximizing rationality among participants, which, if in operation at all in Weston, emerged only in the pursuit of a dream-maximizing strategy. The second is democratic accountability among local institutions and elites. The Weston story illustrates how extremely difficult it is to institutionalize a role for an organized opposition; the anti's were alienated in fact as well as perspective, because Weston was too new and rudimentary to have a method of political conflict in the ordinary sense of the word. The Weston story also illustrates the significance of the elite in a small, local community, despite the renewed sentiment in favor of local participation. Real opposition vanished in Weston as soon as it became clear that the village leadership would be credited with leading their flock into a new era of glory, or into a future without any flock at all.

NOTES TO CHAPTER 10

1. James S. Coleman, *Community Conflict* (New York: Free Press, 1957).
2. David M. Kozak, "ABM and the Grass Roots," unpublished M.A. thesis, University of Chicago, 1972.
3. Intention to move along with Weston in the event of its displacement by the accelerator was fairly closely related to membership in the pro syndrome, as seen in Table 10–4, so we could have included in the syndrome the respondents' intended courses of action in this situation and reduced the groups to 15 members each. On the other hand, one possible response to this question was unrelated to the accelerator: "We're planning to move before that time anyway." Thus to avoid ambiguity this item has been omitted from the definitions of the syndromes.
4. This finding by itself should not be taken as evidence of greater pro-syndromic participation, because the very recent arrival in Weston of many anti syndromics (together with the somewhat greater representation in that group of young people not—or barely—old enough to vote) would legally have prevented them from voting there in the last major election.
5. Clearly, the feeling of helplessness among accelerator opponents may have been an effect of the site decision, but, even if so, this feeling did not absolutely have to suffocate protest, because protest would still have been embarrassing and possibly dangerous in view of the continuing post-announcement national controversy over the site.
6. If this was the case, then the subsequent decision by the accelerator authorities to eradicate the name of "Weston" and everything associated with it was ironic ingratitude, indeed.
7. The very possibility of moving intact was, of course, a peculiarity of the village and not shared with the surrounding farmers. The farmers knew they had no alternative to dispersal if the accelerator took their land. Preservation of their community was impossible because of the huge acreage that they would need if they were to resettle together. Here, perhaps, is one explanation for the early protest by the farmers, which the state and county spent much energy drowning out and discounting.
8. Compare the illusions of independence nurtured by the people of "Springdale," a village that depended on the outside world and that systematically suppressed conflict. Arthur J. Vidich and Joseph Bensman, *Small Town in Mass Society*, rev. ed. (Princeton, N.J.: Princeton University Press, 1968).

CHAPTER ■■ Public Acquisition—In Private

Introduction to an Execution

Nearly $4 billion in land passes from private hands to public agencies each year. Yet no one outside the fraternity of professional appraisers and negotiators has ever looked systematically into the process. The process is called eminent domain—the power to take private property for public use.

Eminent domain is an intrinsic feature of sovereignty. It has a long history; in the United States it was provided for in the original Bill of Rights. The Constitution seeks to protect the citizen by requiring something called "just compensation." But the right of the government to seize property for public uses is never questioned.

Politically, eminent domain is like capital punishment. Even those who agree that the power is necessary for the fulfillment of certain public functions do not want to witness the execution. Consequently, this very large process in the United States is almost invisible.

This virtual invisibility enables its users to play God—or at least lord high executioner. Little people who may run state, local, and county agencies or public utilities and authorities can move vast estates and multitudes of people. Despite this, the process can remain invisible because public land acquisition tends to isolate each property owner. The process is composed of a large number of small, individualized transactions. Only the residuum is large.

Acquisition of the properties within the Weston site area is a very significant case study in the politics of eminent domain. Each individual property owner was atomized by his holdings and by his selfish commitment to them. He was isolated further by his belief that the state would deal fairly with him. He was isolated by his ignorance of what was happening to his neighbors in the village and among the surrounding farms.

The state of Illinois played upon this isolation. It is extremely doubtful that $30 million (minus nearly half of this for fees and administration costs) would otherwise have been sufficient to assemble the 6,800-acre site. Through the DBED the state designed an acquisition process specifically for the Weston project. They separated appraising from negotiating, so that responsibility could be bandied back and forth between the two. A blue-ribbon acquisition committee was set up to review decisions. It was composed of representatives of some of the most hotly involved interests in the metropolitan area; and, as we shall see, it tended to operate mostly as an addition buffer between the property holders and the state.

Each separate role, function, and layer in this process made more and more remote the prospect of "just compensation." Each property holder was inundated with threatening facts about his own situation and deprived of facts about the fate of his neighbors. Responsibility was hidden, the flexibility of the state was maximized, and the bargaining advantages flowed quickly from private individual to public agency. Some instances of intimidation are reported. But of far greater importance was the role played by systematic ignorance of relative property values and personal rights, ignorance of procedures, ignorance of appeals, ignorance of the real agenda of the public agencies. Divided, they were easily conquered.

This chapter deals only with the acquisition of the village properties. In the next chapter the farmers will have their turn.

Compensation: How a Village Becomes an Atomic Gift Horse

From the moment of victory in the site competition Illinois found itself under tremendous financial pressure that was going to require ruthless cost cutting by DBED in the site acquisition process. Ruthlessness was going to be the only way that agency would be able to fulfill its responsibilities.

When Weston was selected as the site, the AEC lost the design team assembled by the Lawrence Radiation Laboratory. Loss of the team meant loss of the AEC-financed $10 million design. A new team had to be assembled and had to develop a new design. This would significantly increase start-up costs at the very time when the Vietnam-induced budget squeeze was beginning to hit the AEC. AEC would have to turn this pressure from itself toward its suppliers, or there would be no new accelerator at all.

The site competition had solved part of AEC's problem. The competitors, including Illinois, had promised outright gifts of land to the AEC. These promises freed AEC from the heaviest initial investment; and freed AEC from having to accept a site on some existing federally owned installation.

AEC officials helped solve their financial problem by still a second method, which developed more slowly during competition and afterward. They began to suggest, and then to establish as a minimum criterion, a site that included buildings usable as office facilities. The politics and economics of acquisition cannot be understood except in terms of the pressure AEC put on Illinois and other states, and in turn the pressure Illinois put on itself by agreeing to AEC's terms in order to obtain the accelerator. The original AEC prospectus clearly indicated a desire for free land, but this first meant land already owned by the U.S. government. Competition changed this until it came to mean that the successful state would have to purchase new territory and offer it free. During a second or third round, AEC spokesmen pressed Illinois to purchase a site in a desirable area. Illinois agreed, but there was confusion on what the agreement meant.

In late April 1966, after the withdrawal of Barrington as a site, the AEC sought clarification of Illinois' intentions. Mr. Graves, heading the Department of Business and Economic Development, moved cautiously, not knowing precisely what the AEC would need, and fearing that any attempt to detail the actual site might unnecessarily jeopardize the Illinois bid. Consequently, the AEC was presented with an area of 7,000 acres and was asked to select the 5,000 acres it wanted from that larger area. The AEC refused to choose and instead demanded the entire 7,000. The director of DBED tentatively agreed and proceeded to produce 8,800 acres from among which the AEC could choose 7,000.

This time Governor Kerner intervened and refused to authorize such an escalation. In order to give the AEC 7,000 acres, the state would have to purchase and replace 4 miles of railroad track without interrupting rail service. This would cost several million dollars. Finally, in November 1966, the governor went personally to Washington to work out concessions and within 3 weeks the deal was made, followed immediately by the announcement that Weston had been chosen as the site. The "concession" the governor got was reduction of the offer to 6,800 acres. A reduction of 200 from the state's maximum made it possible to exclude the expensive railroad trackage. The rest of the governor's agreement with AEC remains secret. Not a trace of it will be found in the available record of the AEC or in the available files of the Joint Committee on Atomic Energy. Here seem to be the only known details: the state of Illinois agreed (1) to convey 6,800 acres to the AEC; (2) to clear this land of all encumbrances; (3) to relinquish all claims in payments in lieu of taxes—payments to which it otherwise had a right according to provisions in AEC's own enabling legislation; [1] and (4) to convey this land to the AEC by a specified date, probably no later than October 1968, and possibly earlier.

These pressures of acreage and time were going to cost a tremendous amount. This is why Illinois sought and got extraordinary condemnation powers to carry out the terms of the agreement —powers it had not used except during World War II. [2] Yet, as the pressures and obligations went up, the legislature refused to increase its support accordingly. The legislature had authorized $12.5 million to acquire the first 5,000 acres and increased this to $30 million for the total 6,800 acres. However, the costs involved in clearing the additional 1,800 acres were not proportionate. There were special encumbrances, which included part of a railway, an oil pipeline, a butane pipeline, vital high-tension electric power lines, three lesser high-tension distribution lines, and, finally, a village of 100 homes plus such improvements as four-lane paved streets, sidewalks, a water plant for 500 homes, and a sewage plant for a like number.[3] This is undoubtedly why the $30 million authorization included nearly $14.4 million for fees. The cost of these items, coupled with the state's promise not to request payment in lieu of taxes, represented a huge saving to the AEC and a huge, and unanticipated, obligation for the state of Illinois.

Federal Needs and the State Agenda

In addition to extraordinary quick-take power, the Illinois legislature granted DBED Chairman Graves tremendous discretion in the selection of land to condemn. The legislature did not require DBED to adhere to any of the condemnation procedures followed by the Illinois General Services Administration or the Highway Department, which together account for most of the state's experience with condemnation.

Quick-take power became especially important. DBED had been granted the regular eminent domain power; however, the right to take these cases to court killed time and could increase purchase prices. With quick-take powers, Graves could confiscate and clear a parcel of land immediately. He had only to file in court for the property and deposit 125 per cent of the appraised value of the parcel—using DBED's own appraisal. The property owner would be required to deliver up his land immediately; under quick-take the owner cannot legally prevent seizure and immediate possession. From that moment, the bargaining advantage would rest with the agency. For this reason, quick-take had always been considered an emergency war power.[4] This kind of power gave all the initiative and flexibility to Graves. Although Graves was accountable to the governor, he was also the governor's chief source of information on the acquisition, and the governor could not really hold him to account.

Despite Graves' tremendous power, he would be able to use it to advantage only so long as he had business support and public acquiescence. Because insiders were already calling the site acquisition a "land grab," it was essential that Graves create and maintain a conflict-free environment. To this end, he adopted a two-part approach. First, he attempted to avoid litigation. This would mean very limited and judicious use of condemnation—leaving it as an omnipresence, but a crude one, like an axe in the corner.

Second, to help deflect whatever criticisms developed, Graves erected a facade of experts and prominent business and civic leaders to assume public responsibility for acquisition. Two groups were established. The blue-ribbon site acquisition committee, mentioned earlier, would take general responsibility for appraisals and negotiations. An appraisers' selection committee was created and designed to take specific responsibility for lining up the actual appraisers to examine each parcel of land. Although no legal authority would be given the two committees, Graves believed that the prestige and qualifications of their members would add legitimacy to any actions the committees approved. The press, he hoped, would be loath to criticize procedures authorized and actions approved by respected, public-spirited business people.

Because DBED would be most vulnerable to criticism in regard to the acquisition of specific parcels, where "human interest" stories could excite public clamor, Graves was especially careful to insure that the selection of appraisers be made in such a manner that they and their actions might be above reproach. Public relations required that appraisers be chosen on the basis of high professional qualifications alone, but a more favorable context for the agency's interests could be created by appointing to the appraisers' selection committee people personally and professionally acquainted with the appraisers. This could lend Graves a friendly atmosphere and at the same time would protect the agency from direct attack. More than likely, this method would also co-opt the appraising profession; they would be more likely to defend the agency in order to defend their colleagues from attack.

Graves began with less than 14 months to assemble the acreage, clear the titles, remove the occupants, and turn over the tract to the AEC. Graves adopted the approach to acquisition used successfully over the years by Commonwealth Edison. That giant utility possesses state eminent domain power to condemn land for rights-of-way for transmission lines. Yet in the course of 30 years Commonwealth Edison had condemned only two parcels of land.[5] Edison's model was to have appraisers evaluate the property and then to follow up that evaluation by sending company agents, independent of the appraisal to negotiate the settlement.

Impressed with the effectiveness of this method, Graves not only chose Edison's method but also "borrowed" Edison's top expert in low-conflict acquisition, Kenneth Reeling, Edison's North Shore director of operations. Reeling was experienced in working closely with local governments throughout the Chicago area. Reeling was made chief site acquisition officer and with Graves adapted Edison procedures to fit DBED's needs. Because DBED was more tightly tied to "fair market value," it could not be so flexible as Edison about negotiating prices. The Graves-Reeling solution was to use not one but two independent appraisals of each parcel. Each field appraiser was to submit his estimate to the chief appraiser, Reeling, who would check accuracy and use the two appraisals as a basis for setting a low and a high offer to extend to the owner. This would set the limits within which DBED would negotiate.

Acquisition of the Village

All but five of the 104 Weston structures were identical.[6] Table 11–1 gives the cost of Weston homes when built and the estimated cost of building the same structures 7 years later when the state acquired them. Costs were up thanks to inflation. Prices should also have been up thanks to the regular improvements that were made in many of these homes during the 3 years they were occupied by purchasers. Owners spent an average of $894 on home improvements.[8] Values were also increased by the community facilities built by the village.

TABLE 11–1 Construction Cost, Lost Costs for Weston Homes (1961–1968) [7]

	1961	1968
Average construction costs ($/sq. ft.)	$ 11.	$ 19.25
Land costs, smallest lot	5,680	7,300
Land costs, largest lot	7,500	9,500
Range of total costs for a Weston home	$14,425–20,700	$22,700–24,900

The state's initial position on property evaluations is indicated by the minutes of the blue-ribbon committee's first meeting.[9] Graves reported to the committee that according to his reading of the law a major cost-saving route was opened by the legal difference between a dead village and a live one. In Illinois, if a village property is taken over but the village relocates, the authority must compensate the village for the loss of public property. In Weston this could amount to more than a million dollars, nearly 7 per cent of all funds available for payments to owners. On the other hand, if the village remained incorporated but was dissolved by the total purchase of all the private properties, the public properties would revert to the state, therefore involving DBED in no expenditure whatsoever. A third route was to block Weston's incorporation, in which case DBED would have to prorate the public facilities to the value of each parcel acquired. As we saw in Chapter 7, the committee selected the second strategy, and Reeling began to work toward the acquisition of the Weston homes.

The state's appraisers and negotiators employed three techniques of pressure to hasten the acquisition process: (1) the state withheld information about what was going on and what was likely to happen; homeowners were kept virtually in the dark; (2) the state rushed through negotiations as soon as appraisals were ready; (3) the state delayed paying the villagers, making it difficult to act on relocation plans. Several additional tactics were brought into play as specific situations warranted. For instance, the negotiators seemed to contact older residents first. Widows were also contacted early. These settlements tended to be quick and at low prices, influencing later agreements. The negotiators refused to make appointments with the villagers; advance notice of a visit was avoided as a part of the strategy of keeping each villager in the dark. In the same spirit, only verbal offers were made; negotiators refused to put their positions in writing. Negotiators advised many of the villagers not to hire lawyers, threatening lower offers and lower final prices if lawyers were so much as consulted. In general, the negotiators badgered the villagers by stressing timing, what others were accepting, the costs of counsel, and so on, just like the hated "blockbusters" of urban neighborhoods in transition. And the tactics worked. Villagers signed quickly, accepted offers, and settled their affairs about as the state had planned. From December

16, 1966, when the site announcement was made, until May 1, 1968, the Weston homeowners did not know when the state would come to take their homes, whether indeed they would come at all, or how much they would be paid, even though the houses were identical except for improvements, which were easy to measure. Between May 1, 1968, and June 16, 1968, 61 of the 67 privately owned homes were appraised and purchased. The entire procedure was accomplished, except for six holdouts, in 6 weeks.

The state could have relieved much of the pressure on the villagers if it had so desired. It could, for instance, have announced its timetable for acquisition, or met with homeowners to work out procedures for appraising and acquiring the property, or made arrangements to close sales in a timely manner, or provided compensation for homeowners' moving expenses, or guaranteed financing for new homes that would replace the Weston homes, or in general worked to anticipate and resolve the difficulties faced by the people forced from their homes. Instead, the state used the pressure of difficulties in each of these areas to gain an advantage in dealing with the property owners. Kenneth Johnson, the chief negotiator for DBED, clearly stated that this was the state's procedure in his report to the blue-ribbon committee on June 11, 1968. Johnson reported that, as of that date, no appraisals had been received on any of the 87 farm parcels, and that he would delay negotiations until the appraisals were completed. Despite the fact that only 4 months remained before the entire site had to be turned over to the AEC, "a good look should be taken at the total picture, not only to see how we stand financially, but also to determine psychologically what would be the expedient course of action to take." [10]

The state's financial condition, an important reason for its delay in beginning condemnation, added more pressure on the DBED agents to cut costs. The state treasury was in a poor cash-flow position at the time of the Weston appropriation. For the biennium for which the $30 million was appropriated, the state faced a deficit of $170 million. DBED received its appropriation on June 30, 1967, but the state's cash position was so poor that no disbursements for acquisition (other than office expenses) could be made before February 1968. Property values in the Weston area had been climbing so rapidly that the state could not proceed with appraisals until it was sure of the date when it could complete transactions. If the appraisals were made even a few months before the transaction was completed, they could be judged invalid by the courts. But because the property values were rising so rapidly, the longer the state waited in making its appraisals the more it would have to pay. The state wished to proceed as soon as possible. Bonniwell, a blue-ribbon committee member experienced in condemnation, pressed the state hardest to proceed. He even qustioned "why the state had to pay for the land immediately. He felt that it should be acquired as soon as possible due to prices possibly inflating, but not necessarily paid for immediately." [11] In this way, the state would have the best of all worlds and only the homeowners would be harmed. The committees consistently viewed their responsibility as one of finding ways to give preference to the state financial problems over the property owners.

Finally, DBED was able to insure success in the village by a deception it played on the villagers (and farmers). Graves announced that the blue-ribbon committee would oversee the site acquisition, and the complaints were to be brought before that prestigious committee—not DBED. But not once in its years of monthly meetings (1967 to 1968) did the committee as a whole meet with a spokesman for the homeowners or the farmers.

The committee's isolation was not accidental. It was a posture chosen by Graves and approved by the members on the grounds that the committee's task was to expedite the acquisition and that consideration of protests against acquisition practices would delay completion of the task. The committee met in places impossible for the public to attend (for instance, Rubloff's office, over 25 miles away in the Loop), shunted villagers' complaints around among its members, and acted as a giant PR organization to stifle objections to the condemnation proceedings or to turn them into favorable points.

The attitude that Graves, DBED, and the blue-ribbon committee took toward their responsibility is epitomized in the following exchange during an early committee meeting. Almost a year after the village was announced as a winner of the site, Village President Arthur Theriault still did not know if it would escape condemnation. In taking steps for its relocation, the village continually ran afoul of DBED. The state's agents refused all cooperation. When Theriault drew up a list of grievances and asked to present them to the blue-ribbon committee, their consideration went this way:

> Mr. Graves said he thought we should reconsider whether or not we should meet with Mr. Theriault at this time. Mr. Graves said if we don't talk to him, he doesn't have much substance if he goes to the press and that in his judgment, it is better to hold in abeyance any meeting with Mr. Theriault until we have some specific information to give him. The Committee concurred in this.[12]

Mayor Theriault indeed had important issues and grievances to bring before the committee. The mayor had faith that the promises he had received from Governor Kerner and Senator Paul Douglas as to the future of the village would be kept, and he believed that the blue-ribbon committee would correct the malicious actions of Reeling and his agents. Further, Theriault was concerned about the timing of the site acquisition and about irregularities he suspected developing in the way in which the village was being appraised, and finally about DBED's reneging on Governor Kerner's promise that the villagers could purchase back their homes. The future would show one other great problem: Graves had promised that the villagers would be able to replace their homes with homes of equal value within 3 miles of the site. The villagers could not replace their Weston homes for homes of equal value 3 miles or 30 miles from the site. The following is a brief treatment of the major grievances:

The problem of incompetent appraisals.

As already described, Graves' official appraisal procedure was to send out two appraisers to each piece of property and from their report established a range of prices within which to negotiate a settlement. But the state did not follow the procedure in the Weston village. Only three appraisers were ever sent into the town; each appraiser visited only one or two homes; none asked questions of the owners. Hence, only a few houses received an actual appraisal. The appraisal was then taken to the villagers individually—not by one of the appraisers but by a negotiator who came without appointment and who, typically, bullied the home-owner into signing a sales agreement. In several cases, villagers reported that the negotiators threatened to lower their offers if the villagers waited or consulted with a lawyer. The procedure re-sulted in gross disparities in settlement prices, with resisters tending to get more. The state did nothing to rectify the causes of the disparity.

So little critical review was given to the haphazard appraisals of the village homes that it was not recognized until after the negotiators began to make offers that two basic prices were being used. One appraiser blindly set values of $14,700 on the homes, another set values at $15,200. Villagers found themselves in a situation where a home that had been vastly improved—painted and paneled, with the addition of a garage—would be appraised at $14,700 at the same time that the state offered $15,200 [13] for the unimproved, poorly maintained home across the street.

The state had not been concerned about the poor appraisals because the DBED officials believed the homes to be equally worthless. At the first blue-ribbon meeting, Graves was asked what types of homes the villagers lived in. Reeling answered that "each $13,000." [14] Reeling implied that the homes were worth, in 1968, home had about 800 square feet of living area and cost about what they cost—that is, sold for—in 1965. Because the prices being paid the villagers were higher than what the villagers themselves had paid, DBED was not concerned about the justice of its actions in terms of approximate market value or replacement cost.

However, when six homeowners demanded—and held out for —the right to repurchase their homes, the state felt compelled to make the individual appraisals they were supposed to make on every house. On June 12, 1968, Graves explained to the committee the difficulty with the last six pieces of property:

> One reason the remaining (six) houses have not as yet been pur-chased is because the (six) owners have asked for a salvage price on their homes, and *inasmuch as the homes have not been appraised separately*, this must not be done. A decision as to price will then be made if the present owners decide that they wish to purchase the homes back from the state.[15]

Only when the state had to resell the condemned homes for salvage was a first appraisal made at all, and then on only six of the homes.

Because the salvage price is given as a percentage of the appraised valuation, evidently the state did not wish to be cheated out of what was due it when it sold the villagers their homes back.

The problem of just replacement value.

The state paid the homeowners an average of $16,797 for the 99 similar homes.[16] Table 11–1 demonstrates that the villagers would have had to spend $24,900 to replace their homes on equivalent lots in 1968, but homes having such lot sizes could not be purchased at all in the area. According to our later survey the villagers' actual experience confirmed this prediction.

All but five Weston homeowners lost money because of the condemnation. Table 11–2, columns 6 and 7, shows that there was approximately $2,300 difference between the average compensation the state paid and the average cost of the replacement homes. Figure 11–1 relates the settlement price to the cost of replacement.[17] The figure indicates that three persons profited from their Weston homes. These persons were able to purchase homes costing less than what the state paid for their old homes. However, only one of these three actually thought his new home to be as good as or better than his Weston home. Three others thought that they were substantially improving their homes in spending more money. In their estimation, a $23,500 house was enough for them to improve their Weston home. All others paid an amount ranging from $250 to $8,000 more for what they believed to be an equivalent or less than equivalent home. One family was locked out of the market by their low settlement price and their inability to meet higher monthly payments. A second family, with a more substantial income, was locked out by a combination of low settlement price and their advanced age, which prevented their obtaining normal long-term financing. The family was consequently forced to buy less expensive, older housing to be able to meet monthly payments. However, the loan market for older housing was such that the family had to pay 50 per cent in down payment. The down payment was so great that the family could afford only a home that cost $10,999 and was in every way inferior to their Weston home.

That the average homeowner spent $2,300 above the state's price to obtain new housing does not mean that the replacement

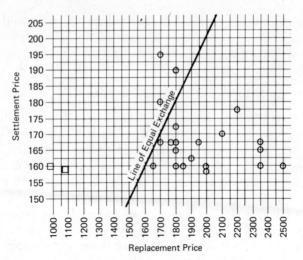

Legend: O = Persons who considered themselves
intentionally improving their housing—
spending more than necessary to replace their
Weston home.
□ = Persons unable to buy a replacement home
due to lack of capital.

FIGURE 11-1 *Settlement price compared to the
cost of the replacement home.*

value of Weston homes averaged $19,100 (that is, $16,797 average
settlement price plus $2,300). Many villagers could not afford to
pay for a home equal to the one they had left. The significance of
the $2,300 average difference was simply that the state's prices did
not come close to being sufficient to replace the homes with ones
of equal value.

Figure 11-2 substantiates our estimate of the value of the
homes. Virtually all homeowners believed their homes to be worth
from $18,500 to more than $25,000, if they were to be replaced
without loss. All but five families considered themselves to be
taking a loss in their move from Weston, particularly in terms of
lot size, utilities, community facilities, and distance from work.

Even if the state had actually paid the price for equivalent
property in the area, it would not have fulfilled its obligation to pay
just compensation. Other factors should have been taken into
account: (1) As we have seen, the state ignored the problem of

TABLE 11–2 Income, Compensation, and Replacement Costs for Selected Weston Families

	FAMILY INCOME	SAVINGS	ORIGINAL PRICE	EQUITY	VALUE OF IMPROVEMENTS	SETTLEMENT PRICE	COST OF NEW HOME	PERSONAL EVALUATION OF HOME	PER CAPITA INCOME
COLUMN NO.:	1	2	3	4	5	6	7	8	9
VA	$10,000	0	$13,200	$1,050	$1,000	$17,850	$22,000	$20,000	1,428
VB	13,104	0	13,200	650	400	16,500	23,500	16,500	3,276
VC	5,100	0	13,200	1,000	100	16,500	18,000	18,000	1,275
VD	10,400	0	13,200	1,050	2,500	19,000	18,000	25,000	2,500
VE	13,000	0	13,200	4,700	800	17,250	18,000	21,000	2,166
VF	6,000	0	13,200	1,000	400	16,000	16,500	17,500	1,500
VG	9,100	0				NA			1,820
VH	9,900	0				16,000	Rent	*	4,950
VI	13,000	$5,000	13,500	1,500	3,500	(22,750)	b	(29,000)	4,333
VJ	12,000	0	(16,500)	200	200	16,000	20,000	20,000	3,000
VK	16,800	0	13,200	3,000	1,000	16,700	19,000	20,000	8,400
VL	8,000	0			1,000	NA			1,333
VM	13,000	0	13,200	1,700	750	19,450	16,900	22,500	2,167
VN	9,600	0	13,000	1,200	500+	17,930	17,000*	18,000	1,600
VO	10,200	0	13,200	900	750	16,000	23,500*	20,000	1,457
VP	12,000	4,500 *	13,200	850	550	16,750	17,700	20,000	4,000
VQ	11,000	4,200 *	13,200	1,300	750	17,000	20,500	19,000	2,750
VR	6,000	3,200 *	13,200	1,300	1,200	16,000	18,500	19,500*	857
VS	18,000	5,000	13,200	1,000	1,000	16,000	25,000*	16,000	6,000

TABLE 11-2 Income, Compensation, and Replacement Costs for Selected Weston Families—Continued

COLUMN NO.:	FAMILY INCOME 1	SAVINGS 2	ORIGINAL PRICE 3	EQUITY 4	VALUE OF IMPROVE- MENTS 5	SETTLE- MENT PRICE 6	COST OF NEW HOME 7	PERSONAL EVALUATION OF HOME 8	PER CAPITA INCOME 9
VT	8,280	0	13,200	3,000	0	15,800	20,000	16,000	1,183
VU	12,500	4,400	13,200	1,200	1,000	16,750	16,900	23,000	2,500
VV	6,000	0				NA	NA		750
VW	8,500	3,300	13,200	1,000	510	16,250	18,800	18,500	2,833
VX	8,000	0	13,200	2,600	1,600	16,000	NA	21,000	4,000
VY	9,100	0	13,200	1,100	400	16,750	18,000	20,500	1,820
VZ	10,000	0	13,200		25	16,750	23,000*	19,000	3,333
VA1	5,100	0		2,016		NA			1,275
VB1	9,200	0	13,500		100	16,000	18,000	19,000	1,840
VC1	8,000		13,200		500	16,200	10,900*	24,000N	2,667
VD1	15,000	0	13,200		2,600	18,500	*b*	21,000	2,142
Average					894	16,797	19,087	19,791	
	N = 30				N = 27	N = 25	N = 22	N = 25	N = 25

N = 30; total population = 67.

Column 1: Incomes were the total family incomes and were obtained in interviews.

Column 2: Savings information was obtained in interviews. Asterisk (*) denotes savings that were actually capital gains from the sale of the Weston home to the state.

Column 3: The FSLIC sold all homes to the villagers. Homes were sold on purchase contract at interest rates of 6 to 6.5 per cent. The one home in parentheses was a different model from all the other Weston homes. It was two stories high and had a full basement, whereas the rest of the homes were one story built on a slab (cf. Chapter 6).

Column 4: "Equity," refers to the portion of the purchase contract that had been paid off. The different equity positions of the owners were caused by the different lengths of time the owners had held the property, and by the fact that the equity position developed at a faster rate the longer the owner held the property. The homeowner could expect to have available for the purchase of his new home the sum of his equity in the old property and the capital gains derived from the sale.

Column 5: The value of improvements included only major maintenance and upkeep items that would tend to increase the value of the property. Such items would include new water systems, gutters, shrubs, driveways, garages, wall-to-wall carpeting, and paneling.

Column 6: The value in parentheses refers to a different model home than the rest (see column 3).

Column 7: Asterisk (*) indicates homes that the owners described as significantly better or significantly worse than the Weston home. Otherwise, the owner considered the new home to be as good as the Weston home, and the cost of the new home equals, for these people, the cost of replacing the Weston home with its equivalent. In fact, the new homes were rarely equivalent to the Weston homes in all respects. Most people lost the large lots they had enjoyed in Weston, even though they paid more for their replacement home. Small b indicates that the owner bought back his Weston home and moved it.

Column 8: The owner was asked what he thought his Weston home was worth. All persons asked had been searching for a replacement home in the area for the past 1 to 6 months. The owner was asked what he would have to receive for his home from someone who could not force him to move before he would move willingly. "For instance, if a supermarket needed your property to build on, what would it have to pay you before you would move?" This example was used after it was discovered that some homeowners indicated that the price they would require depended on the use the property was going to be put to. They would sell at a lower price to a school than to a store. Replacement home was often of less value—for instance, smaller lot, smaller house, no utilities. Persons who salvaged their Weston home and moved it are not included (6). Nor are persons who were renting in Weston (4) or who moved to a different state (3).

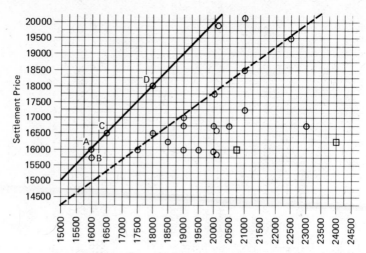

Legend: Solid line represents line on which owner would be charted if he
received what he estimated to be a just price.
Broken line indicates a relationship: the more the owner thought
his home was worth, the more he received.
☐ = Owner who would sell at any price, but estimated that this
was a just price.

FIGURE 11-2 *Settlement price compared to owner estimate of
just price.* An explanation of those (A through D) who were satisfied:

A. Owner moved to Weston for speculative reasons after
announcement that the accelerator might come. He looked down on
other residents as belonging to a lower class.

B. Owner replaced the home with a $20,000 home that was
similar but had a basement and was on a smaller lot. That is, the new
home was an approximately even trade, but the owner paid $20,000
and received only $16,000. He had anticipated leaving Weston within
2 years even without the accelerator.

C. Owner was a Southerner who liked the renter community of
early Weston and did not like the buyer community at the time of
condemnation. He would have moved in 1 year anyway. He moved to
a bigger house, costing $23,000.

D. Owner was one of the last to sign. He received what he
estimated his home was worth. More importantly, he felt he had won
his fight.

financing for the families. The case cited above is typical of the
Westonites' difficulty in finding new financing, particularly for
those who were older. (2) The state ignored the difference in

interest rates for those who could finance (a difference no sound business investor would have ignored). (3) The actual expense of moving from the Weston home and the lost time spent looking for a new home (300 hours was not unusual) were not considered.

The problem of inequitable variation in settlements.

Because there were not individual appraisals (except for the last six homes), there could be no reasonable basis for variation in settlement prices. Nevertheless, a glance at Table 11–2, column 6, shows there were wide variations in settlement prices, ranging from a low of $15,800 to a high of $19,450 (several families had settled with the state at $14,700, but moved before they could be interviewed and so were excluded from the survey). The state paid the five villagers receiving the highest compensation an average of $18,546. It paid the five in our sample receiving the lowest compensation an average of $15,960. It paid the FSLIC owners of 33 one-floor homes and four of the promotional two-story homes an average of $12,968 per house.[18] The state claimed each of these prices was the appraised value. But of course there were no individual appraisals on any of these!

Tests controlling for the value of the improvements made on the property and for variations due to lot size show that these factors do not explain the price variation. The last six families to sign—the holdouts—received an average of $2,500 more for their homes than the average given to the 61 other villagers.[19] They owned the only homes individually appraised. And even though there would be good reason to think that the rest of the homes would have received higher settlement prices if they had been similarly appraised, as is required by law, no other appraisals and readjustments of the sale price were made. This fact alone reveals much of the relationship between the villagers and the state: *the state acted consistently as if it were in an adversary relationship with the villagers.* The trouble with that posture here is that the two were not equals, nor were they presenting their cases before some judge or jury where full disclosure could be pursued through cross-examination or other means. It was deliberately adverse, but not truly adversary.

Indeed, one fact explains why the last six received their

appraisals: they were the only villagers to have lawyers. They got better prices and they got the option of repurchase. A large number of families had wanted to buy back their homes and move with the village, but only six were able to do so. Lawyers had forced the state to sell the six homes back; lawyers had forced the state to do what it was legally required to do. Neither the blue-ribbon committee nor all the other experts called in to oversee or carry out the state's task protected the barest legal rights of the villagers. Only the lawyers were effective, and they were because they simply knew the rights of the property owners.

One member of the village planning commission had been an employee of the AEC-duPont Corporation during the building of the Savannah River Project in South Carolina in the early 1950s. There he witnessed the evacuation of over 6,000 persons from the area (315 square miles) in a period of 1 year, and he recalled the human crises caused by the forced evacuation. He had seen similar activities on a smaller scale at the AEC Paducah, Kentucky, installation, and fully expected the same events to befall Weston. He was the only villager who openly criticized the pursuit of the accelerator. When the announcement was made that the village would definitely be condemned, this man called together his neighbors and told them of the problems they would have, and that only a lawyer could adequately handle their affairs. None of the low-income residents heeded his advice.

Most villagers refused to engage lawyers for three reasons: (1) The state negotiators actively discouraged people, particularly the less educated, from talking with a lawyer, as recounted above. (2) The legal profession maintains a high fee structure in condemnation cases. The Weston homeowners were informed they would have to pay a basic fee plus 50 per cent of the compensation received in court over and above the state's initial offer. Thus it could easily cost a homeowner $1,500 to recover $2,400 additional compensation for his home. If he lost his case, he would have owed several hundred dollars in legal fees. Given Weston's experience before the local courts, the villagers could not have any great expectations of winning their cases. In any event, the lawyers would gain more from the action than the homeowners. (3) The most serious reason the villagers did not seek lawyers was that they failed to understand that the state was taking an adversary stance toward them. They trusted the state and its negotiators, as they had been asked to do. They believed the state would not offer them anything but a fair price, and that a lawyer was in no way necessary. Moreover, for many villagers and farmers, hiring a lawyer to squeeze money from the government contradicted the patriotic aspect of a project the country so badly needed.

Not all owners of site property were treated badly by DBED and the AEC. The 6,800-acre site included 4 miles of high-tension towers belonging to Commonwealth Edison Company and a major pipeline belonging to Northern Illinois Gas Company, both represented by members of the mayor's committee active in winning the accelerator for Illinois. The consequences of condemnation for these companies were not, in any degree, as serious as they were for the farmers and villagers. In fact, Edison could be said to have profited from the acquisition of its land, and to have known that it would benefit in this well before the enlarged site was firmly established.

Acting under federal statute, the AEC granted Commonwealth Edison a right-of-way along the eastern boundary of the site, approximately ½ mile (2,740 feet) east of the former right-of-way, just east of the village. Moreover, Edison was paid for its towers and property and then paid the difference between the value of the old towers and the value of the new, upgraded ones it had long planned to install in the first place. The gas company moved its pipeline to Edison's new right-of-way, and so was saved the expense of acquiring new right-of-way on its own. Finally, the two utilities were the only property owners on the site that the state or the AEC bothered to help relocate.

This list of the problems and grievances is far from exhaustive, but it is illustrative. The pressure continued throughout the acquisition. In fact, it did not end when the settlements were made. After signing and closing, the homeowners had to wait an additional 1 to 2 months for their money. This meant absolute delays in purchasing other homes, and several villagers reported losing purchase opportunities as a consequence.

DBED also delayed and blocked repurchase in all but the last six cases. It is normal in condemnation proceedings for the government to sell for salvage prices whatever buildings remain on the condemned land, and the governor had promised the villagers that they would indeed be able to buy back their homes. However, none of the state negotiators would budge on this issue, and they were supported in this by DBED and the blue-ribbon committee. Only when it was clear that the villagers would not be able to move as a group to a nearby place on which to found a new Weston did the state begin to cooperate. And even then the asking salvage price was an unwarranted and unprecedented 20 per cent of sale price. Standard salvage prices run from 6 to 10 per cent, and at 20 per cent moving a house is not economically feasible. At the very end, rather than go to court, the state sold back the homes to the six holdouts for salvage prices ranging from 6 to 13 per cent. No explanation of the range was ever given or could be discovered.

Whatever the needs of the state, and whatever the pressures under which the state and its agents were working, the villagers had grievances. That is hardly worth remarking upon. What is remarkable is the acquisition of this entire village of 100+ homes in 6 weeks without any public clamor at all. The unpublic character of the acquisition is attributable almost entirely to the strategies and tactics of the DBED staff and committees. The Weston campaign was a PR triumph. And it was no accident. The entire proceeding was established to achieve this result. Almost nothing was left to chance. There were a few slip-ups. The rest was sheer genius.

When alleged injustices were brought up, individual members of the blue-ribbon committee handled them on a case-by-case basis, and neither they nor the committee at large was ever in a position to look at the entire process to see if the grievances, if true, were systematic rather than haphazard. Thus on two occasions the representative on the committee from Continental Illinois Bank extended help from his bank to Weston residents. But their coming to his attention was accidental, and meanwhile the compassionate banker continued to support the process that was giving rise to the need and the grievances.

Even some of Graves' own colleagues had misgivings. Attorney General William Clark expressed his concerns in a letter discussing the original acquisition plans:

> It is apparently contemplated that the full amount the state is willing to pay as just compensation would not be offered immediately to the landowners, but some type of "discounted offer"

would be made initially and the negotiators would have a range within which to make a final settlement.

I appreciate that the discounted offer system is used most successfully by industrial development corporations seeking to acquire real property, but it should be remembered, however, that the Department is acting as a governmental body of all the people, including the landowners whose property is sought to be obtained, and not as a profit-making corporation accountable to shareholders.

If you begin negotiating on price by offering the landowner a lesser amount than he is entitled to, what happens if the landowner accepts unwittingly, a lesser amount, on the mistaken belief that he is being treated fairly by his government? Such a settlement would be, in my judgment, unconscionable and contravene the Constitution, which places the obligation, if not the burden, upon the government, to provide just compensation. A landowner of this state should not have to horsetrade with his government in obtaining the full amount his government is prepared to pay for his property as just compensation and the full amount of the offer should be made known to him immediately.[20]

Graves lamely replied that because the range would be set by two independent appraisals, and because the negotiator would receive a simple percentage fee and no bonus for lower settlements, DBED's proposed procedure differed significantly from the older discount system. He argued that his system would have a great appearance of fairness. But we have seen that the two major premises in that reply were false. Most of DBED's success was erected over such false premises.

The first false premise was that two independent appraisals would be made. We have already seen how overwhelmingly false that premise was.

The second false premise, albeit never fully articulated, was that there was knowledge among the property owners as to prices and rights. Exhibit A, a portion of a state information brochure deleted prior to the brochure's publication, shows that the state officials were actually banking on just the opposite condition of intelligence among the property owners in the site area. The authors of the draft were DBED staff people responsible for developing DBED routines and policies. Elimination of the draft page from the final publication reveals the inherent contradiction in DBED's position on land acquisition in the Weston site project.

It proved impossible to join the idea of a fair price to the idea that each property owner should be able to deal properly with the state for his fair price. DBED faced this dilemma squarely and made its decision accordingly.

EXHIBIT A: Instructions proposed in a draft of the state information brochure for property owners.

COPY D
WHEN THE PUBLIC WANTS YOUR LAND:
Consider carefully the offer you receive. You may do better through agreement than through eminent domain proceedings.
If you honestly feel that a fair price has not been offered, ask for a better settlement.

(These instructions were deleted from the final version of the publication.)

NOTES TO CHAPTER 11

1. 42, U.S. Code, sec. 2208.
2. This version of the manner in which the village became included within the site relies heavily on the testimony of Charles Schrader, DBED's Chicago director at the time of the site acquisition. The interpretation is admittedly generous to the state, wherein the state appears inept and foolish, but does not appear to have designs against the village of Weston. Some evidence exists that the state acted with more purposefulness against Weston. See later.
3. We encountered a disagreement among the county legal authorities concerning the true size of the village water and sewage systems; some claim 250-home capacity, others a 500-home capacity. We are accepting the larger figure.
4. The request for quick-take power was guided and influenced by the AEC, whose direct experience with the power was extensive and successful. This had to be true in their acquisition of the Savannah River Project site, a project comparable to Weston. Although some argument can be made that Savannah had occurred during something of a national emergency, none existed in the Weston case. AEC appears to have become accustomed to using these extraordinary powers for convenience and not just necessity. See F. Stuart Chapin et al., *In the Shadow of a Defense Plant* (Chapel

Hill, N.C.: Institute for Social Science, 1954). For more on the character and use of condemnation in Weston, see Chapter 12.

5. Interview, Lawrence Trimble, vice-president of Commonwealth Edison.

6. See Chapter 6. The precise number of homes in Weston is not absolutely settled. Of the 105 homes started, 100 were the 40- by 20-foot rectangles on slabs, five were more elaborate model homes, two stories high with basements. Only one of the five model homes was ever completed and occupied. One of the 100 rectangles was destroyed in a tornado that struck the village on April 21, 1967. Hence, discussions of the value of the homes may refer to 100 homes—the 99 rectangles plus one model home—or to 99 homes—eliminating the model home. The context will make the reference clear.

7. Keith Smuckler Agency, Aurora, Illinois. Mr. Smuckler sold the homes for the FSLIC in 1965–1967. Also, Professor Oldenberg, DuPage County Engineer during Weston's construction; and Chicago Real Estate Board, *Chicago Building Costs Manual* (Chicago: CREB, 1968).

8. See footnotes to Table 11–2 for information on the collection of data from the village. The owner's word was taken for cost of painting, wiring, plumbing, and so on. Costs were found to be relatively constant for similar work. Some major improvements were obvious to the interviewer—wall-to-wall carpeting, paneling, landscaping, driveways, garages, and so on. Visual inspection verified that the large improvements had been made. Because many villagers were skilled tradesmen, and because almost all did their improvement work themselves, their estimates of improvement investment were conservative.

9. Minutes, Site Acquisition Committee, October 1968.

10. Minutes, Site Acquisition Committee, June 11, 1968.

11. Ibid., October 1968.

12. Ibid., June 12, 1968.

13. A third type of price, evidently unappraised, was paid the FSLIC for the houses it still owned. These prices were generally lower, and that reduces the average paid. Without figuring in the FSLIC houses, the average was $16,797; with those houses included, the average was $15,446.

14. Op. cit.

15. Ibid. Emphasis added.

16. See note 13.

17. The cost of the new home, as used in Figure 11–1, is considered to be only the cost of the principal required for the home, and not the principal plus the interest that the purchaser would actually have to pay. If the interest charges were included, the difference between the price the state paid for the Weston homes and the

price that would be required to replace the home would be greater since the villagers had to pay at least 2 per cent higher finance charges in 1968 than in 1965.

18. The state also purchased 41 lots at $2,500 each from FSLIC.
19. They received 33 per cent more than the federal government received for its 32 homes.
20. DBED files.

CHAPTER **12** **Enemy**

of the People

The rural occupants of the site area were distinctly unlike the Weston villagers. They knew their way around; they knew one another; they had some self-esteem. The rural way of life was still widely esteemed in DuPage County.

The rural residents had departed from the villagers on almost everything, including their attitude toward the accelerator. They had doubted the value of the accelerator, had opposed it, and had been vociferous about rights and prices when acquisition finally did prove unavoidable. Yet all that is left of rural people and of farming in this area is a model farm—erected by the scientists to honor farming but not to farm, erected in the memory of farming once all real farms had disappeared.

By 1965, the rural way of life had become the enemy of suburbia. The village of Weston stands for virtually all the reasons for the suburban change of attitude toward farming. The village of Weston had once been a farm. Most remaining farm owners and operators expressed strongly their intention to stay forever in the area. But given the pressures of urbanization and the pressures of high taxation and low farm incomes, how many owners could promise that they would never be forced to yield their land to a developer, just as the Krafft family had yielded their land for the

261

building of Weston? And even if 100 per cent of the present occupants held the line, how many could effectively bind their heirs?

The rural families had to go, each and every one. Taken as a single instance, the village of Weston was only a somber presence. Conceived altogether, these farms were a threatening omnipresence. How many additional farms would have to yield to the developer, for the area was irreversibly committed to urbanization? The overwhelming majority of the suburban DuPage County citizens would best be served by declaring war on the farmers as well as the villagers. The chosen instrument of war was, once again, eminent domain.

The State vs. the Farmer: 6,800 Desirable Acres

As reported in the preceding chapter, the Weston villagers did not heed a report of one of its own leaders of the operations of the AEC leading toward the acquisition of property to build the Savannah River Project in South Carolina in the early 1950s. But the experience with that project was not lost on the AEC or on the state of Illinois. A published study of the Savannah project indicated a variety of problems, ranging from extreme difficulty of obtaining loans for any eligible families to long delays in the appraisal process and to a variety of inequities and injustices.[1] But the actual lesson learned by the AEC was not how to prevent injustices in future acquisitions but how to avoid getting involved directly in the acquisition process at all. The AEC adopted the position that the land was to be a gift from the state of Illinois, and when the farm operators and owners approached the AEC to inquire or to complain the AEC officials insisted that they had no responsibility whatsoever. The complaints were referred back to the state officials. The land was to belong to the AEC. But the case was state of Illinois versus the farmer. The consequences of this arrangement were even more devastating for the farm population than for the villagers because of the greater value of each parcel of land and also because of the deeper ties of the people to that particular area and to a particular piece of land.

Because of its extremely desirable characteristics, DuPage County land values were soaring as farmers were refusing to sell their land. These rural occupants of DuPage County were keenly aware of the benefits they enjoyed. Rather than being beset by the traditional rural problem of isolation, they were on the fringe of an exciting metropolitan area. As a group, these rural residents were literate, sophisticated, and articulate. Most of them were aware of the various dilemmas that their proximity to an urban center posed but so far had steadfastly stood up to them. The sale of Weston had jolted the suburbanites; nevertheless, only one tract of land had been sold for development. Ancestry and heritage were in fact cherished. The land had formed the basis of family life and was not going to be relinquished lightly. It would be difficult if not impossible to sell this type of land to a highest bidder, because it would be impossible to transplant these specific characteristics of the property and the specific characteristics of the rural community to another area.

This kind of resistance to sale was contributing to soaring land values. In order to gain an independent picture of the market value of this land, we made a study of land sales in this area during the period 1968–1969, around the time of the real beginning of the accelerator development.[2] The following pattern is based strictly on land exchanges in western DuPage County near the actual accelerator site [3]:

East of the NAL site

1. Land in the immediate vicinity of the site from Chicago.
   a. Without good frontage: $2,300 to 3,000 per acre.
   b. With good frontage (e.g., access to arterial highway): $3,000 to 4,000 per acre.
2. Land located in immediate vicinity but outside of Wheaton.
   a. Without good frontage: $5,000 to 6,000 per acre.
   b. With good frontage: $6,000 to 8,000 per acre.
3. Land located in immediate vicinity but outside incorporated limits of Lombard: all property sold had good frontage and sold at $11,000 to 12,000 per acre.

West of the NAL site

1. Immediate vicinity of the site.
   a. Without good frontage: $2,000 to 3,000 per acre.
   b. With good frontage: $3,000 to 3,500 per acre.

2. Immediate vicinity of the site (closer to Chicago), all good frontage: $11,000 to 13,000 per acre.

When several of the farmers later contested the evaluation of their land as appraised by DBED, they would bring forth these comparable sales in the area to oppose the state's appraisals. Sales cited in actual cases were at the following prices per acre: $2,900; $2,537; $3,000; $3,500; $5,000; $5,000; $5,541; $7,000; $7,000; $10,500.[4]

In order to analyze and assess the pattern of acquisition, it is necessary first to identify the various types of occupancy in the rural part of the site. "Weston farmers" is a term used in reference to all nonvillagers who had their land taken for the accelerator site, but it is an oversimplification. The Weston farmers should be divided into six groups:

I.   The farmers: those who own more than 10 acres of land, live on the land, and farm the land (farmers $N = 29$).

II. The gentlemen farmers: those who own more than 10 acres of land, live on the land, but do not farm the land (gentlemen farmers $N = 17$).

III. The absentee farmers: those who own more than 10 acres of land, but neither live on the land nor farm the land (absentee farmers $N = 7$).

IV. The exurbanites: those who own less than 10 acres of land, who live on the land, but who do not farm it (exurbanites $N = 6$).

V.   The tenants: those who own no land, but who live on the land and farm it as tenants (tenants $N = 9$).

VI. The unclassifiable ($N = 3$).[5]

Although most of the farmers were very reticent about their personal finances, certain conclusions can be drawn from the financial information gleaned in interviews. Most of the farms were small and were, under even the best of circumstances, inefficient. The farms were taxed at an urban rather than a rural rate because of general county zoning regulations defining the entire area as residential and industrial rather than as farmland. In approximately half of the known cases, rent did not cover the taxes.

Of the active farmers (group I), 60 per cent had outside employment to supplement their income from their farms. All gentlemen farmers (group II) rented their land to tenant farmers and none called this rent his primary source of income. All of the absentee farmers (group III) rented to a tenant, and none depended on this rent as his chief source of income. Thus only 30 per cent of the total membership in these three groups (63) depended on their farm for their chief source of income.

As an indication of income derived from the land, it is useful to look at rent levels. Rent was paid in the form of either cash or a 50-50 share of the crops. The straight cash rent ranged from approximately $25 an acre to $35 an acre. Because several landowners rented their land to tenants on a 50-50 basis, one might assume that the landlord's share was roughly equal to the average rent of $30 an acre. This means that a 100-acre farm would yield an income of $3,000. A quick glance at the size of farms (Table 12–1) suggests that land incomes were low. When farmers were asked "Do you feel you made a *good* living from your farm?" only 12, or 41 per cent, answered affirmatively.

The Weston farms were not profitable, but it is important to note that for approximately three fourths of the farmers profit was of minor importance. Although only 51 per cent said they made a "good" living, another 20 per cent said their income was sufficient, although not good. It was not unusual for a farmer to say to the interviewer, "Well, you probably wouldn't think the income is good, but it's okay with me." And, whereas 39 per cent felt their income was insufficient to live on, 90 per cent of this group held

TABLE 12–1   Number of Farms
According to Size

FARM SIZE	NUMBER
Under 50 acres	12
50–100 acres	16
101–150 acres	13
151–200 acres	8
Over 200 acres	3

Source: Township Platt Maps, Sexton Engineering Service, Ottawa, Ill., revised April 9, 1967.

outside jobs in order to make enough money to continue farming.

Clearly, the Weston farms were not profit-oriented businesses. Moreover, the farmers displayed little interest in selling their profitless farms and moving on. Four fifths of the farmers intended, prior to the coming of the accelerator, to remain on their land "forever" or "indefinitely." This strong desire to stay on the land was demonstrated by approximately one third of the farmers who had declined concrete offers made by private parties for their land. Their attachment to the land and firm roots in the community help explain what led them to resent the coming of the accelerator and to resist vigorously the acquisition of their land by the state of Illinois.

Like the residents of Barrington, the farmers believed the accelerator threatened their valued way of life. Unlike the Barrington residents, however, the farmers were ignored by the state and the AEC and were outnumbered by the united and vocal village.

In 1965, when the Weston farmers first discovered that their land might be taken for the accelerator site, they organized the Weston Landowners Association to prevent such an occurrence. The association began its activities when the state of Illinois made public its offer of a DuPage County site and continued until individual farmers were defeated in the courts. But the association's efforts were to no avail. A petition against the location of the accelerator was reportedly signed by the owners of 95 per cent of the site land, but the local newspaper would not print it.[6] A bus trip to Springfield was organized to lobby against the "quick-take" legislation. The trip, like other farmer efforts to contact political leaders, produced no results. Approximately 70 landowners had attended meetings of the Landowners Association, but by the time of our study many of them had stopped trying to fight and most had already signed sales contracts.

Eminent Domain in Action

There was no real need to take these objections into account. Once the AEC had decided the United States should smash atoms, and once the Illinois legislature decided to authorize an acquisition for the accelerator site, the "public purpose" required in order to give the state the right to acquire the land was beyond question.

Following *Berman* versus *Parker* (348 U.S. 26, 1954), the leading Supreme Court decision in this area, "public purpose" was interpreted to be roughly equivalent to "public interest," which could mean anything a legislature said it meant. Thereby the judiciary virtually eliminated itself from the eminent domain process. It was no longer going to be possible to get judicial review of the question of whether any acquisition, including a university-operated atom smasher, was sufficient to qualify as a public purpose.

This lack of judicial review was strongly resented by the farmers. They had appealed in vain to local political leaders, to county officials, to state legislators, and to United States congressmen. Their discovery that they were also without judicial recourse appeared to them to be another indication that they were on the outside of a closed governmental system, totally powerless.

The U.S. Supreme Court in *Berman* versus *Parker* also affirmed that "just compensation" exhausted the rights of the property owner. But what is just compensation? Traditionally, it has been defined as "market value," but there are several problems in determining market value in eminent domain cases. The most persistent problem is that it involves a fundamental contradiction in terms. The bible of realtors, the *Appraisal Terminology and Handbook*, defines market value as the "price at which a willing seller would sell and a willing buyer would buy, neither being under abnormal pressure." [7] But how can one determine such a price when the seller under normal conditions would not sell at any price, and the buyer virtually alone is the final arbiter of the price? Quite clearly any forced sale that occurs in an eminent domain case is entirely different in nature from a willing sale. When a man makes a willing sale, his motive is presumably one of self-betterment. Usually a willing sale is made because the purchase price exceeds the value that the seller has placed on the land. However, a forced sale lacks a willing seller, so it would seem that if the seller is to be justly compensated he must receive more than the "market value," for at mere market value the satisfied owner—such as a Weston farmer—would probably not sell. Further, the problem becomes particularly acute in those instances in which quick-take is used. For quick-take permits the state to acquire title to the land, over the objections of the owner, and argue the merits of the case later in court. At no point is there any question where title rests. It rests with, and will continue to rest with, the condemning agency.

There are several additional problems with the exercise of forced sales at "market value" near the accelerator site. First, farmers could not replace their land in the area. Yet the definition of "market value" can be understood to mean that price that a buyer must pay to purchase an equivalent piece of property in the same area. If a farmer was paid $2,000 per acre for his land, but must pay $2,500 for an equivalent piece of property in the same area, was he paid market value or fair value? None of the farmers was able to replace his farm in the area, and the bulk of the farmers moved 100 to 150 miles away. Only at this distance could they find a farm equivalent to their Weston farm at a price approaching the price paid them by the state. Only by relocating at a considerable distance could a man continue farming, as Table 12–2 demonstrates. One of the farmers testified in court, "I didn't see anything that I wanted that I could have touched for a minimum of $3,000–$3,500 per acre" in the area.[8]

Next, in calculating just compensation the state failed to recognize that the removal of 6,800 farm acres from farm utilization caused the area land market to tighten. Sellers in the vicinity recognized the predicament Weston farmers were in and raised their prices when the farmers sought to purchase new farms. For financial reasons they had to replace their land immediately and for personal reasons they wished to replace it in the area; but as buyers the Weston farmers were at the sellers' mercy. Thus, because of state policy, the farmers were first impotent as sellers and later impotent as buyers. This complaint of higher than normal prices was made by 14 farmers who were seeking new farms. Indeed, sellers of farms seemed to have made little secret of their increased prices. At an area auction, an auctioneer began the bidding with, "Okay, boys, let's bid the price up there where it belongs. There are some desperate Westies [Weston farmers] in the crowd." At another auction, the auctioneer said, "$2,500 more if he's from Weston." These remarks were not in jest.

Moreover, although moving expenses for farmers were high, the state refused to provide any compensation. Most of the Weston farmers had to move a considerable distance, and because movers

TABLE 12–2 Relocation Distance in Relation to Opportunity to Continue Farming

	UNDER 25 MILES	26– 50	51– 100	101– 150	151– 200	200 MILES
Will continue to farm	None	None	16	21	14	3
Will not continue to farm	9	6	9	None	None	None

charged fees by the mile the high costs forced many of them to move themselves rather than hire professionals. One farmer, who had moved his family unassisted, estimated that the total man-hours expended went up into the hundreds. Although their labor was "free," the farmer and his wife (both over 60 years old) paid a steep price in nervous and physical exhaustion. Machinery and livestock often had to be sold at a loss because the expense of moving them was too great. Different farmers estimated they took losses ranging from $250 to $11,000. The state also refused to compensate farmers for their buildings, yet the buildings' unwieldy size and construction made it impossible to move them. Indeed, the value of the buildings was not lost on the AEC, for some rather charming farmhouses on the site are now occupied by NAL employees.

Many farmers were unable to secure loans or mortgages because of the tight money market. Those who did obtain mortgages were able to do so only at high interest rates. Those who were old, or ill, or less prosperous, could borrow nothing.

Business interruptions and loss of clientele were not compensated. Yet some men were destroyed financially because they were forced to leave clients and establish business elsewhere. Farmers and other businesses in the area, such as dog kennels, were dependent on professional reputations, which take years to establish and which cannot easily be transferred from place to place. An egg farmer estimated that once he moved to a new location it would take him 3 years to build a clientele similar to his Weston clientele. Grain farmers estimated that it would take them 2 to 3 years to adjust to a new farm and reach their maximum efficiency.

Finally, and perhaps most importantly, the state in taking the Weston land destroyed a community and its way of life. This way of life and the communal interdependencies on which it was based could not survive the taking of the land.

From the logic of the situation alone, "market value" bears little resemblance to "just compensation." Further, even if market value were paid, certain factors not encompassed by the market value concept would militate against the compensation being a "just" one. The actual facts, to which we now turn, will help determine the degree to which the state of Illinois compensated the farmers justly.

Market Facts and Illinois Values

By mid-1968, when the actual acquisition of land for the accelerator site was begun, the state found itself in the midst of a financial crisis. Because of (1) an Illinois Supreme Court decision that declared unconstitutional a section of the Illinois sales tax and (2) a revocation by the legislature of a tax on insurance proceeds, the state had significantly less money to spend than it had anticipated. Suddenly the $30 million appropriated for land acquisition loomed larger with the state's budget than it would have under less critical circumstances.

Land in DuPage County had been increasing in value as rapidly as 20 per cent per year between 1964 and 1969. In addition, Commonwealth Edison industrial development experts had pinpointed this area as a prime industrial site.[9] If the state bargained in good faith and bought the land at market value, there was good reason to believe that land acquisition would cost more than the budget provided.

Thus the state was financially unprepared to bargain in good faith, and the first few steps taken by the state did not bode well for the farmers. When DBED was authorized to employ "quick-take" powers in its condemnation proceedings, the die truly was cast. DBED's responsibilities made it absolutely necessary that they play a high-pressure game.

The DBED was aware of the importance of hiring appraisers

who were familiar with the unique conditions in the area. In a letter to Paul Ronske, Chairman of the DuPage County Board of Supervisors, Gene Graves (Director of DBED) wrote:

Pursuant to this Act (House Bill 2243) the Department of Business and Economic Development will . . . engage the services of competent real estate agents from the Weston area to acquire, by negotiation, the lands required for the facility. . . . The real estate agents and appraisers will be firms of outstanding integrity and reputation, who are familiar with the Weston area.[10]

Yet the state hired farmland appraisers from downstate Illinois who knew little of land values in rapidly urbanizing DuPage County. The two appraisers who, according to farmers, appraised the largest number of parcels were from Ottawa (downstate, rural Illinois). The appraiser who appears to have done the follow-up appraisals was from the South Side of Chicago. He was primarily an appraiser of big-city urban property, rather than urbanizing property in exurbia. A fourth appraiser was from Libertyville (a semirural town in Northern Illinois, famous for having been the country home of Adlai Stevenson and more recently famous for successfully opposing another federal site, the ABM). Two other appraisers were from La Grange and Wheaton in DuPage County, and one seems to have done a minimal amount of appraising, which was then reappraised by the Chicagoan; the other quit very early in the procedure.

It is widely recognized within the appraisal profession that the appraiser does not offer expert scientific judgment, but rather knowledgeable opinion.[11] Nonetheless, the courts recognize the appraiser's opinion as holding great weight. When an appraiser from downstate Illinois appraises land in the metropolitan area, the court does not question his competence as an appraiser; thus the state would be legally safe if it chose men whom it knew to be unqualified. Furthermore, appraisers often have become the tools of their employers. Depending on whether he is employed by the condemnor or the condemnee, an appraiser can make a good case for any of a wide range of "market value" prices on the same piece of property.[12]

It is difficult to determine precisely what procedures appraisers used on the rural Westonites. Despite the DBED's constant reiteration of the promise that each farmer would be able to show his land to the state appraiser and discuss it with him, over 40 per cent of the farmers interviewed by us had never seen or spoken to their appraiser. One farmer recalled that he was working on his land when he spotted a stranger walking on his neighbor's farm. When the farmer asked him what he was doing, the man replied he was appraising the land for the state. When asked why he had not informed the land's owner of his presence, the appraiser replied that he had neither the time nor the inclination to do so. Nevertheless, it is standard professional procedure for the appraiser to see the property owner. As the prominent appraiser Joseph R. Smith states, "You have to have the facts and the owners have them. Often they cannot be obtained in any other way." [13]

Furthermore, those appraisers who spoke to farmers made it clear that they were appraising the land as farmland despite the fact that the land was taxed as residential or industrial land. This policy of appraising the land as farmland ran counter to the professional stipulation that "highest and best use" should be paid. Highest and best use is defined as "the most profitable use, . . . that use which produces the greatest net return in money to land during the foreseeable future." [14] The county had already defined highest and best use for the Weston land, for purposes of zoning and taxation, *as residential or industrial, not farming.*

The appraisers also chose land in rural southern and western Illinois as comparables. This made a complete farce of the appraisal process. To be "comparable," two pieces of property must be identical in all value elements, and two important value elements are time and place. Properties must be sold at approximately the same time in the same location, or in separate but highly similar locations. Nevertheless, the state's appraisers argued to the court that land sold in 1964 was "comparable." [15] This was 4 years before the condemnation, and in a rapidly urbanizing area this was an absurd comparison. When the lack of sound comparables is coupled with the many other shortcuts, such as frequent failure to see landowners, the only possible conclusion is that the appraisers performed inadequately. No elaborate concept of justice has to be defined to see this.

These abuses were carried over from appraisal to negotiation. The negotiator is an agent hired by the condemning authority to determine what price the landowner will accept for his property. The negotiator is often a real estate agent but rarely an accredited appraiser. The negotiators in this instance were apparently instructed to obtain the lowest possible price by any available method. They often made offers to the rural residents that were less than the appraised value. They concentrated on the old, the sick, and the poorly educated, who were more readily intimidated by official representations. Those who were well educated, or who were represented by counsel, were left alone. To create something of a bandwagon or a "blockbusting" effect, negotiators misrepresented to some farmers the number and identity of others who had signed; accepted prices were either kept secret or misrepresented. The most persistent and insidious form of intimidation was the threat made to many of the farmers that if they resisted and went to court their land would eventually be taken at a much lower price.

All of this was made more effective by the fact that the negotiators, like most of the appraisers, were unknown to the area and were themselves professionally ignorant of the area. This had the effect of lossening still further the state's already loose procedural standards. Despite Graves' assurances, reported earlier, that negotiation would be conducted by competent realtors from the Weston area, the two most active negotiators were from DeKalb, and others were, respectively, from Chicago's South Side, from St. Charles, and from Wheaton. Only the last two were, in any sense, from the "Weston area."

Actual prices offered by the state reflect the effectiveness of their procedure. Data on approximately two thirds of the state's original offers were obtained from interviews with the farmers. The prices offered by the state ranged from $850 per acre to $4,000 per acre, a difference of 470 per cent. Although some parcels clearly were more valuable than others from the standpoint of farming, no parcel was worth 470 per cent more than another from the standpoint of the accelerator site, where rural value elements, such as fertility of soil, are of no relevance. And it is difficult to conceive of the 470 per cent differentiation being due to road frontage, because the site was going to be treated as one complex whole.

And surely the distribution of offers shows that all of this was irrelevant anyway. The lowest price was offered to an old, seemingly illiterate, foreign-born man; the highest offer was made to a client of the prestigious Chicago law firm of Lord, Bissell, and Brook. These two are the limiting cases. Other offers range between.

The offers to the actual farmers (group I) covered the full range. Of the 29 households in this category, 26 were willing to divulge the first offers received from the state. The median first offer was $2,040 per acre, somewhat lower than the median for all six categories of $2,065 per acre. But the range was from a low of $850 to a high of $4,000 per acre. In an effort to discover the causes behind this range, farms were grouped according to tillable acres per farm, frontage, soundness of buildings, and productivity (productivity was based on interview replies). These groupings—which were admittedly rough—revealed that a few good farms were offered high prices and a few mediocre farms low prices; but there were no discernible patterns.

An effort also was made to correlate first offers with each appraiser and negotiator, but this yielded conflicting patterns. Although all the appraisers seemed to have appraised fairly low, one appraised at a particularly low level. Similarly, certain negotiators seemed to have made consistently low offers, whereas others at times made somewhat higher ones.

Several farmers alleged that two negotiators in particular had lied to, insulted, and intimidated them and their neighbors. However, two families who dealt with these same negotiators found them to be charming and reasonable men who made them *high* offers. Here may have been the key to the whole mystery, because these two families were different from all other families who dealt with the two negotiators. They had considerable wealth, education, and prestige. The other families, although by no means poor or uneducated, nonetheless made a weak first impression on our interviewers, and perhaps also on the negotiators.

Among the farmers, 12 had made a very strong first impression on the interviewers. Among these, ten were given offers ranging from $2,400 to $4,000 per acre. The median for this group was $2,435 per acre—considerably higher than the median for the group as a whole.

Those nine farmers who had made a weak first impression

had received offers ranging from $850 to $2,156 per acre. Their median was $1,800 per acre, or considerably lower than the overall median.

Data were available for 12 of the 15 gentlemen farmers (group II). Again with the respondents arranged impressionistically, for the eight who made a strong impression the median was $2,300. For the weaker ones, the average was $1,261.

Thus it seems highly probable that the state consistently offered prices according to the impression made by the people with whom it was dealing, not according to the value of the land it was purchasing. The lowest prices were offered to those who did not appear clever enough to oppose the state. To those who seemed more capable of offering opposition, higher prices were offered, apparently because the state wished to avoid the costs of court proceedings and publicity.

This thesis is supported by the treatment of the exurban homeowners (group IV). Because this group had considerably less property than any other group, and the total value of their property also was correspondingly less, they were placed in a serious dilemma. As each negotiator pointed out, they could not afford to go to court, because it would cost them more in lawyers' fees than they could gain by an increase in the state offer. This dilemma was exploited by the state, as the following case illustrates:

One of the homeowners was a carpenter, who had built an eight-room ranch-style home with an attached two-car garage. Because of the extensive meticulous handwork and the abundant use of exotic and expensive woods, the owner believed $100,000 to be a fair price for his home. The state's negotiator offered him $37,500. When the carpenter complained that the offer came nowhere near the value of his house, the negotiator admitted that the offer was low, but he then proceeded to show the homeowner that he could not afford to reject the state's offer. The negotiator told the carpenter the most a court would be likely to give him was $60,000 and probably $50,000; at the same time, argued the negotiator, lawyer's fees would come to at least $7,000. Therefore, the negotiator proposed a compromise of $44,000, which was equal to the amount of money the homeowner would probably end up with if he went to court. Clearly, this state negotiator's definition of "just compensation" was the minimum compensation that a property owner could be induced to accept.

In another incident, a homeowner had been offered $28,500 for a home that had been privately appraised at $40,000. Again, the negotiator pointed out that legal fees of at least $7,000 would be prohibitive if the matter went to court. The owner would have to get $34,000 from the court to break even with the state's offer. The negotiator said he would therefore increase the state's offer to $35,500. This was still $4,500 short of the privately appraised value.

An interesting footnote to these incidents is the story of the church located within the site. The church had been appraised by the state at $37,500, which was also the state's first offer. The pastor of the church said he would go to court if he did not receive $50,000. The negotiator finally offered $47,500—$10,000 more than its appraised value—because the negotiator said the state had to be careful about public relations. The American people, he claimed, did not approve of attempts to cheat churches.

In short, the bargaining situation was immensely aided by the status of the individual owner and by the image of potential bargaining resolve he presented. However, that was very much tempered by his behavior during the entire course of events. Those who actually joined the farmers' resistance movement were severely punished, no matter what their status or reputation was. It appears to be the case that those who appeared at all capable of hard and knowledgeable bargaining were given offers consistently higher than those who made a poor impression as to status or willingness to fight a personal battle on property values. But among the sophisticates differences in treatment did emerge, and those differences reveal the true nature of the whole process, as shown dramatically in Figure 12–1.

The sophisticates, following the figure, tended to divide fairly evenly according to whether they had been nonresisters, partial resisters, or diehards during the site competition and early appraisal history. The numbers in Figure 12–1 clearly portray the results. The lower line shows only a little variation among first offers received. At that point, the record of resistance was less

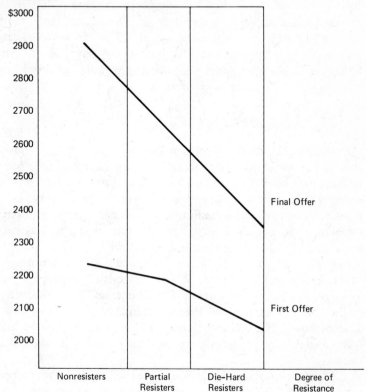

Average Per Acre
Prices Offered

FIGURE 12-1 *The sophisticated and their behavior: degree of resistance vs. prices offered.* (Source: *Weston questionnaires*)

clear, and the identity of the resisters had not yet become a factor in the negotiations. By the time the final offers were made, the effect of having resisted the site began to show up clearly in the final offers received by each type of sophisticated, high-status owner. Those higher-status owners who had shown a cooperative side to the state got consistently the highest offers of all. Any history of resistance pushed final offers downward, in direct correlation with the degree of resistance.

Reflections on Eminent Domain

Our two accounts of the acquisition process for the village and rural occupants of the accelerator site have not been constructed as a brief against eminent domain. Power to take private property for a public purpose is inherent in sovereignty itself. Eminent domain simply reaffirms the ultimate public character inherent in all private property, and we can respect that as long as the public authorities respect it.

Nor is our account a brief against a specific science project as a case of a public purpose. We are not qualified judges.

Rather, our brief is against two fundamental errors committed in the name of science and the public interest. These two errors have corrupted the eminent domain process in this instance and will corrupt any public agency process involved in the same manner.

The first of these errors resides in the mythology of "just compensation." Our studies overwhelmingly documented the charge that "market value" is an impossibility in any context in involuntary exchange. Our studies also show that no approximation of just compensation can result from an acquisition process based strictly on negotiation between the authorities and single, isolated individuals. Indeed, it should be immediately granted that individual owners should not be allowed to gouge the public. Once a commitment has been made for a particular highway direction or a particular site for a public function, prices for the land involved in such a project would rise at an exponential rate without some kind of controls. Nevertheless, our cases show that the eminent domain process is far too important to the cause of justice and to the legitimacy of public agencies to be left to professional negotiators and appraisers, no matter how profession-alized their skills may appear to be to the layman. This process is also too important to be left entirely to the discretion of each of the acquiring agencies. The agencies will continue to use ap-praisers in the narrowest possible way as long as no public con-siderations are imposed upon the process. Professional reputations and narrowly defined agency responsibilities simply perpetuate the myth of just compensation.

It is not our place to define just compensation. Our respon-sibility is fulfilled by bringing this agonizing and myth-filled nonsense to the public's attention in the hope that courts and legislatures can determine appropriate criteria as a matter of high public policy.

The second source of error that corrupts the eminent domain process is the belief that "public purpose" is a fact inherent in any action taken or any end sought by a public agency. Portia said that "God made him, therefore let him pass as a man." With-out seeing the tragic irony, Americans tend to accept a similar proposition, that the public has an interest, therefore let it pass for a public interest. But unfortunately, "public" is not a fact; it is a criterion in desperate search of proper definition by proper authorities. Therefore, everything done in the name of the "public" is problematic—that is, it requires elaborate and constant justi-fication. In the realm of the public, nothing could be more prob-lematic than eminent domain. Yet almost nothing is quite as invisible from popular awareness and no public activity is any further removed from serious attention by the most responsible levels of government.

NOTES TO CHAPTER 12

1. Gerald L. Breese, *The Impact of Large Installations on Nearby Areas* (Beverly Hills, Calif.: Sage Publications, 1968), pp. 441–586.
2. *The Wheaton Journal,* Wheaton, Illinois, reported all major real estate transactions in DuPage County for most of the period we are concerned with.
3. The difficulties in establishing true market value are discussed in a later section. Here it is sufficient to indicate that market value is

at best a rough estimate—for the professional appraiser as well as for other analysts.

4. *Department of Business and Economic Development* v. *Pioneer Trust and Savings Bank* (Kane County Circuit Court, 69 C1–22); *Department of Business and Economic Development* v. *Fredrickson et al.* (DuPage County Circuit Court, C-69-1495).

5. Specifically the unclassified were a church and its pastor, a small businessman, and a family who had bought an acre on which to build a house in the future.

6. See Chapter 7.

7. American Institute of Real Estate Appraisers, *Appraisal Terminology and Handbook,* 4th ed. (Chicago, 1962), p. 31.

8. Depository of Eugene Mack as found in record of *Department of Business and Economic Development* v. *Pioneer Trust* (Kane County Circuit Court, #69 C1-22).

9. Interview with Lawrence Trimble, vice-president of development for Commonwealth Edison.

10. DBED files.

11. For a discussion of the inexactness of appraising, see Fred M. Lange, "The Advantages and Pitfalls of Appraisal Techniques," *Institute on Eminent Domain* (Dallas: Southwestern Legal Foundation, Matthew Bender & Co., 1969), p. 83.

12. An appraiser who acknowledges this problem is Robert L. Free, MAI, "Preparing a Condemnation Appraisal," in *The Appraiser's Job in Eminent Domain,* proceedings (Pittsburgh: Bureau of Business Research, 1957), p. 1.

13. Joseph R. Smith, III, "Preparation and Presentation of Condemnation Cases from the Viewpoint of the Appraiser," Mimeo, p. 75.

14. George L. Schmutz, *Condemnation Appraisal Handbook* (Englewood Cliffs, N.J.: Prentice-Hall, 1963), p. 19.

15. *DBED* v. *Pioneer Trust* (Kane County Circuit Court).

13 **Aftermath and Afterthoughts: Building on a Solid Base of Ignorance**

The Weston accelerator was a prestigious industry, and it had involved eminent participants. Mayor Daley's original planning group for Chicago and the metropolitan area was composed of the top businessmen and intellectuals in the community. Governor Kerner, despite the financial indiscretions that later put him in jail, had been considered a good governor, especially where state industrial development was concerned. His Department of Business and Economic Development was composed of people unusually dedicated and unusually qualified to sell the state to the nation and to sell the nation to the people of DuPage County.

Illinois senators and congressmen ranked second to none in competence and distinction among state delegations to Congress; those members of the state delegation who had concerned themselves with the accelerator were particularly distinguished. Even DuPage County officials were several cuts above the ordinary run of political operative.

Most outstanding among all these participants were the representatives of the national science community. Scientists, especially in high-energy physics, belong to an important international elite.

However, our respect for these participants is equaled by our astonishment at their ignorance. During a period of over 30 months they were involved in a public works project worth more than an ABM site or a large automobile assembly plant. There was no way to usher the accelerator in on little cat's paws. Publicity had in fact been encouraged by the Washington participants. The scale of participation in the original decision was far more extensive than is typical in public works decisions. But knowledge of the whole situation did not increase with size and publicity. Ignorance was of epidemic proportion.

Ignorance turned out to be a major result of specialization. Decision makers give up their knowledge of the whole as they seek full and complete knowledge of their particular piece of the whole. But ignorance is not merely a correlative of specialization. It is almost a condition for peaceful coexistence among specialists.

Ignorance tends to be meaningfully distributed throughout the hierarchies. There was more ignorance at the center than at the periphery. There was more ignorance in Washington than in Wheaton. There was more ignorance in Congress than in Chicago. And there was more ignorance among physicists than among politicians.

This brings our particular concern into focus. Ignorance on the scale we have observed could not have occurred by chance alone. Ignorance on this scale involving scientists—that is, men otherwise dedicated to knowledge above all else—had to be deliberate.

Until they read this book, they will almost certainly be ignorant of most of the factors behind the development of the village of Weston. They will be ignorant of the motivations back of making this area a candidate for the accelerator, and they will be ignorant of the motivations back of the massive effort by the county to prevent the building of the village. Thus they will not be able to grasp the extent to which the national government and the scientists had been a pawn in a larger strategy of county planning and development.

Until they read this book, they will remain ignorant of how it was possible for the Weston villagers to make an eager show of support for the accelerator. The scientists may go on thinking that the project was welcome. They may even remain ignorant of the intense desire of the villagers and the farmers to retain their homes.

Unless they read this book, they will remain ignorant of the many community ties unnecessarily destroyed by the project. They will be ignorant of the traditional community in which the rural residents were longstanding members. They will be ignorant of the new middle-class community that had already begun to develop in the village of Weston. They will remain ignorant of the special problems created by the sudden displacement of so many families; ignorant of the barriers to relocation in a manner that allows maintenance of communal and friendship ties.

Until they read this book, they will also be ignorant of the unusually harsh methods used by their agents in state government to assemble the 6,800-acre site. They are probably not ignorant of the fact that slight changes in the definition of the site might have reduced the number of households affected by the acquisition, because they were determined from the beginning to receive as a gift the houses and facilities that made up the village. But they have almost certainly been ignorant of the methods of acquisition. And they probably remain ignorant of the degree to which the real plan to acquire all of the structures as well as the land was kept hidden from the local residents.

Until they read this book, they will probably be ignorant of the extent to which the present development of that region accords with the original plans made by officials in the region and generally approved by an overwhelming majority of the suburbanites. After more than 7 years on the site, the scientists cannot fail to see that the region is more middle class and lily white than it was in 1960. They cannot fail to see the development in the worst tradition of McDonaldized suburbia, with strip after strip of garden apartments alternating with strips of raw commerce and enclaves of country clubs and bridle paths. They cannot remain ignorant of the fact that an area west of the site has been acquired for a community college—despite local assurances in 1966 that the accelerator itself could not have been placed on this western site because of the impossibility of land acquisition. But they are very probably ignorant of how much all of this accords with the original "plan for the orderly development" of the region.

Tolling the Bell for the Farmer in the Dell

How difficult would it have been to replace ignorance with knowledge? Could the scientists have gotten the knowledge if they had wanted? Were the information costs prohibitive?

Readers who go back over this book will not find much evidence of effort to gain full knowledge. And this is lamentable because the costs of information were quite low. For example, our book, which is based completely on unpaid research power, already contains a great deal of the requisite information. And we can assure Washington that still further knowledge would have been easy to get, inasmuch as the local officials were extremely cooperative. Virtually every local participant we talked to was confident that he was carrying out his responsibilities according to broad popular support. No one had very much to fear from full exposure; most were eager to provide details. For the centers in Washington to be ignorant, ignorance itself had to be a policy.

One more look at the rural residents of the site—who were clamoring to tell their story—will help in an assessment of how difficult, or how easy, it is to learn relevant things at relevant times in the decision process. These data will also begin to suggest that relevant knowledge, although usually easy to get, makes decisions harder to make. This tells us something more about the function of ignorance as well as the necessity for knowing.

Between January and May 1969, we conducted interviews of more than 1 hour in duration with 85 individuals in 60 of the rural households in the site area. Seventy-six per cent of the respondents had lived on or had been associated with land in the site area for more than 10 years. Thirteen were actually born on the site, two were the fifth generation in residence on this site area, and 9 were beyond second generation. Of the others, 43 had resided in that place for more than 10 years.

Over 40 per cent of the respondents were related to each other. Almost all of the residents and their children could report that they were welcome on friendly terms in three or more homes in the area eventually acquired for the site.

On the basis of this kind of attachment, almost 80 per cent of the respondents said that no monetary offer alone would encourage them to leave this area and live elsewhere. Yet money was a matter of immediate concern to most of them. They had other jobs to meet taxes, because for over 10 years it had not been profitable to live in this area on farming alone.

Once the boundaries of the site were established and the acquisition arrangements were gotten under way, virtually all the farmers and other rural residents expressed confidence that the state would deal fairly with them. This in fact helps explain why the group organized to represent these residents went only once to Springfield to protest. During the acquisition, spokesmen for only six families could report that they were satisfied with the arrangement. Spokesmen for nine families expressed no attitude, and spokesmen for the rest—45 families—expressed extreme bitterness.

The farmowners were given verbal assurances by the negotiators that they could remove personally valuable objects from their land. (They were turned down on requests for written assurances.) Some were given assurances on the right to remove their houses. None was ever told that the AEC had demanded all of the homes and movable objects; in return, the AEC was apparently never told that contrary verbal assurances were given during the process of negotiation.

It is clear from our research in the whole area, as well as from the interviews, that the decision makers had kept themselves completely ignorant of marginal shifts in the definition of the site that might have minimized the impact on families committed to remaining in this area. The results of this kind of ignorance are extremely clear and compelling. The 17 families who chose to continue farming moved an average of 100 miles away to find comparable land at prices they could afford. Moreover, they are scattered in every direction. It is doubtful that the typical public works project by the typical highway engineer or political hack leaves such a residue of community destruction and ill feeling. Yet, the scientists were lucky inasmuch as most of these residents were generally favorable to the government and loath to gouge agents of the government. For example, 28 of the 60 heads of household reported that they had accepted the sale at the government's price because the accelerator was "for the greater good." Only three of these 28 heads of household had resisted or bargained with the state at any time. To us, this indicates that acquiescence without a long court battle was due largely to patriotism and a faith that science equals progress.

Because the land was acquired by forceful means before the owners could profit from suburban development, and because the owners were neither law violators nor offenders of public order, it would seem they had a right to expect removal on the basis of an airtight case that the accelerator absolutely had to go on that specific piece of earth with that specific amount of surrounding acreage. No such justification was ever offered. Because the national decision makers did not know the character or history of the people they were removing, there never existed any obligation to justify this site as the very best one among all the possible sites in that region, or elsewhere. This site was best only because it was the best bid made among all the bids offered by the state planning officials in the United States.

The science personnel who operate the accelerator are apparently pleased with the physical features of the site and have been eager to preserve everything left by the departing rural residents:

> Contrary to what many of us thought when we first came to these cornfields, there is a real potential for beauty here. We need to conserve every tree, every bush, every patch of grass, and every body of water. . . .[1]

As already reported, the NAL went to great lengths to preserve the sense of the agricultural heritage by setting aside several unneeded acres of the site as a model farm to be run by "Farmer Bob," a farm manager with a Ph.D., to help preserve "the only vestige of rural living in this area. . . ." The plan was to include "a historical display of past and present memorabilia, probably housed in one of the beautiful large barns on the site." The director urged the NAL employees to lease land on the site to raise vegetables.[2] The director and his associates are proud to report that they have installed a herd of buffalo and are allowing them to roam over a great deal of the unused farmland, land that was acquired and cleared of farmers apparently years before there was a scientific need for the land.

We juxtapose the scientific present with the bucolic past not out of any overwhelming sense of sympathy for the past or antagonism toward scientists or the present. We juxtapose these two situations because we are certain that the scientists themselves would not have been able to abide the contrast—if they had known it. Their values, not ours, are the appropriate values by which to judge the situation. And the more we judge by their values, the more we are led to conclude that ignorance is one of the most intolerable yet ubiquitous features of modern government. If ignorance is the correlative of specialization, modern government may have created more problems than it can ever hope to solve.

Bad Processes, Bad Regimes

From the standpoint of good government the accelerator project was a failure. It did not just fail to make more than a narrow contribution to fundamental national goals; it provided valuable resources to local influentials for the maximization of local, distinctly not national, goals.

Many apologists will argue that there are better ways to change social habits or to fill economic needs than to freight public works with public policies. But, as we have argued frequently in this volume, when a public works project is large enough to have a community impact, the project will have the effect of a policy and will attract those whose private policies will best be served thereby. The question then is not whether public works should be freighted with public policies but *who shall make the policies.*

When project designers admit to their responsibility as policy makers, they are doing more than behaving responsibly toward their positions of authority. They are also setting limits on the extent to which the local recipients of the project can abuse and misappropriate these resources. That is, the policy is a standard of responsible conduct for local authorities as well as a means by which local land use and social habit might be changed.

There is still another advantage to attaching policies explicitly to public works projects. The larger policy works as a limit on the designers and the congressional budget makers themselves. At the present time we regularly find ourselves wondering if the next science project or space probe or bomber series is necessary, or is instead an expression of Senator X's need for reelection or Suburb Y's need to maintain a style of life to which it would like to grow accustomed. Requiring that each project fit into some larger social plan works as a very effective limitation against an otherwise boundless and ever-expanding domain—a domain that we in the United States, for good reason, call the pork barrel.

We cannot say what those policies ought to be, although we

do feel there are ample guidelines toward the most fundamental national goals. What we can do is to insist on a principle of good government: *the governmental unit that authorizes the project ought also to make the policy the project is to serve.* Time after time, our accounts in this volume illustrate the wisdom of that principle and the unwisdom of disregarding it.

In the past decade, states' rights rhetoric has shifted from the conservatives who oppose national government to liberals who are enthusiastic about a large and growing national government. Oddly enough, the rhetoric on both sides of this question is almost the same. The argument is that the local units of government and local residents are best qualified to decide the policies applicable to that level. Our accounts bring that seriously into question: *when a central government authorizes a project or delegates any kind of powers that are not accompanied by some rather explicit standards of conduct, these powers are implemented according to the values of the localities where the implementation takes place.* And in public works projects, where actual central resources are made available to help implement central decisions, these almost inevitably become resources in the hands of local interests to carry out goals that are irrelevant to, often contrary to, national goals. Often, as in the case of Weston, such local goals as the elimination of a working-class village and all land on which future subdivisions might go would probably not have been successfully fulfilled without the intervention of federal resources.

Given these tendencies, it does not matter whether the decision makers are amateurs, scientists, or philosopher kings. When the goals of government action are not provided for as a matter of policy—where the goal is simply a project that can be implemented according to local discretion—the institutions of government are likely to be misused regardless of the composition of the elites.

We feel these are universal tendencies. A large federal system simply takes these tendencies and increases their probabilities, and the involvement of high-quality personnel such as scientists seems not to reduce the probabilities at all.

Public works projects, including expensive accelerators, are part of a larger system of modern irresponsibility. They are part of a system in which governments collect money they do not spend and spend money they do not collect. This kind of a specialization of function must inevitably involve the end of responsibility and therefore of good government.

In the United States, the question of public responsibility is usually resolved into personal terms. *Who* was responsible? *Who* should pay? *Who* deserves election or defeat? Perhaps only in America could there have been two recent presidents to vow that they would never be first of whom the public could say "He lost the war." Lyndon Johnson and Richard Nixon may have been colossally arrogant men; but they were not unique in their tendency to translate a very large war into highly personal terms. This to us is part of a general American cultural tendency to denounce the man and exonerate the system.

We insist that the system can be at fault; moreover, we feel that is the only adequate approach to understanding the behavior of the scientists and the other role players in our story.

Political science has contributed to the American practice of exonerating the system and of defining public responsibility in personal terms. To many realists in the field, the question of responsibility hardly comes up at all, and when it does it is largely a question of electoral or administrative accountability from someone to someone. There is little room in political science for anything but personal responsibility because of the "process" orientation in the field. At least since Arthur F. Bentley at the turn of the century, political science has visualized politics as one or more processes within which individual activity takes place. A process is a course of events or time; but ordinarily it implies in addition a series of actions or continuous operations leading to a result. In biology the term connotes a "natural or involuntary operation, natural and unchanging." In the law, a process is something specified and usually unavoidable under relevant conditions. In political science, a process is virtually an amalgamation of these special meanings.

We do not object to the importance of the notion of process in political science. We tend to agree that such notions helped free American political science from the old European fallacies of reifying the state and being unconcerned with social forces in politics. The idea of a political process helped free political science from naturalistic and animistic fallacies and gave the discipline an opening toward a more comprehensive as well as a more scientific analysis of politics and government.

However, there is always danger of overreaction, and some types of overreaction end up incorporating some of the worst traits of earlier practices and patterns. This we feel is what has happened to process in political science.

The field is divided into certain subdisciplines, such as "the electoral process," "the governmental process," "the administrative process," and "the legislative process." Then there are the lesser and more specific occasions for its use, such as "the pork barrel process," "the budgetary process," "the taxing process," "the socialization process," or "the decision-making process in committees," "the decision-making process in juries," and so on and on. Again, up to a point we find this effort a very sound one, because we recognize that there is a tremendous amount of repetition in politics and that some of it amounts to a regularity deserving of separate recognition as a process.

However, for every formulation of a process there is also a potential for falling into naturalistic and animistic thinking. Without careful and well-cultivated self-consciousness, it is but a short step from the hypothesis of regularity to the assumption of immutability.

In politics, many regularities worthy of the name "process" are distinctly unnatural and not necessarily immutable. The observed regularities of behavior and regularities of result may flow "naturally" as long as that process exists; but the process itself was very probably the result of some kind of structure or procedure deliberately contrived at an earlier point in time by the fertile mind of political man. "The administrative process" can be almost any behavior series set in train by a man-made agency. There are of course some continuities among all administrative agencies; but that is more likely to be due to the limited number of ways an agency can be contrived than to anything inherent and natural about some process called administrative. Or for that matter, if we take "the American political process" as a whole, it is almost certain that federalism has had a tremendous amount to do with what is American about the American political process, and yet nothing is more man-made and contrived than federalism. "The legislative process" is another example of a highly repetitive and predictable series of behaviors that could be made very different by slight changes in the committee structure or the procedural rules.

If anything we call a process is at all attributable to human contrivance, and if it is at all susceptible to being changed by deliberate action, then it would seem that we are obliged not to accept it as natural or respect it as immutable. It would seem to us that the contrary perspective is the obligatory one.

In that spirit, we find ourselves committed to a still older American tradition, constitutionalism. From this perspective, ordinary man can be good or bad depending on the constitution—that is, the structures and processes—within which he operates. Within a large political system such as our own, there are many structures, many constitutions. This is only a way of specifying the large number of regularities within established political processes. And this is still another way of saying that as a modern industrial state we are politically, as well as economically and socially, differentiated. As constitutionalists we go still a step further and attempt to judge each of these processes and each of the structures that give rise to it. From the constitutionalist or formalist view a process can be good or bad depending on whether it produces good or bad actions.

It is from this perspective that the Weston accelerator decision was a failure. The decision was the result of a series of bad actions, and these bad actions are largely attributable to a bad process.

Few would disagree with our designation of our account as a case of "the public works process." Few would disagree when we go further to say that the popular or vulgar name for this is "the pork barrel process," and that this is an appropriate label for it. It is generally agreed also that the process refers to all public decisions that allocate public resources on a case-by-case, project-by-project basis. The very imagery of the pork barrel is one of a collection of very discrete units that can be drawn out one at a time, each in isolation from each of the others.

This means that the public works process is distinguished by decisions that embody no rule of conduct, no conditions or standards that tie together the various discrete units. In fact, to say that each unit is discrete is tantamount to saying that no rule or condition binds any of the recipients.

This is the characteristic common to all public works decisions. Except in terms of outward style, it does not matter very much whether the decision makers are political hacks, career bureaucrats, politically appointed lawyers, congressmen, or high-energy physicists. Once a statute sets the pork barrel process in train, the behavior series is predictable. It is pretty much as we have described it in our account of one major public works decision in the science and technology field. As we put it earlier, the public works decision-making process is tantamount to a conspiracy to keep larger social questions from becoming issues of public policy. Possibly the most explicit, certainly one of the most dramatic, statements about the *modus operandi* of the pork barrel process was made by Senator Dirksen against the efforts of the Eastern Seaboard senators to apply civil rights considerations to the selection of the accelerator site. As he put it, "If Congress in its wisdom undertakes at any time to draw that line [applying a civil rights condition to a specific public works project], then I want to say . . . that line is going to be firmly drawn, and it is going to be equally firmly held" (see Chapter 5). No one, not even the Eastern Seaboard senators, wanted advances in civil rights at the price of putting an end to the pork barrel process. And it took only one utterance from one senator to remind them that the application of policy conditions to a pork barrel allocation would put an end to the pork barrel process.

As we have also had occasion to emphasize already, the evil of the pork barrel process does not stop merely with the absence of general public policy guidance. That is certainly important, but only the beginning of the bad aspects of the behavior series that comprises the process. When the initial decision makers refuse to consider the larger context within which each public work will fit, then someone else will take that project and have it serve quite different kinds of goals and ideals. In the absence of the rule or condition of performance, it is certainly true that each federal project is a delegation to a local unit to make the decision locally as to what purposes the national project will serve. But the local unit is distinctly not composed of "the people," regardless of the present rhetoric of decentralization and local control. Local control means control by people who are privileged to be at the right place at the right time. This process placed within a federal system is even worse, because that simply means greater distances of removal between the original level of responsibility and the ultimate point of implementation. This to us is a more reliable and meaningful measure of "closeness to the people." Distance should not be measured by mere physical proximity; we have only to recall the enormous distance between people and city hall. Distance should rather be measured in terms of the number of levels of government between the point at which the people, by voting, give their consent and the point later on when those same people must accept the consequences in terms of the imposition of controls and the allocation of privileges.

The public works process is certainly one of the worst processes in the American system from almost any and every perspective. It is bad in terms of the absence of laws and rules. It is bad in terms of the narrowness with which decision makers can allocate public resources. And it is measurably the worst in terms of the remoteness of the citizen from the points of ultimate responsibility, despite the fact that the final implementing decisions are made in close geographical proximity to *some* citizens. It is in the typical public works decision that we can best see the practice and the consequences of governments that collect money they don't spend and spend money they don't collect.

Finally, the public works process is a bad process because of the effect it has on the participants. We have in our account the ultimate test in our time, because we have observed here how the public works process has had a bad effect even upon our best citizens, the pure scientists in government.

Exit: The Institutionalization of Second Thoughts

None of this leads to a rejection of federalism, of Congress, of science projects. The whole system is not at fault, only one particular political process.

The public works process can be transformed by the elimination of pork barrel, and this can be done by rules, laid down at the point of origin, that attempt to plan for some of the social consequences of each project. This does not require the specification of

294 THE POLITICS OF CONQUEST

every detail, nor does it require a detailed accounting of all spill-over effects years before they are expected to take place. It requires a recognition of the variations in goals and perspectives among the intervening levels of government, and it makes absolutely necessary some kind of continuous central planning (pre-audit) and a never-ending supervisory process (post-audit).

This kind of federal responsibility is not as difficult as it may at first sound. Granted, a science project or a regulatory program may be extremely complex. On the other hand, local officials who can bend federal programs to their own localized perspectives can also bend those same programs toward national perspectives if those perspectives are spelled out clearly enough. Most officials are eager to live according to the responsibilities of their offices. But if these responsibilities are not spelled out for an official he is very likely to try to define them for himself, taking his guidance from his own professional norms and from his immediate environment —meaning from his clientele. But this means that there are un-exercised opportunities to influence administration toward the implementation of larger priorities and toward central responsibility. Apologists claim that totally unguided delegation is inevitable because life is too complex for central guidance by rules and standards. Close observation of local elites reveals that they already have magnificently detailed goals and plans. Are we to admit that only obscure local elites have the capacity to plan?

We should not attempt to replace congressional or AEC wisdom with our own. But we are able to propose some means by which Congress, through the president and the AEC, might exercise its wisdom rather than allow it to be displaced by local elites.

We must begin again with recognition that the failure of this science project to pursue any larger national social or economic goals is not a personal failure of scientists or of the science point of view. At the personal level, our story only proves that scientists, alas, are human. We must look to the points of origin where policies ought to be made: Congress, the president, the AEC, and the JCAE. These are the points of origin where each political process is set in train according to the structure of policy set for it. When some kind of rule is attached to a project at the origin, the various specialized agencies are more likely to be obliged to co-ordinate with each other as behaviors inconsistent with the rule are exposed by clients or other agencies. A rule will increase the probability that agencies will feel obliged to collect all data on prospective sites, the unpleasant with the pleasant. The rule itself exposes the areas of ignorance. The rule gives the citizens potentially removed or heavily affected by a prospective site a calculus of their rights and of their causes of action. How can we say that any project is superior to these considerations?

Thus it is the rule that makes the difference. When a policy is attached to a project, the "public works process" is transformed. The transformed process is a better one because it requires more "search behavior" on the part of the specialized agencies. It imposes—without of course guaranteeing—a more regular and nationally consistent consideration of social issues. It institutionalizes second thoughts. Let the technologies be decided by technological specialists. But give them an institution that gives them second thoughts.

Prospects

The full story of the National Accelerator Laboratory does not suggest a favorable outlook for a politics dominated by science, science projects, and scientists. We say this not because we find ourselves and our political society worse off as a result of activities such as the accelerator. We say it because we find ourselves no better off.

The problems of government seem to transcend the types of personnel who occupy the elite posts. Elites change, perhaps for the better. Styles of politics change. Agendas change, with new problems or new priorities among the old problems. But in pursuit of those problems there are always the higher-order problems of how that pursuit will advance justice and whether it will keep elites responsible and circulating. These problems seem always to be just beyond the reach of the old bourgeois elites, the pluralistic influence brokers, the professionals, the bureaucrats, and the scientists; and they will also be beyond the reach of the new and future ethnic elites. For it was never a question of better people but of understanding government.

Thus we must end our inquiries with an admission that our real problem all along was not with communities and scientists but with public institutions. Can we arrange our political and governmental structures in any way to bring out the best in officials and politicos? Are there ways we can institutionalize a broader view? Is there a way to throw the many parochialisms together into a larger perspective? We end as we began: can big governments really govern, or are we doomed to see government submerged, value free, into our natural environment?

NOTES TO CHAPTER 13

1. An exclamation by the director of the National Accelerator Laboratory for the NAL's own publication, *The Village Crier*, 1: No. 3 (June 1969).
2. Ibid.

Index

Accelerator laboratory, site selection for
committee for, 67–69
competition and expanded participation in, 57–58
criteria for, 3–4, 58–59, 65–67
  extension of, guidelines in, 76–78
process of, change in, 50–51, 52–53
  by AEC, 50
  by JCAE, 49–50
proposals for, to AEC, 60
repercussions of, 51–53
results of, 69–72
  analysis of, 72–75
in Weston, Illinois
  cooperativeness in, 219–20
  decision for, by AEC, 78–80
  economic advantages in, 162–63
  explanation for, 163–65

interests in, analysis of, 216–19
involvement of officials in, 4–6
opposition to, analysis of, 220–29
preservation of physical features in, 286
scientists' decision in, creation of illusion for, 14–17
support of, explanation of, 229–32
withdrawal of Barrington from, 159
Ann Arbor, Michigan, features of, for site selection of laboratory, 69–70, 71–72
Appraisal Terminology and Handbook, 267
Arado, Joseph, 169
Argonne National Laboratory, 3, 41, 95, 117

Army Corps of Engineers, 27

Associated Universities, Incorporated (AUI), organization of, 40

Atomic bomb, development of, 36

Atomic Energy Act, 38

Atomic Energy Commission (AEC), 1, 2, 3, 14, 16, 27, 42, 44, 49, 57, 58, 60, 61, 65, 94, 119, 120, 124, 159, 172, 196, 294

assignment of construction of "Bevatron," 40–41

consideration of civil rights issue, 110–14, 126

decision for site selection of Weston accelerator, 78–80, 124

establishment of, 37

function of, 41

NAS and. See National Academy of Sciences

performance of, use of outside organizations for, 37

plan of, for basis of fellowship among physical scientists, 3–4

policy of, influence of JCAE on, 38–39

proposals to, for site of Weston accelerator, 60–61

reassembly of design team, 237

Atomic policy, formulation of, agencies concerned with, 39

Bane, Jack, 94

Barrington. See South Barrington

Battaglia, Sam "Teetz," 149

Bauer, William, suit against village of Weston, 144–45

Bentley, Arthur F., 289

Berkeley Radiation Laboratory, 40

Berman vs. Parker, 267

Berry, Brian, grid of, for mapping towns of a metropolitan area, 198–200

"Bevatron." See Electron volt (bev) accelerator

Beverly Savings and Loan Association, 140

Blacks, residing in DuPage County, 111

Block, Harold, 189

Briggs Committee, 36

Brooke, Edward, 120

Brookhaven National Laboratory, 37, 40, 51, 98

features of, for site selection of accelerator laboratory, 70, 71–72

Bureau of the Budget, 63

Bureaucracies, operation of, 110

Bush, Vannevar, 36

Chicago, Illinois

interest in for site selection of accelerator laboratory, 92–94

metropolitan area of, counties of, 187

municipal incorporations in, 181t., 183t.

"orderly development" of, comparison of, 187–90

population of, 176t., 177t

unincorporated areas in 183t.

Chicago Better Business Bureau (BBB), 6

William Riley and, 146–47
Chicago Sun-Times, 148
Chicago Tribune, 145, 146
Civil rights, consideration of in site selection
  by AEC, 110–14, 126
  arguments on, 119–20
  by Congress, 114–19, 124
Civil Rights Act, on fair housing, 112
  arguments on, 122–24
Commercial establishments, patronized by Weston residents, location of, 205*t*.
Committee on Economic Development, support of Midwest for site selection, 91–92
Commonwealth Edison Company, 87, 92, 94, 166, 255
  compensation to, 255
  interest in Illinois as site of accelerator laboratory, 88, 89
  rate reducation for Weston, 98
Communities, of Weston, Illinois
  categories of, comparison of, 206–211
  failure of conflict in, 215–16
    related to site selection of accelerator laboratory, 216–19
Compton, Arthur, 40
Congress. *See* United States Congress
"Consensual assessment," process of, 13–14
Constitutionalism, commitment to, 291
Continental Illinois Bank and Trust Company, 87
Conyers, John, 119

Cook County, Illinois, 95
Corplan Associates, 89
"Cosmotron," construction of, 40
Counties, government of, influence on development of metropolis, 22–23
Cyclotron cycle, between East and West
  breaking of, by MURA, 43–47
  establishment of, 40–41

Daley, Richard J., 74, 100, 281
  interest in Chicago as site of accelerator laboratory, 88, 89, 92
DBED. *See* Illinois Department of Business and Economic Development
Decision making
  "consensual assessment," 13–14
  by scientists, analysis of, background for, 62–64
Denver, Colorado, features of, for site selection of accelerator laboratory, 70, 71–72
Design team, reassembly of, 237
Development. *See* "Orderly development"; Research and development
Dirksen, Everett, 74
  deletion of Weston authorization and, 122–23
Douglas, Paul, 8, 75, 97, 100, 117
  urging of Johnson for Illinois as site of accelerator laboratory, 101–102
DuPage County, Illinois, 131, 198, 200, 201, 219
  building and zoning regulations of, 133–34
  citizens of, profile of, 175–80

DuPage County, Illinois (*cont.*)
  desirable characteristics of, 262–63
  industrial development of, 176–77
  land sales in, 263–64
  plan for "orderly development," 177–80
  population of, 176*t.*, 176
  vs. Weston, for site of accelerator laboratory, 185–87
DuPage County Comprehensive Plan, 177
DuPage County Forest Preserve District, 186
DuPage County Mayors and Managers Conference, 161
DuPage Magazine, 186

East Coast coalition, 100
Electron volt (bev) accelerator, construction of, 40–41
  federalism and, 27
  in Weston Illinois
    history of scientists' involvement in, 2–4
    impact of, 1–2, 6–7
    outlook for, 31–32
    participants and perspectives in, 8*t.*–12*t.*, 13
    scientists' decision in "consensual assessment," 13–14
Elgin, Joliet and Eastern Railway (EJ&E), 132, 168, 169
Eminent domain
  corruption of, 278–79
  operation of, in acquisition of farm property in Weston, 266–70
  politics of, in Weston, 236

Employment
  opportunities opened in, 125–26
  of Weston residents
    place of, distance of, 201*t.*, 201
    types of, 203, 203*t.*, 204
Erlenborn, John N., 117, 120
Evans, Philip, 149
Extension Service, 27

Farmers, attitude of, in acquisition of land, 283–85
Farms, in Weston, Illinois
  income derived from, 264–66
  number of, 265*t.*
  occupancy of, patterns of, 264
  sale of, 261–63
    patterns of, 263–64
Federal government, policies of, implementation of
  layering in, 27–29
  local subversions of, 25–26
Federal Housing Authority (FHA), 141, 142
Federal Savings and Loan Insurance Corporation (FSLIC), 140, 143, 144, 196
  role of, in ownership of village of Weston, 149–50
Federal system, outline of, 8*t.*–12*t.*
Federalism, in United States, 27
Fermi, Enrico, 40
FFAG, 42
  canceling of, 49
Financial support
  to research, 35
  to science, 35
First National City Bank, 99
Forest service, 27

Fox River Valley, 131, 198, 219
   change in, 131–32
Fricken, Raymond, 94

General Advisory Committee
      (GAC), 37
   history of, 37–38
General Advisory Committee of
      the Atomic Energy Com-
      mission (AEC-GAC), 46
   strategy of, 44
Geneva Conference on the Peace-
      ful Use of Atomic Energy,
      42
George Pearce Realtors of Aurora,
      149, 151
Ghetto, comparison of, to Wes-
      ton, 209–211
Goetz, Donald, 171
Government, problems of, 295
Graves, Gene, 87, 92, 162, 165
   efforts of, to eliminate village
      of Weston, 166, 167, 239–
      41
Grodzins, Morton, 27
Groves, Leslie, 39, 40

Hart, Philip, 120
High-energy physics, user groups
      of, distribution of, 73, 73t.,
      74t.
Holifield, Chet, 119, 120
Homes, in Weston, Illinois
   building of, developers involved
      in, 141–44
      illegal activities of, 137–41,
         144–48
   financing of, 132–37
   rehabilitation of, 149–50
   selling of, 151–52

Hoover, Herbert, 35
Hosmer, Craig, 66, 119
Housing and Urban Development,
      agencies of, 27
Huitt, Ralph, as spokesman for
      MURA, 47–48
Hydrogen bomb, development of,
      38

Illinois
   counties of
      "orderly development" of, in-
         corporation and, 180–85
      plan for development, 178–
         79
   interests in, coalition of, 88–91
   population of, 177t.
   site selection for accelerator
      laboratory in, 93, 94
Illinois Appellate Court, ruling on
      incorporation of village of
      Weston, 161
Illinois Department of Business
      and Economic Develop-
      ment (DBED), 14, 87,
      90, 91, 95, 97, 100, 169,
      243, 255
   acquisition of village property
      in Weston, 239–41
   cost cutting by, 237
   fight against annexation of vil-
      lage of Weston, 169–170
   pressure of, 270–71
Income, compensation of, for
      Weston residents, 249t.,
      250t., 251
Incorporation, of new municipali-
      ties, limiting of county
      control of "orderly devel-
      opment" by, 180–85
Indiana, offers to AEC, 90

Javits, Jacob, 120
Johnson, A. B., 148
Johnson, Kenneth, 243
Johnson, Lyndon B., 4, 49, 75, 99, 289
    role of, in site selection of accelerator laboratory, 101–102
Joint Committee on Atomic Energy (JCAE), 2, 44, 63, 75, 79, 92, 100, 101, 294
    influence of, on AEC, 38–39
    members of, consideration of civil rights issue by, 115–16

Kane County, Illinois, 131
Keir, Arthur, 151
Kennedy, David, 92
    letter to Mayor Daley, regarding Chicago as site selection, 92
Kennedy, John F., 45, 49
Kerner, Otto, 75, 89, 100, 143, 167, 281
    agreement with AEC on financial compensation for property, 238
    meeting with Chicago businessmen, 93
King, Martin Luther, 122

L and H Builders, fight to incorporate village of Weston, 188–89
Laboratory. See Accelerator laboratory
Lake County, Illinois, 188, 190
Lawrence, Ernest O., 40
Lawrence Radiation Laboratory, 62, 237
    site criteria of, 165
Liberty, Illinois, Sentinel ABM site in, 218
Lilienthal, David, 38
Lofgren, Edward, 53
Los Alamos, 37, 100

McDaniel, Paul, 93
McGrath, Kyran, 100
Madison, Wisconsin, features of, for site selection of accelerator laboratory, 70, 71–72
Manhattan Project, 37, 39
"Marble cake," 27
Maryland, offers to AEC, 90
Mayor's Committee on Economic and Cultural Development (Chicago), 87
Metropolis, development of, influence of county on, 21–26
Midwest Governors Conference, 91
Midwest University Research Associates (MURA), 3, 44, 57, 90, 91
    breaking of, 43–47
    building of FFAG by, 42–43
    members of, 41
    pressure by 47–49
        change in site selection for accelerator laboratory from, 50–51

Naperville Chamber of Commerce, 97
National Academy of Sciences (NAS), 2, 3, 36, 51, 58,

61, 64, 96, 124
assistance to AEC, in process of site selection for accelerator laboratory, 64–65
criteria for, 65–67, 75–76, 76–78
evaluation committee for, 67–69
results of, analysis of, 69–75
evaluation of site contestants, 61
National Accelerator Laboratory (NAL), 1, 14, 28, 32, 171, 186, 286
employment practices of, 126
Policy Statement of Human Rights, 124–25
National Association for the Advancement of Colored People (NAACP), 111
National Defense Research Committee (NDRC), 36
National Science Foundation, 42
Newport Mortgage Company, 150
Nixon, Richard M., 289
Northeastern Illinois Planning Commission (NIPC), 132
Northern Illinois Gas Company, 255

Oak Ridge, 100, 126
Oppenheimer, J. Robert, 38
"Orderly development," of counties of Chicago metropolitan area
comparisons of, 187–90
county control of, limits in, incorporation and, 180–85
of DuPage County, plan for, 177–80

Panofsky, W. K. H., 43
Pastore, John O., 115, 120
examination of civil rights issue, in site selection of accelerator laboratory, 118–19
urging of postponement of project, 121
rejection of, 123–24
Percy, Charles, consideration of civil rights issue, 117
Physical scientists, harmony of, basis for, 2–4
Physics, high energy
priority list for, 46
research and development of, 63
Piore, Emanuel R., 71
panel of, 44
Planning, methods for, 190–93
Policies, for public works projects, 287–88
Political science, process of, 289–90
Politics, patterns of, 22
"Pork barrel," 110, 287
practice of, in Weston, 127
Power, costs of, in Weston, 98
President's Science Advisory Committee (PSAC), 44, 46, 63
strategy of, 44
Price, Melvin, 100, 115
Princeton, Illinois, 93
Process, formulation of, 290–91
Property(ies), in Weston, Illinois, acquisition of
errors committed in, 278–79
rural, 261–62
appraisers for, incompetence of, 271–72
compensation for, inadequacy of, 266–67

Property(ies) (*cont.*)
  rural (*cont.*)
    negotiators for, incompetence of, 272–73
    price offers for, ranges of, 273–78
    relocation of owner of, 268–70, 269t.
    See also Farms
  village, 236
    appraisals in, incompetence of, 245–47
    compensation for, 237–39
    by DBED, methods for, 239–41
    replacement costs, losses in, 241t., 247–48, 249t., 252–53
    settlements for, inequitable variations in, 253–58
    by state, procedure for, 241–44
Public institutions, problems of, 295–96
"Public purpose," interpretation of, by Supreme Court, 267
Public responsibility, resolution of, 289
Public works process
  evils of, 291–93
  transformation of, 293–95

Quo warranto suit, 144, 184

Rabi, I. I., 40
Raby, Al, 122
Ramey, James T., 111
Ramsey, Norman F., 46
Ramsey panel, 46
  recommendation for high

energy physics, 46
Reeling, Kenneth, fight against annexation of village of Weston, 168–69
Research and development (R&D), 92
  budget for, 30
  financial support of, 35
Riley, William G., 167
  involvement of, in construction of homes in Weston, 141–44
    failure of, 144–49
Rolvaag, Karl, 92, 99
Ronske, Paul 178
Roosevelt, Franklin D., 36
Rostenkowski, Daniel, 92, 100, 101
Rural hamlet, features of, 208–209
  comparison of Weston to, 209

St. Louis, site team of, letter of dissent from, 99–100
Savannah River Project, problems of, 262
Schrader, Charles, 90
Science
  American ideology of, 29–30
  involvement of federal government in, 28–29
Science public works, outline of, 8t.–12t.
Scientists
  attitude of
    toward government-scientific complex, 33–35, 36
    toward private support, 35–36
  ignorance of, related to project, 279–83

participation of, for accelerator laboratory site, 57–59
benefits from, 57
Seaborg, Glenn, 50, 51, 64, 97, 168
Seitz, Frederick, 64, 67
Self-government, need for, 109
Sentinel ABM, site of, 218
Shopping, patterns of, of Weston residents, 204
factors in, 204, 205–206
Sierra foothills, features of, for site selection of accelerator laboratory, 70, 71–72
Site selection. See Accelerator laboratory
SLAC, 43, 63
construction of, 44, 45
Smukler, Keith, 149
Social goals, failure in pursuit of, 127
Society, involvement of politics in, 21–22
pattern of, 22
Soil Conservation Service, 27
South Barrington, Illinois, for site selection of accelerator laboratory, 94, 218
features of, 70, 71–72
opposition to, 94–96
withdrawal of, 96, 159
Stanford High Energy Physics Laboratory, 43
State governments, interpretation of policies by, 25–26
Subcommittee on Research, Development and Radiation, 115
Suburbia, ideal of, 195
Weston and, 195–96, 206–207
Suburbs, development of, 131
Swartout, John, 94

Tape, Gerald, 87
Teolis, Matthew, 189
Theriault, Arthur, 97, 150, 159, 166, 167, 168
efforts of, for location of accelerator laboratory in Weston, 160–61, 166, 167, 168
Ticho, Harold, 94
Tinley Park Savings and Loan Association, 135, 138, 140

USSR, building of accelerator by, 42
United States Congress, 2
consideration of civil rights issue, in site selection of accelerator laboratory, 114–19, 124
power of, 109, 110
United States government. See Federal government
United States Post Office, 6
United States Supreme Court, interpretation of "public purpose," 267
University of Chicago, 41, 87, 219

Vernon Hills, village of, incorporation of, 188–89

Warrenville, Illinois, 169
fight against annexation of village of Weston, 169–70
Westfield Construction Company, 136, 137, 138
Weston, Illinois
community of. See Communities

Weston (*cont.*)

  economic portrait of, 200–206

  future of, 215

    opinions on, by citizens, 220–26

  history of, 197, 207, 216

  incorporation of village of

    advantages in, 161

    battle for, 168–72

    court ruling on, 161

  independence of, 207–208

  move to, reasons for, 202*t.*, 202–203

  physical features of, preservation of, 286

  removal of village of, 166–68

  residents of

    employment of. *See* Employment

    previous residences of, in 1967, 199*t.*

  social portrait of, 196–200

  vs. DuPage County, 185–87

Weston Development Corporation, 138, 139

Weston Nuclear Laboratory, 171

Wolfson Development Corporation, 136, 137

Work. *See* Employment

Young Men's Christian Association (YMCA), 126

Zaininger, William, 166

Zero Gradient Synchrotron, building of, 42–43